RECORDED VERSIONS GUITAR

AUTHENTIC TRANSCRIPTIONS WITH NOTES AND TABLATURE

Transcribed By
KENN CHIPKIN

BLUE ÖYSTER CULT

Cult Classic

ISBN 0-7935-6130-2

HAL•LEONARD™
CORPORATION
7777 W. BLUEMOUND RD. P.O. BOX 13819 MILWAUKEE, WI 53213

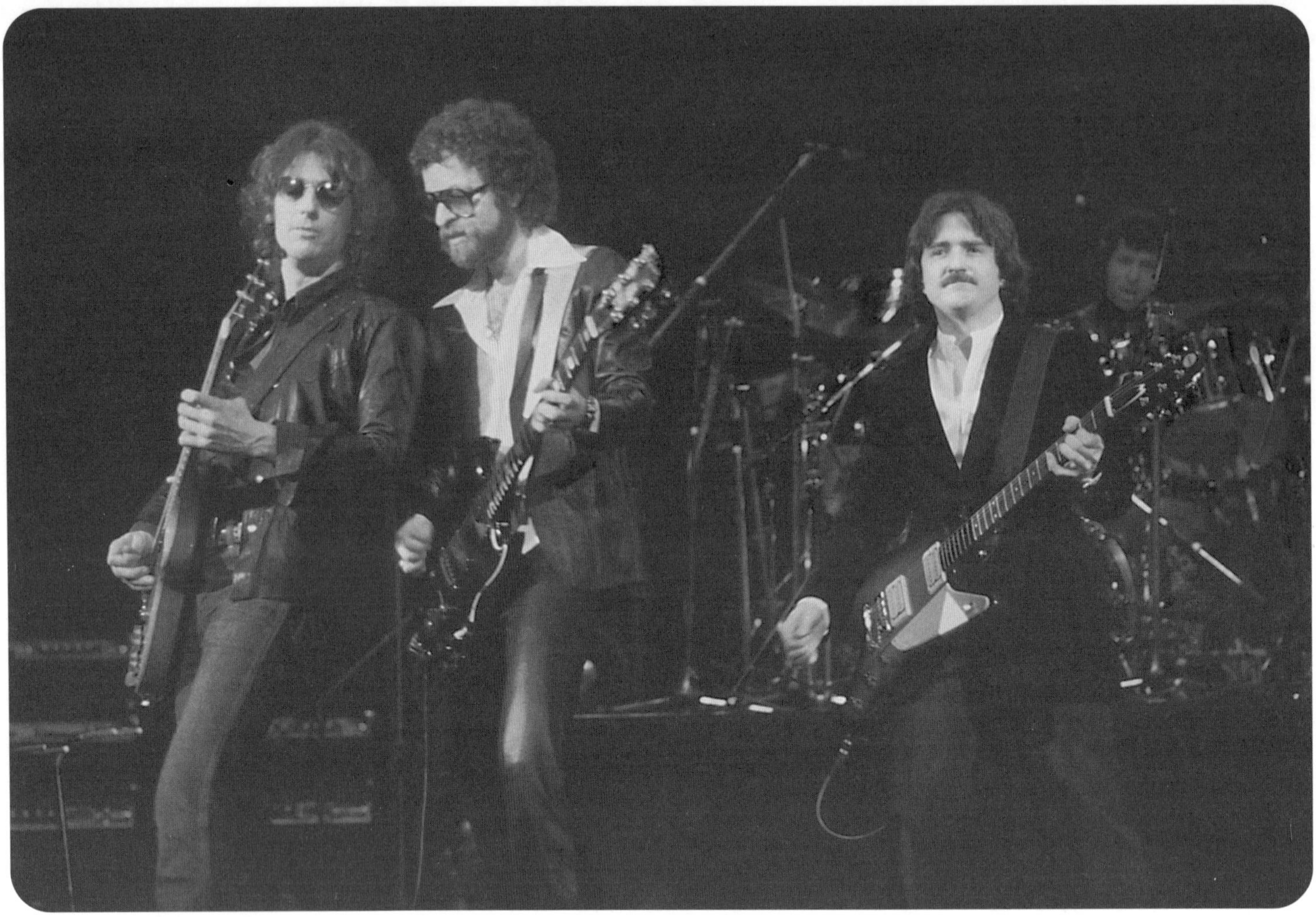

Photo by Chuck Pulin/STAR FILE

BLUE ÖYSTER CULT

Cult Classic

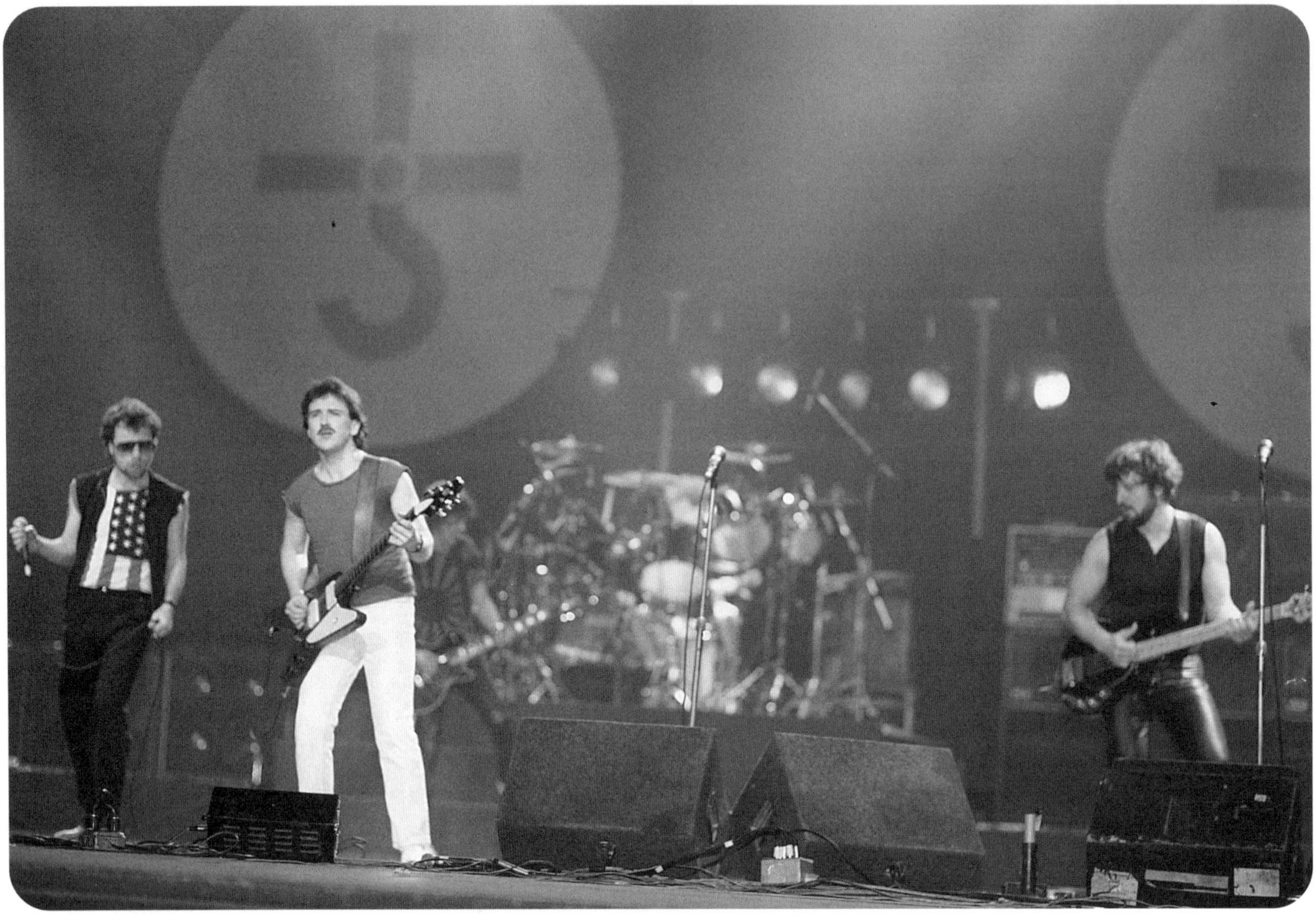

Photo by David Seelig/STAR FILE

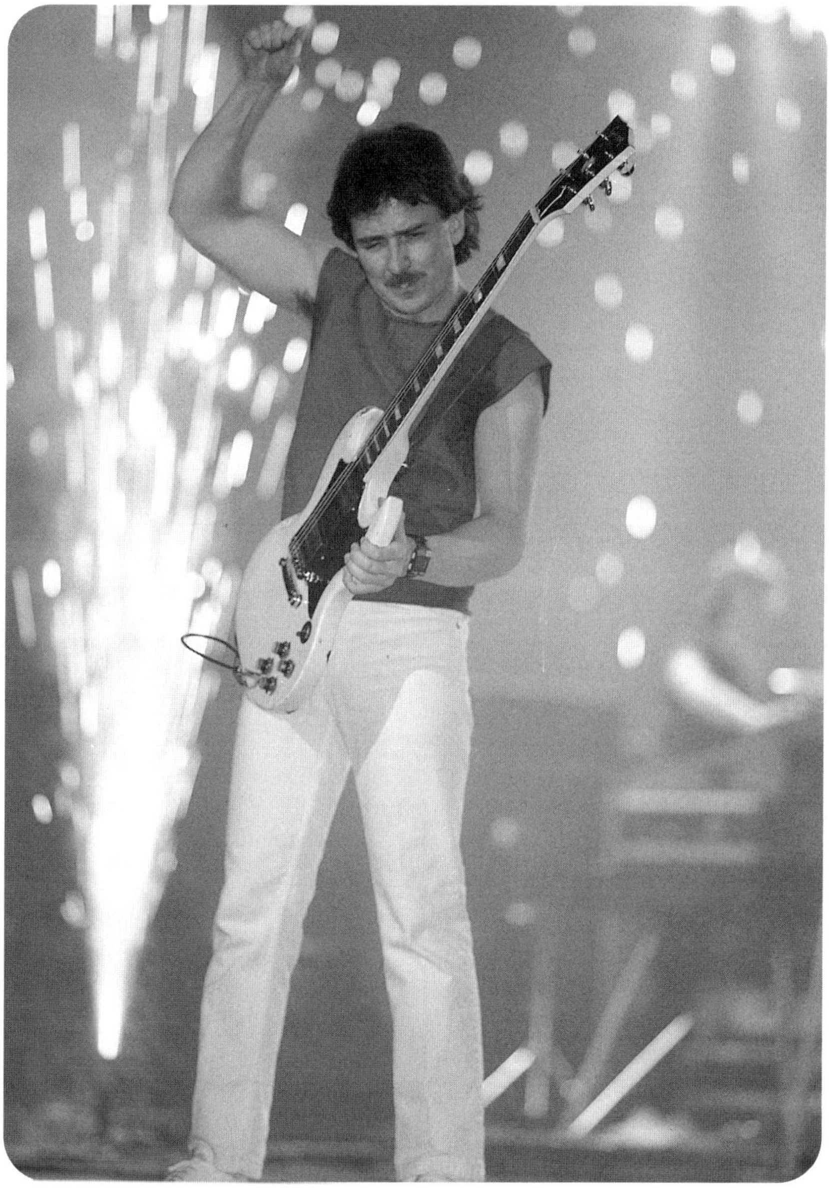
Photo by David Seelig/STAR FILE

Don't Fear The Reaper

Words and Music by Donald Roeser

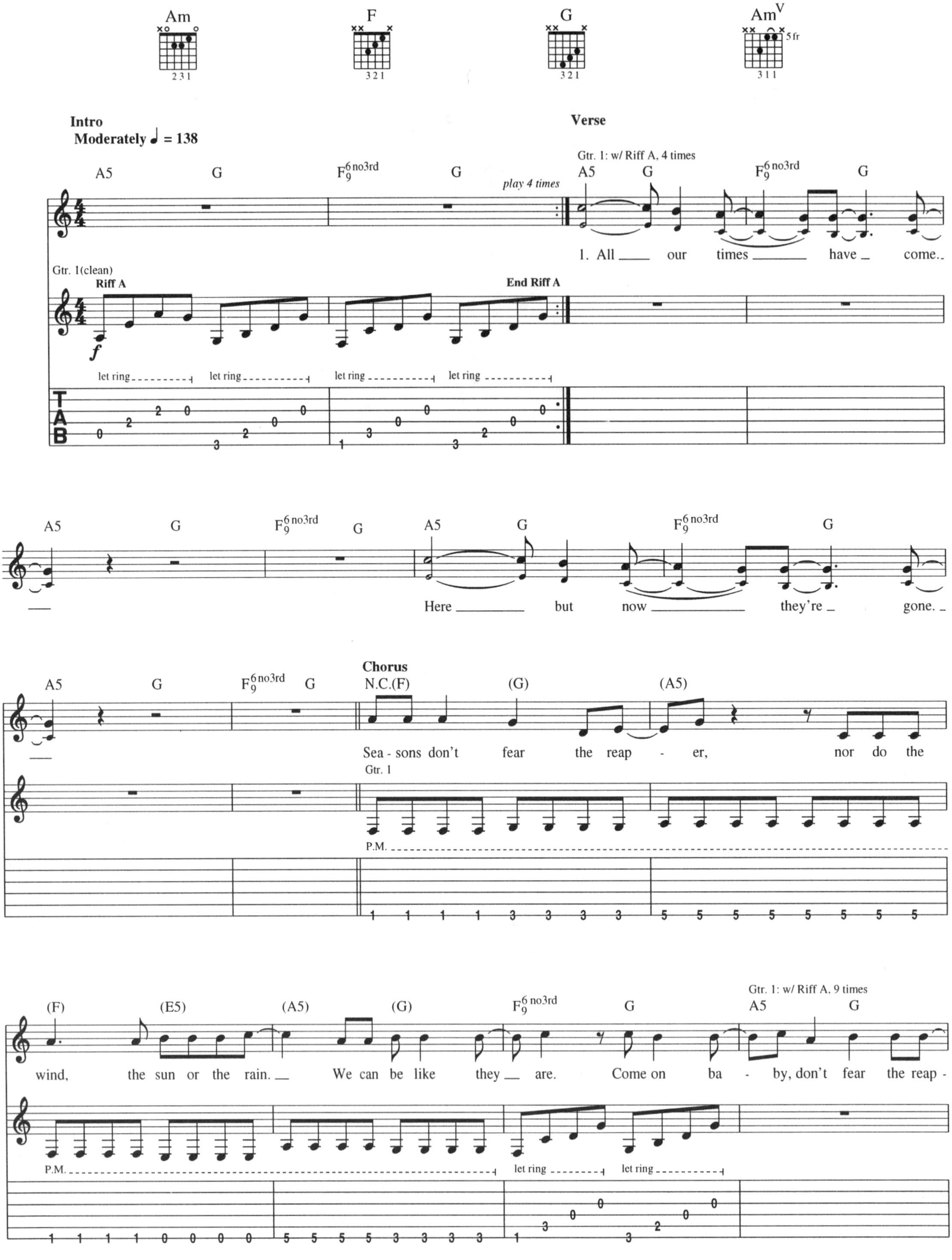

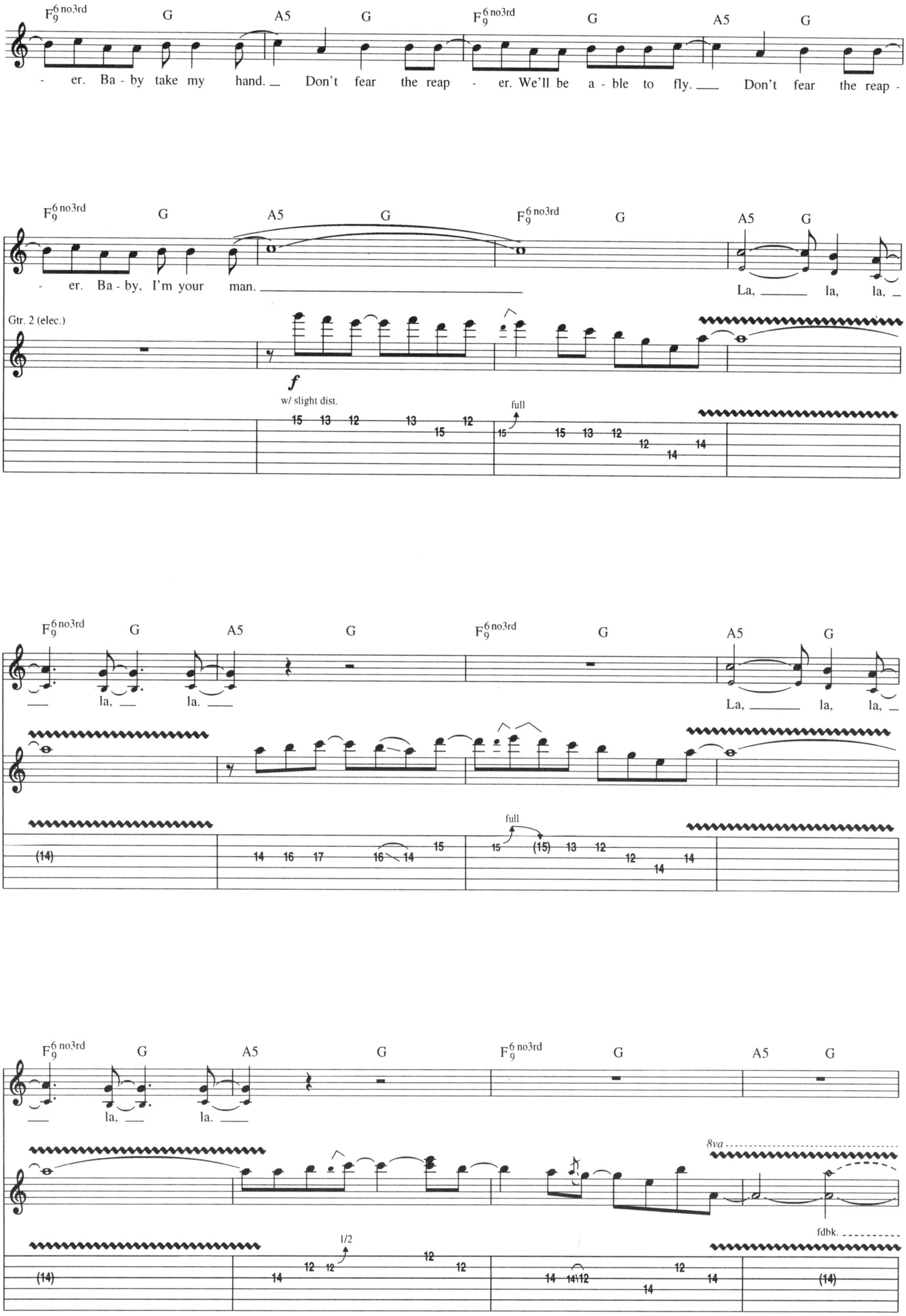
F6/9 no3rd G A5 G F6/9 no3rd G A5 G
- er. Ba - by take my hand. Don't fear the reap - er. We'll be a - ble to fly. Don't fear the reap -
F6/9 no3rd G A5 G F6/9 no3rd G A5 G
- er. Ba - by, I'm your man. La, la, la,
Gtr. 2 (elec.)
f
w/ slight dist.
full
F6/9 no3rd G A5 G F6/9 no3rd G A5 G
la, la. La, la, la,
full
F6/9 no3rd G A5 G F6/9 no3rd G A5 G
la, la.
8va
1/2
fdbk.

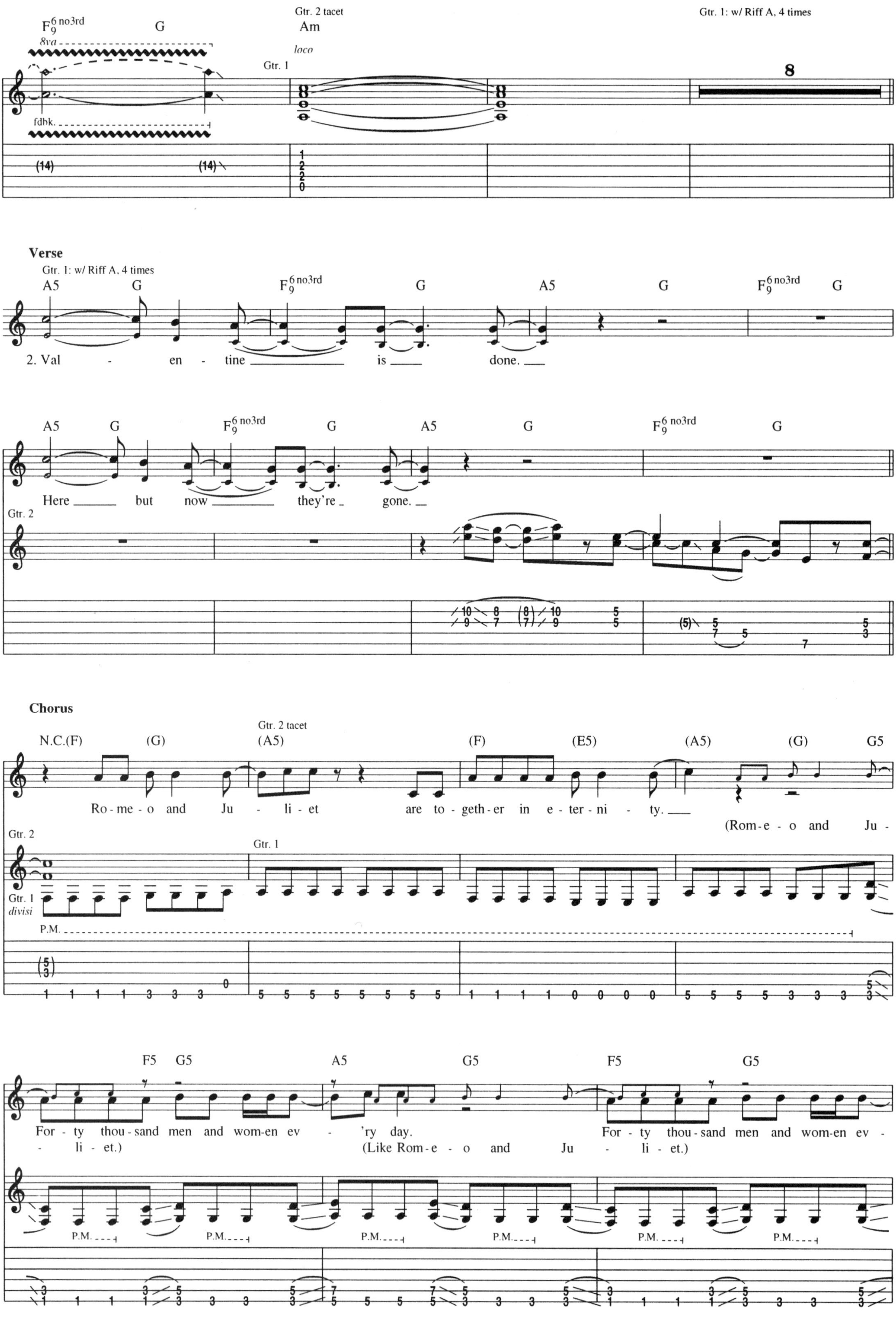
Gtr. 2 tacet
Gtr. 1: w/ Riff A, 4 times
8va
loco
Gtr. 1
fdbk.
Verse
Gtr. 1: w/ Riff A, 4 times
A5 G F6/9 no3rd G A5 G F6/9 no3rd G
2. Val - en - tine is done.
Here but now they're gone.
Gtr. 2
Chorus
N.C.(F) (G) (A5) (F) (E5) (A5) (G) G5
Gtr. 2 tacet
Ro-me-o and Ju - li-et are to-geth-er in e-ter-ni - ty.
(Rom-e - o and Ju -
Gtr. 1
divisi
P.M.
F5 G5 A5 G5 F5 G5
For - ty thou-sand men and wom-en ev - 'ry day.
- li - et.)
(Like Rom-e - o and Ju - li - et.)
For - ty thou-sand men and wom-en ev -

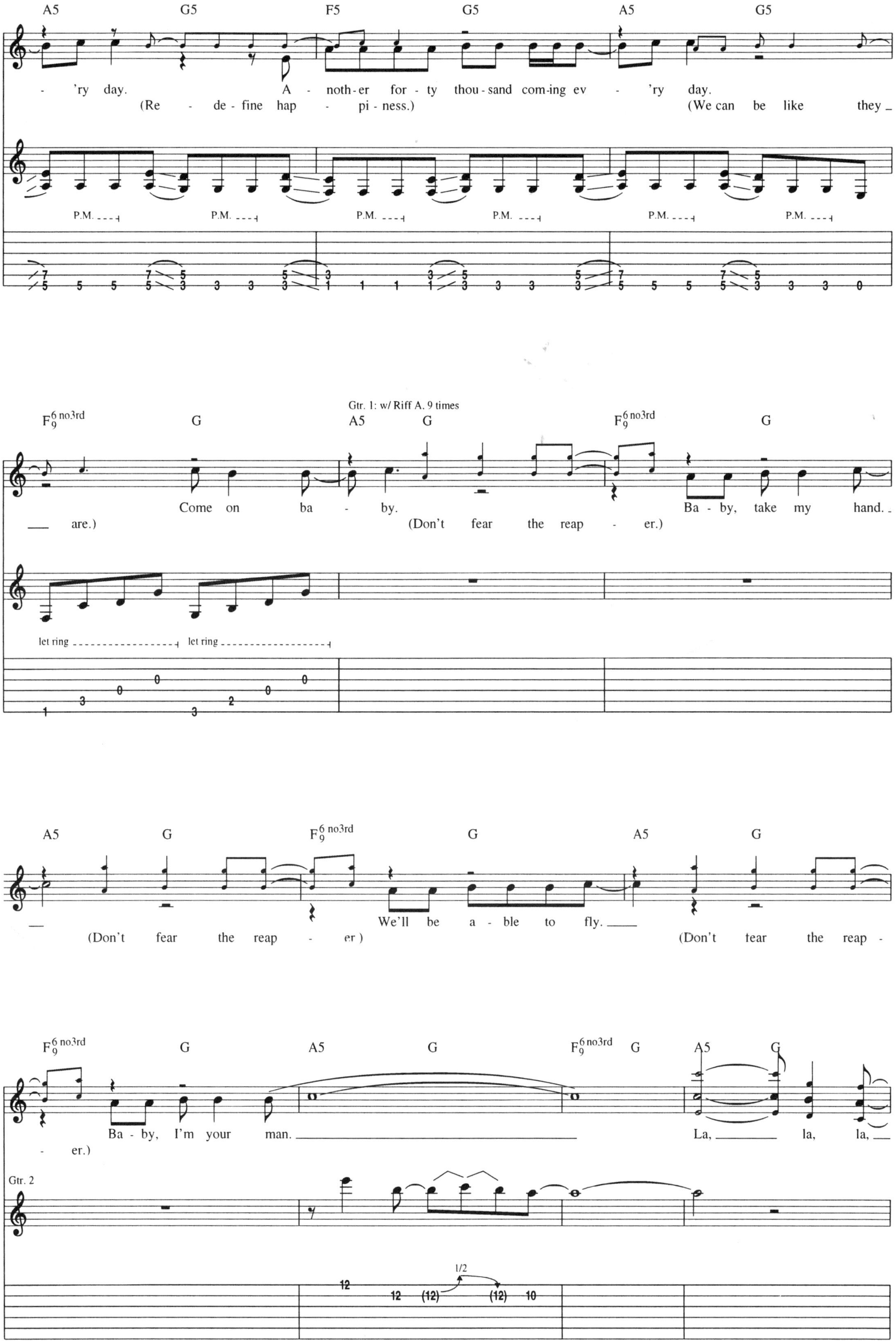
A5 G5 F5 G5 A5 G5
-'ry day. A - noth-er for - ty thou-sand com-ing ev - 'ry day.
(Re - de-fine hap - pi - ness.) (We can be like they
P.M.
F6 no3rd 9 G A5 G F6 no3rd 9 G
Gtr. 1: w/ Riff A, 9 times
Come on ba - by. Ba - by, take my hand.
are.) (Don't fear the reap - er.)
let ring
A5 G F6 no3rd 9 G A5 G
We'll be a - ble to fly.
(Don't fear the reap - er.) (Don't fear the reap -
F6 no3rd 9 G A5 G F6 no3rd 9 G A5 G
Ba - by, I'm your man. La, la, la,
- er.)
Gtr. 2
1/2

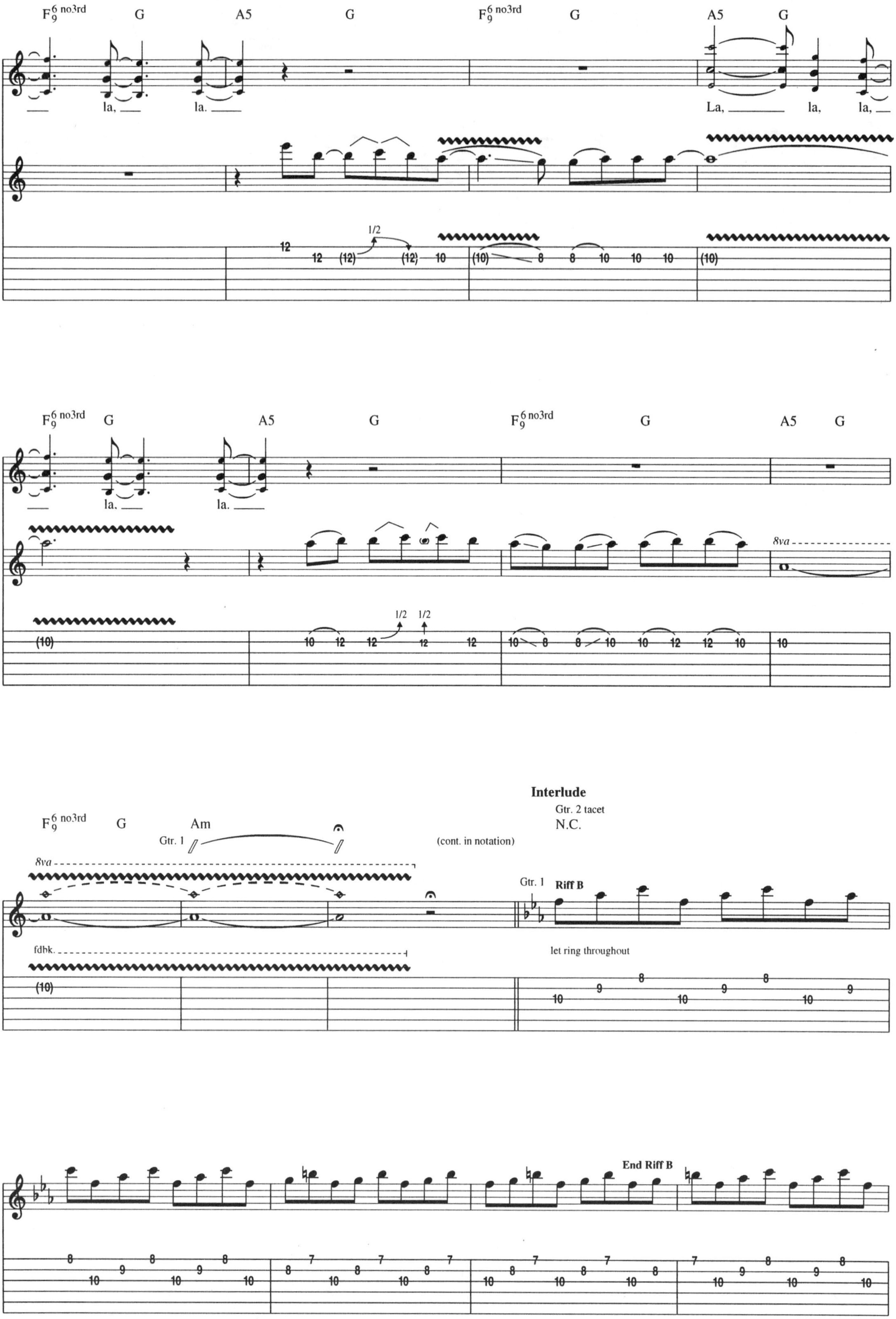
F6/9 no3rd G A5 G F6/9 no3rd G A5 G
la, la. La, la, la,
1/2
F6/9 no3rd G A5 G F6/9 no3rd G A5 G
la. la.
1/2 1/2
8va
F6/9 no3rd G Am
Gtr. 1
(cont. in notation)
Interlude
Gtr. 2 tacet
N.C.
fdbk.
Riff B
let ring throughout
End Riff B

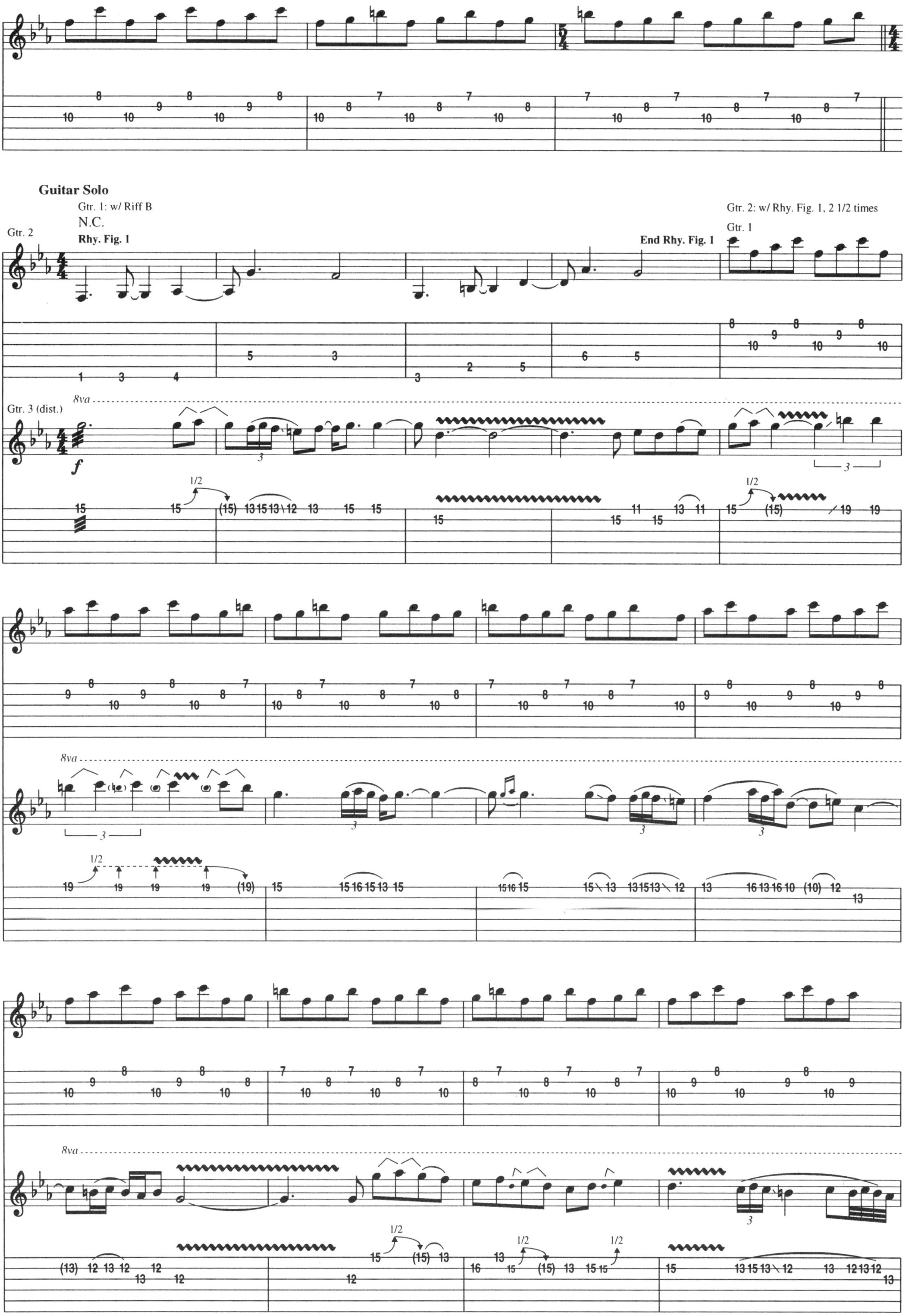
Guitar Solo
Gtr. 1: w/ Riff B
N.C.
Gtr. 2
Rhy. Fig. 1
End Rhy. Fig. 1
Gtr. 2: w/ Rhy. Fig. 1, 2 1/2 times
Gtr. 1
Gtr. 3 (dist.)
8va

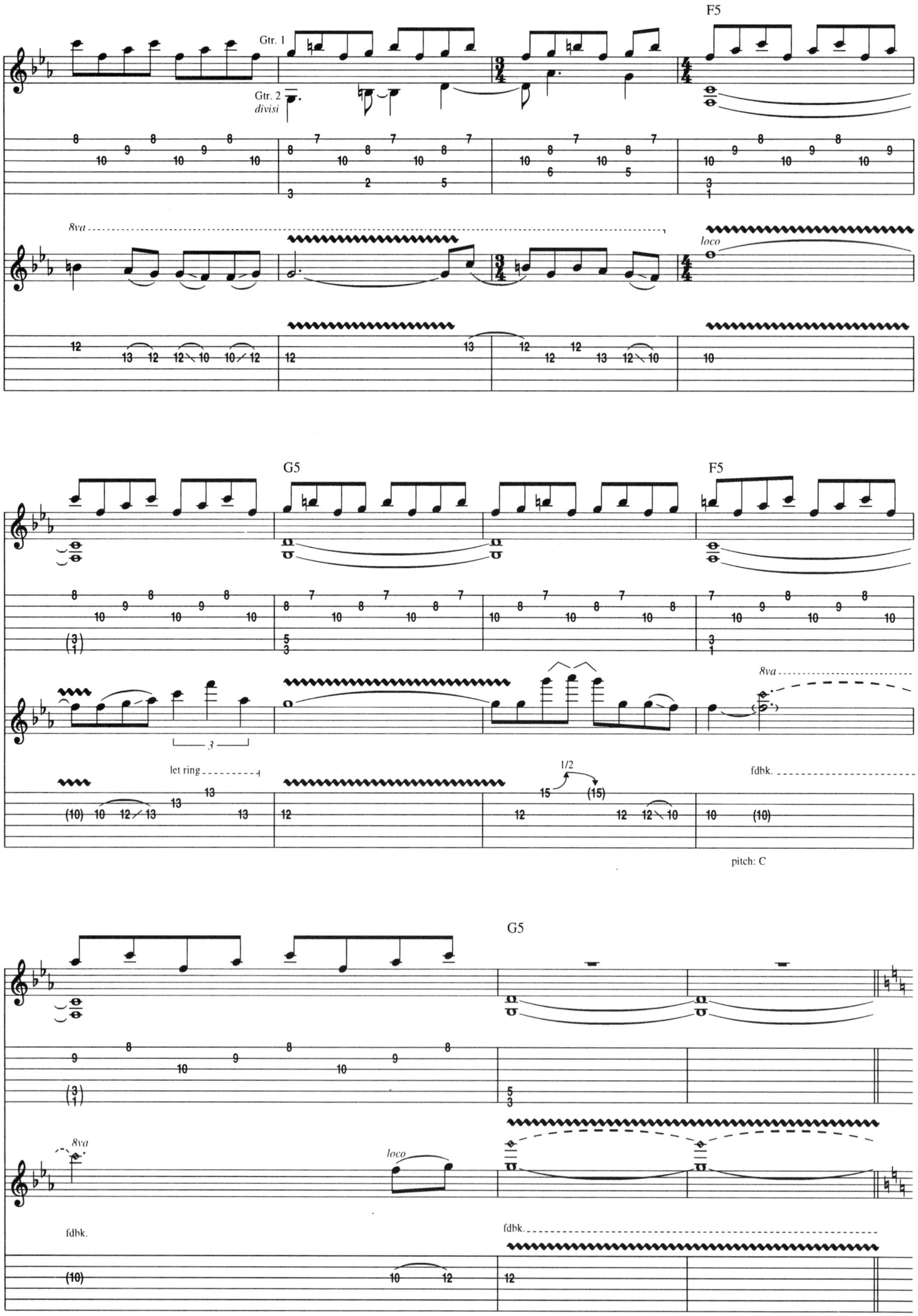
F5
Gtr. 1
Gtr. 2
divisi
8va
loco
G5
F5
let ring
1/2
8va
fdbk.
pitch: C
G5
8va
loco
fdbk.
fdbk.

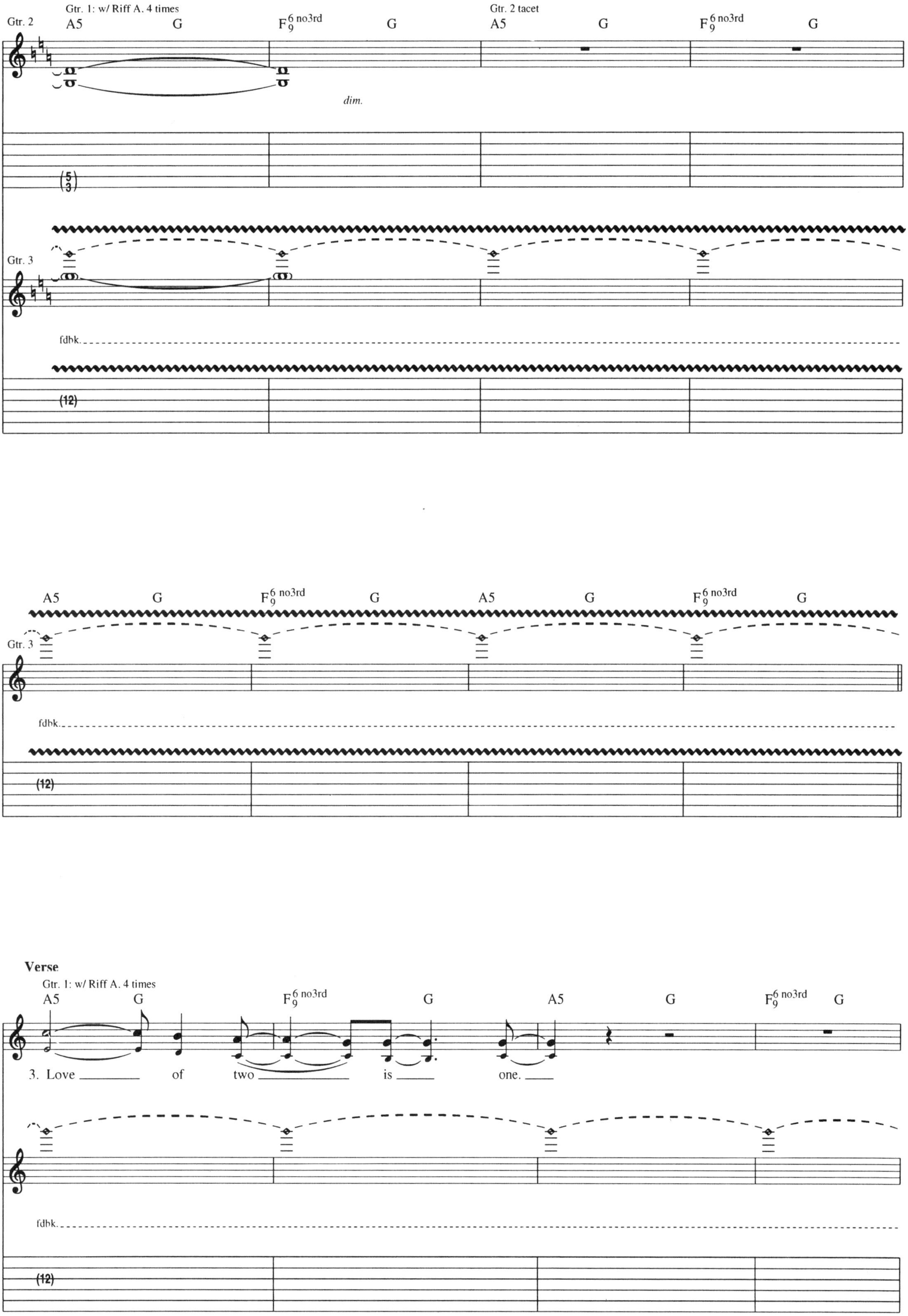
Gtr. 1: w/ Riff A, 4 times
Gtr. 2
A5 G F6/9 no3rd G
Gtr. 2 tacet
A5 G F6/9 no3rd G
dim.
(5)
(3)
Gtr. 3
fdbk.
(12)
A5 G F6/9 no3rd G A5 G F6/9 no3rd G
Gtr. 3
fdbk.
(12)
Verse
Gtr. 1: w/ Riff A, 4 times
A5 G F6/9 no3rd G A5 G F6/9 no3rd G
3. Love of two is one.
fdbk.
(12)

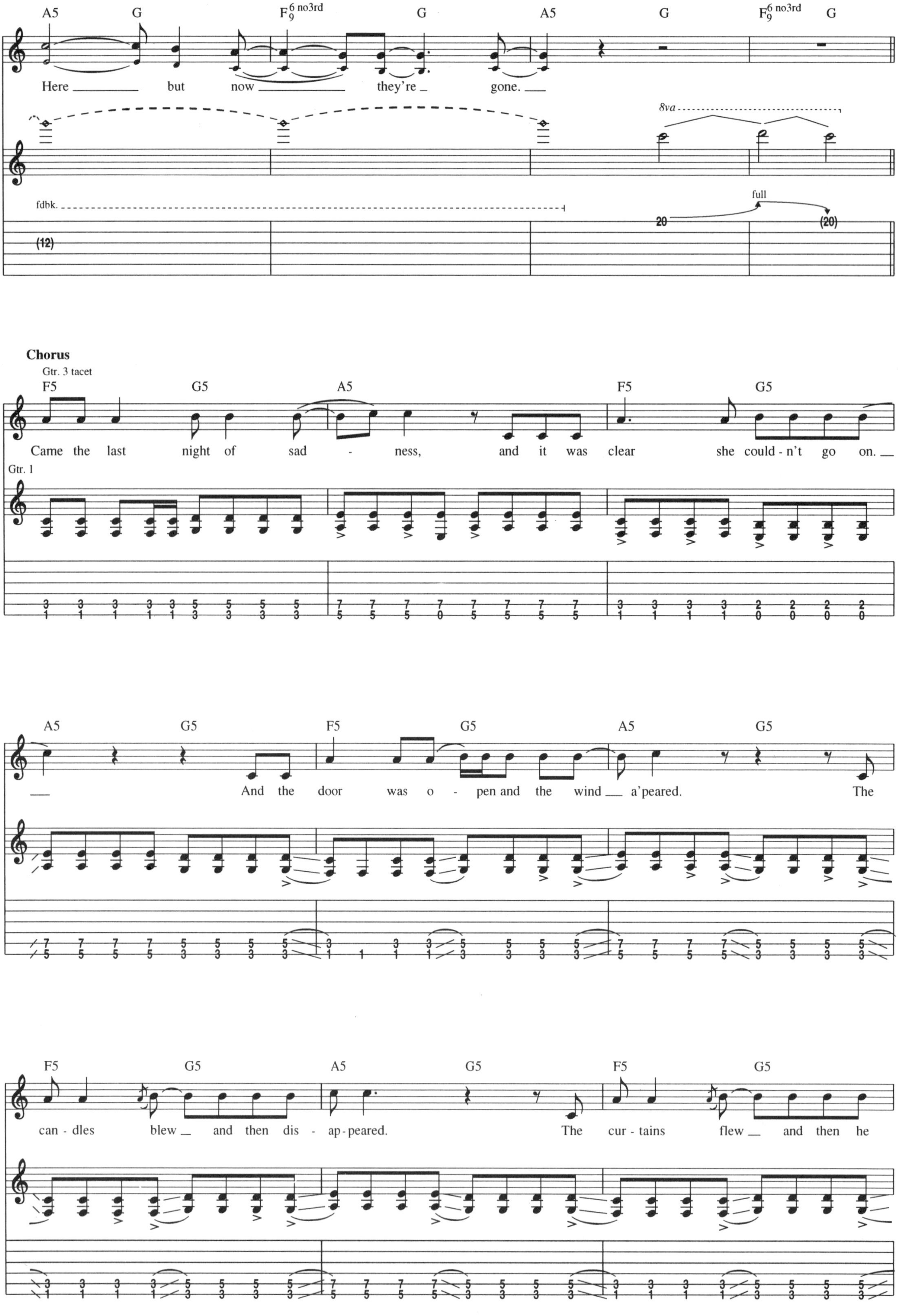
A5 G F6/9 no3rd G A5 G F6/9 no3rd G
Here but now they're gone.
8va
fdbk.
full
Chorus
Gtr. 3 tacet
F5 G5 A5 F5 G5
Came the last night of sad - ness, and it was clear she could - n't go on.
Gtr. 1
A5 G5 F5 G5 A5 G5
And the door was o - pen and the wind a'peared. The
F5 G5 A5 G5 F5 G5
can - dles blew and then dis - ap - peared. The cur - tains flew and then he

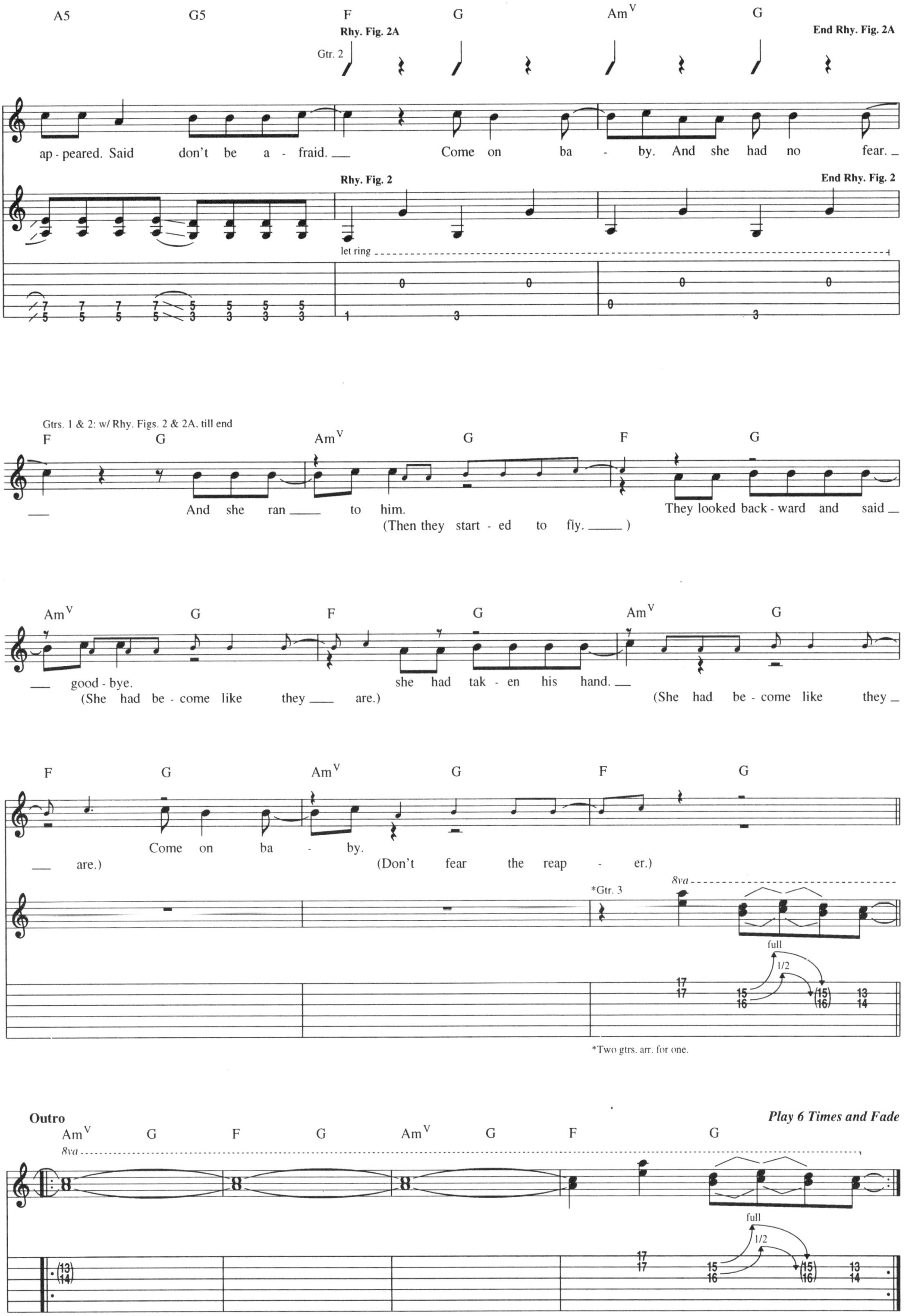
A5 G5 F G Am V G
Rhy. Fig. 2A
Gtr. 2
End Rhy. Fig. 2A
ap - peared. Said don't be a - fraid. Come on ba - by. And she had no fear.
Rhy. Fig. 2
End Rhy. Fig. 2
let ring
Gtrs. 1 & 2: w/ Rhy. Figs. 2 & 2A, till end
F G Am V G F G
And she ran to him. They looked back - ward and said
(Then they start - ed to fly.)
Am V G F G Am V G
good - bye. she had tak - en his hand.
(She had be - come like they are.) (She had be - come like they
F G Am V G F G
Come on ba - by.
are.) (Don't fear the reap - er.)
*Gtr. 3
8va
full
1/2
*Two gtrs. arr. for one.
Outro
Am V G F G Am V G F G
Play 6 Times and Fade
8va
full
1/2

Extraterrestrial Intelligence

Words and Music by Samuel Pearlman and Donald Roeser

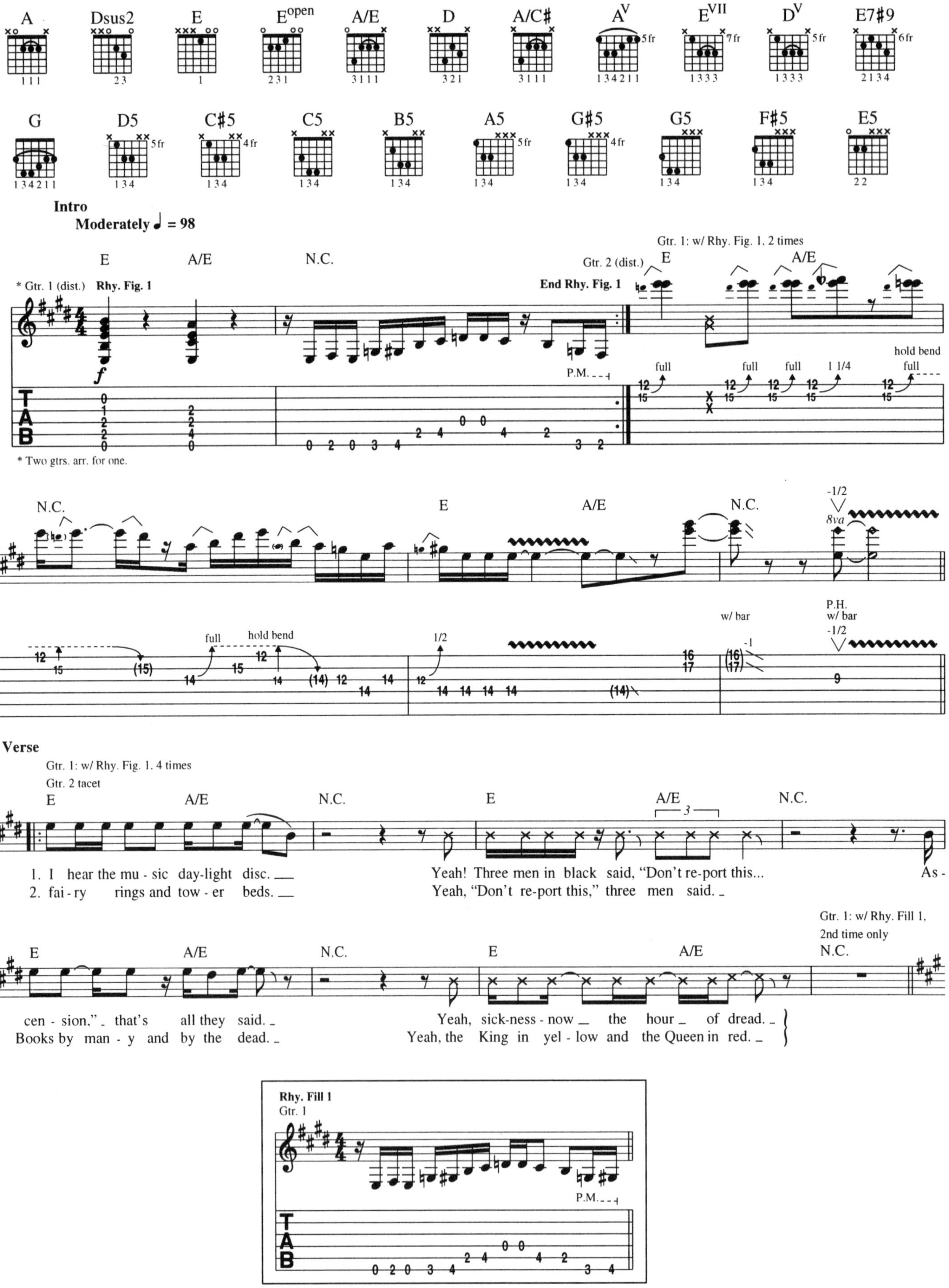

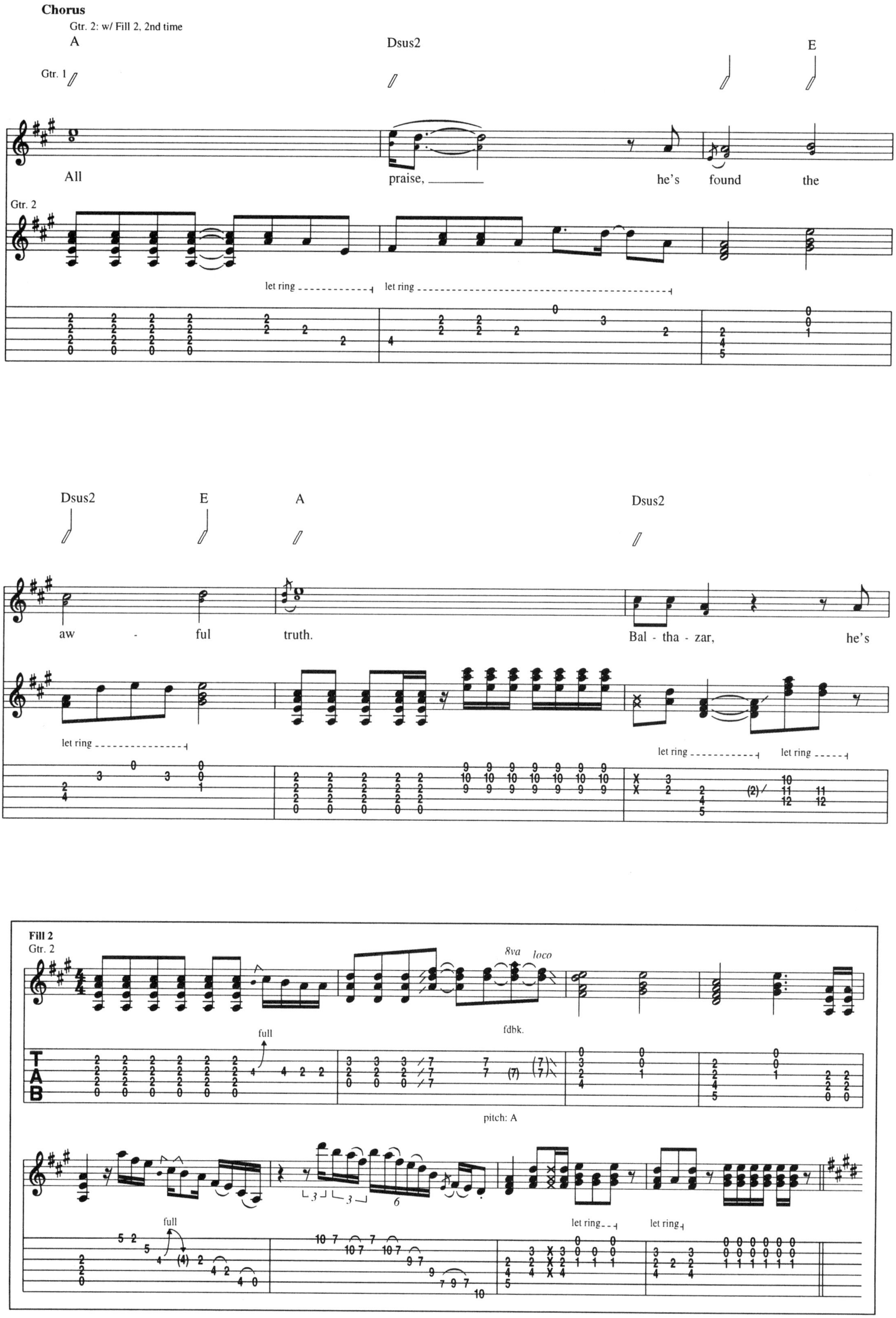
Chorus
Gtr. 2: w/ Fill 2, 2nd time
A
Dsus2
E
Gtr. 1
All praise, he's found the
Gtr. 2
let ring
let ring
Dsus2
E
A
Dsus2
aw - ful truth.
Bal - tha - zar, he's
let ring
let ring
let ring
Fill 2
Gtr. 2
8va
loco
full
fdbk.
pitch: A
full
let ring
let ring

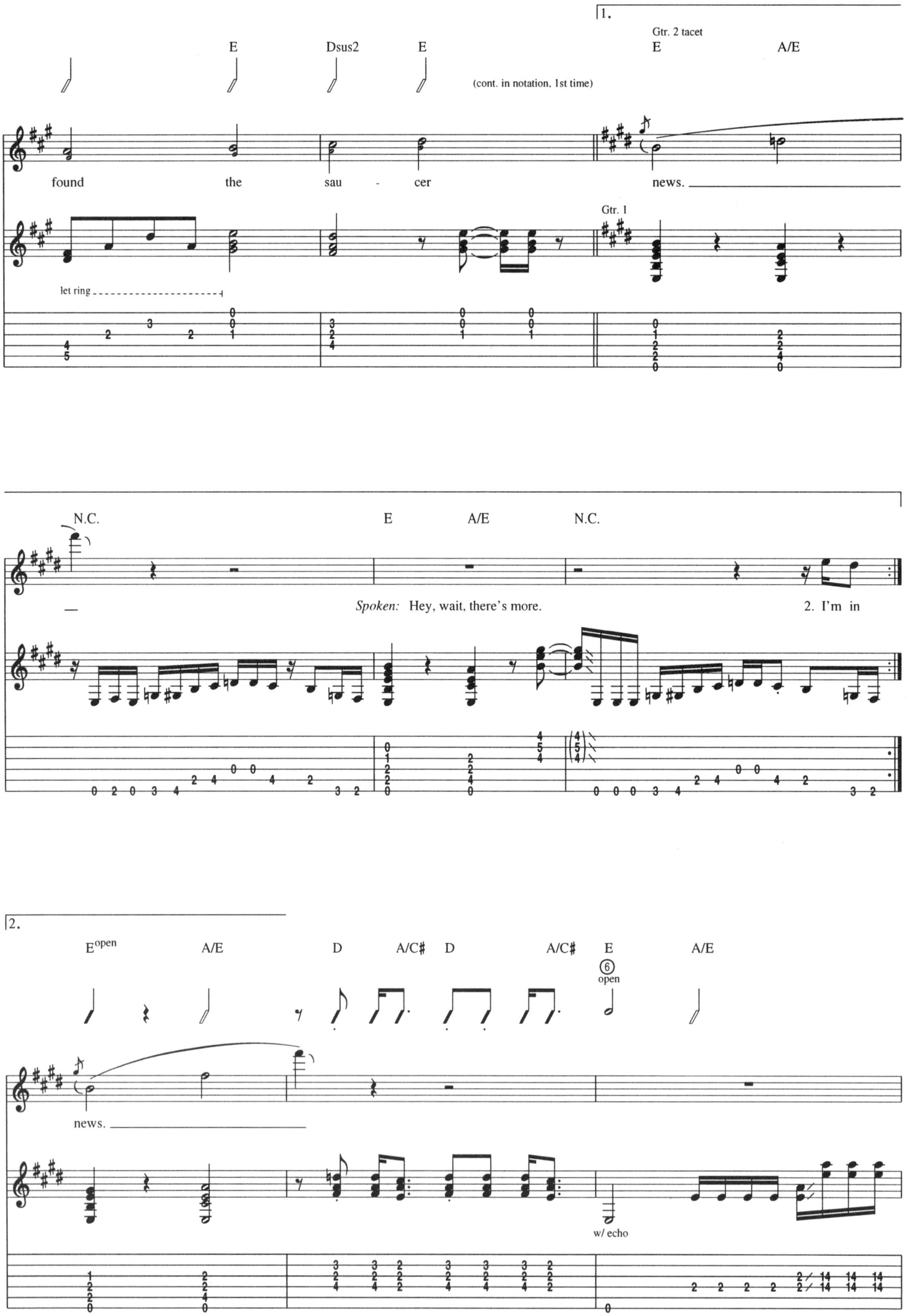
1.
Gtr. 2 tacet
E
Dsus2
E
E
A/E
(cont. in notation, 1st time)
found the sau - cer news.
Gtr. 1
let ring
N.C.
E
A/E
N.C.
Spoken: Hey, wait, there's more.
2. I'm in
2.
E open
A/E
D
A/C#
D
A/C#
E
6 open
A/E
news.
w/ echo

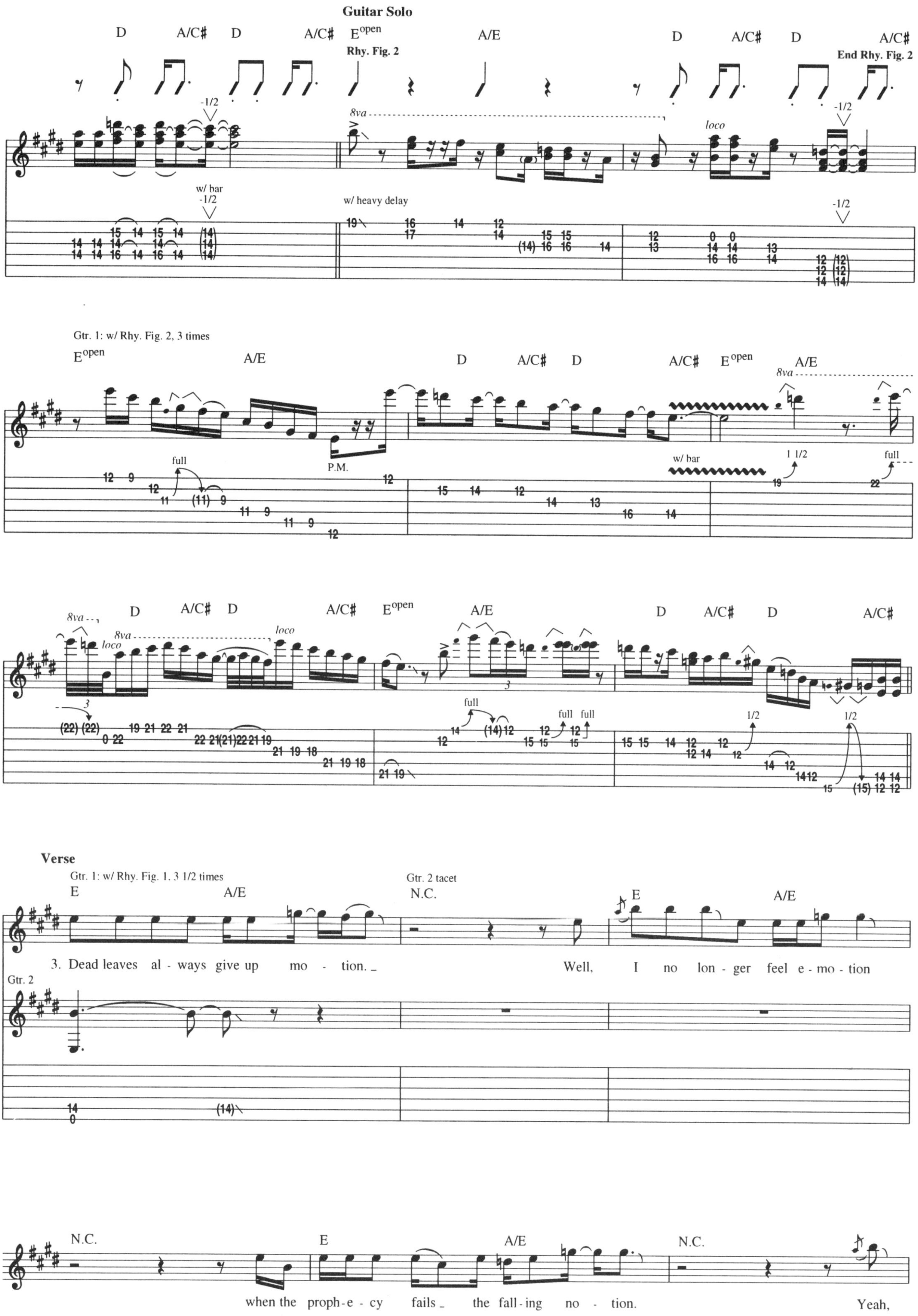
Guitar Solo
Rhy. Fig. 2
End Rhy. Fig. 2
8va
loco
w/ bar
w/ heavy delay
Gtr. 1: w/ Rhy. Fig. 2, 3 times
P.M.
full
1 1/2
Verse
Gtr. 1: w/ Rhy. Fig. 1, 3 1/2 times
Gtr. 2 tacet
N.C.
3. Dead leaves al - ways give up mo - tion. _ Well, I no lon - ger feel e - mo - tion
Gtr. 2
when the proph - e - cy fails _ the fall - ing no - tion. Yeah,

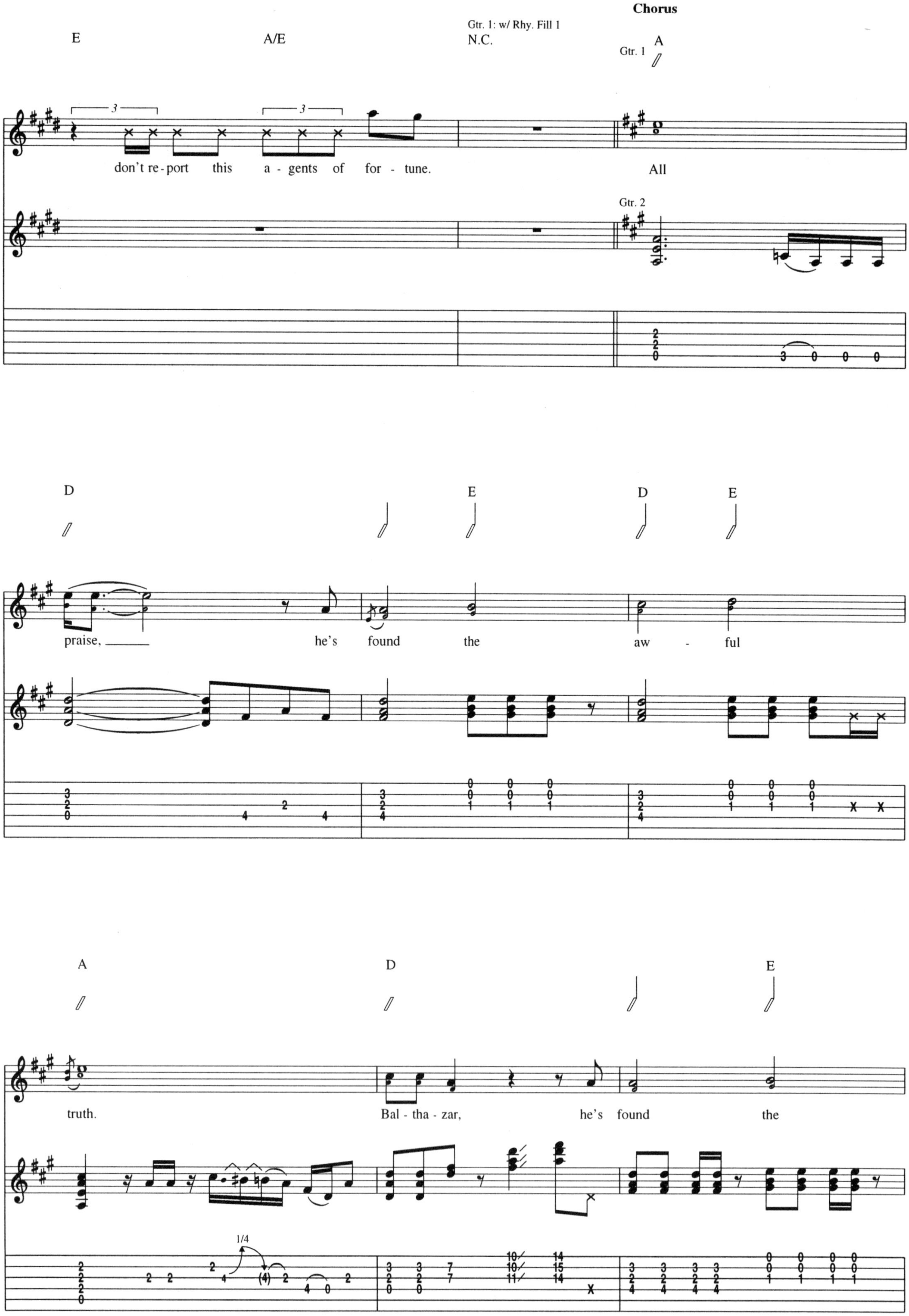
Chorus
Gtr. 1: w/ Rhy. Fill 1
E A/E N.C. A
Gtr. 1
don't re-port this a-gents of for-tune. All
Gtr. 2
D E D E
praise, he's found the aw - ful
A D E
truth. Bal - tha - zar, he's found the
1/4

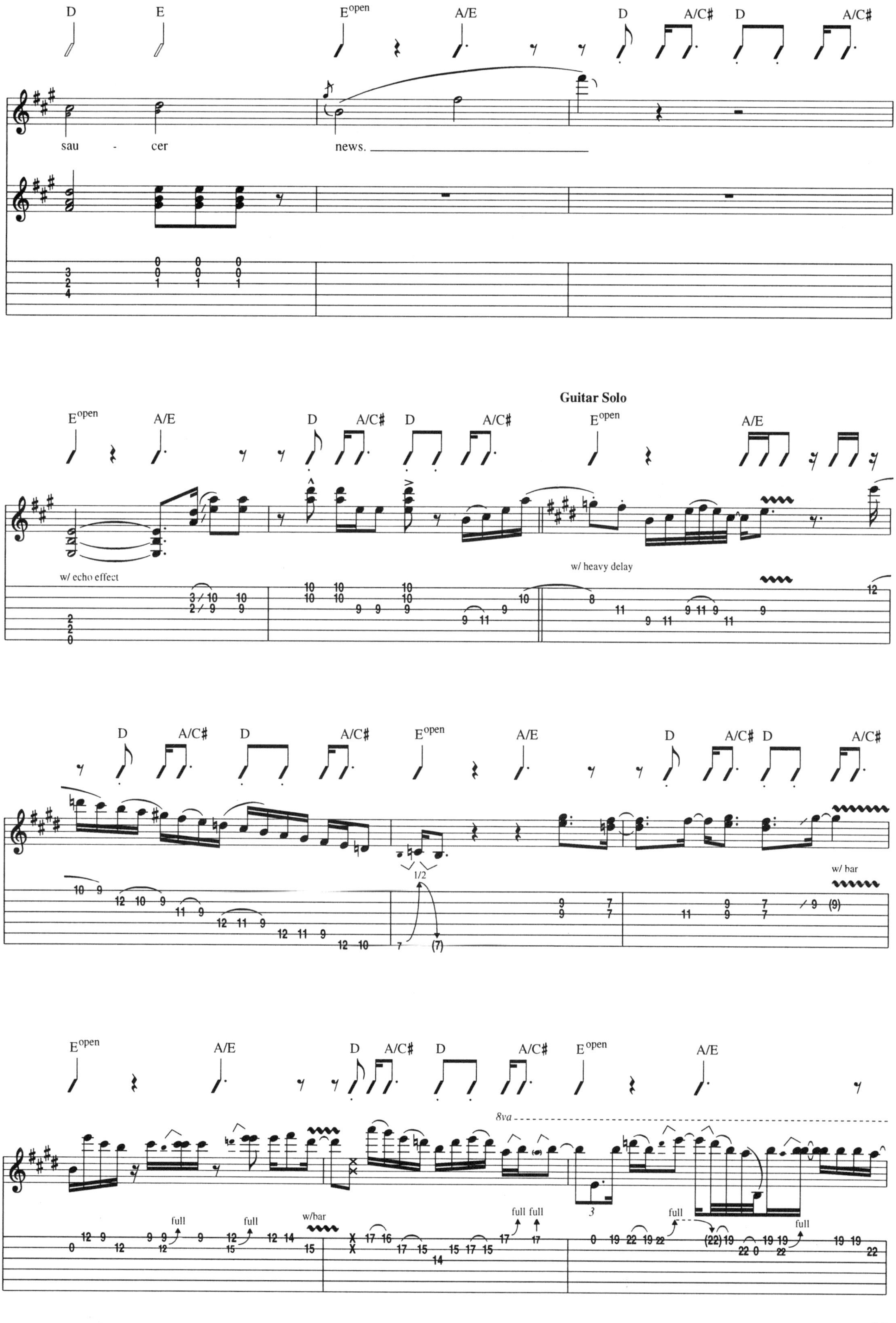
D E Eopen A/E D A/C♯ D A/C♯
sau - cer news.
Guitar Solo
Eopen A/E D A/C♯ D A/C♯ Eopen A/E
w/ echo effect
w/ heavy delay
D A/C♯ D A/C♯ Eopen A/E D A/C♯ D A/C♯
1/2
w/ bar
Eopen A/E D A/C♯ D A/C♯ Eopen A/E
8va
full
w/bar
3

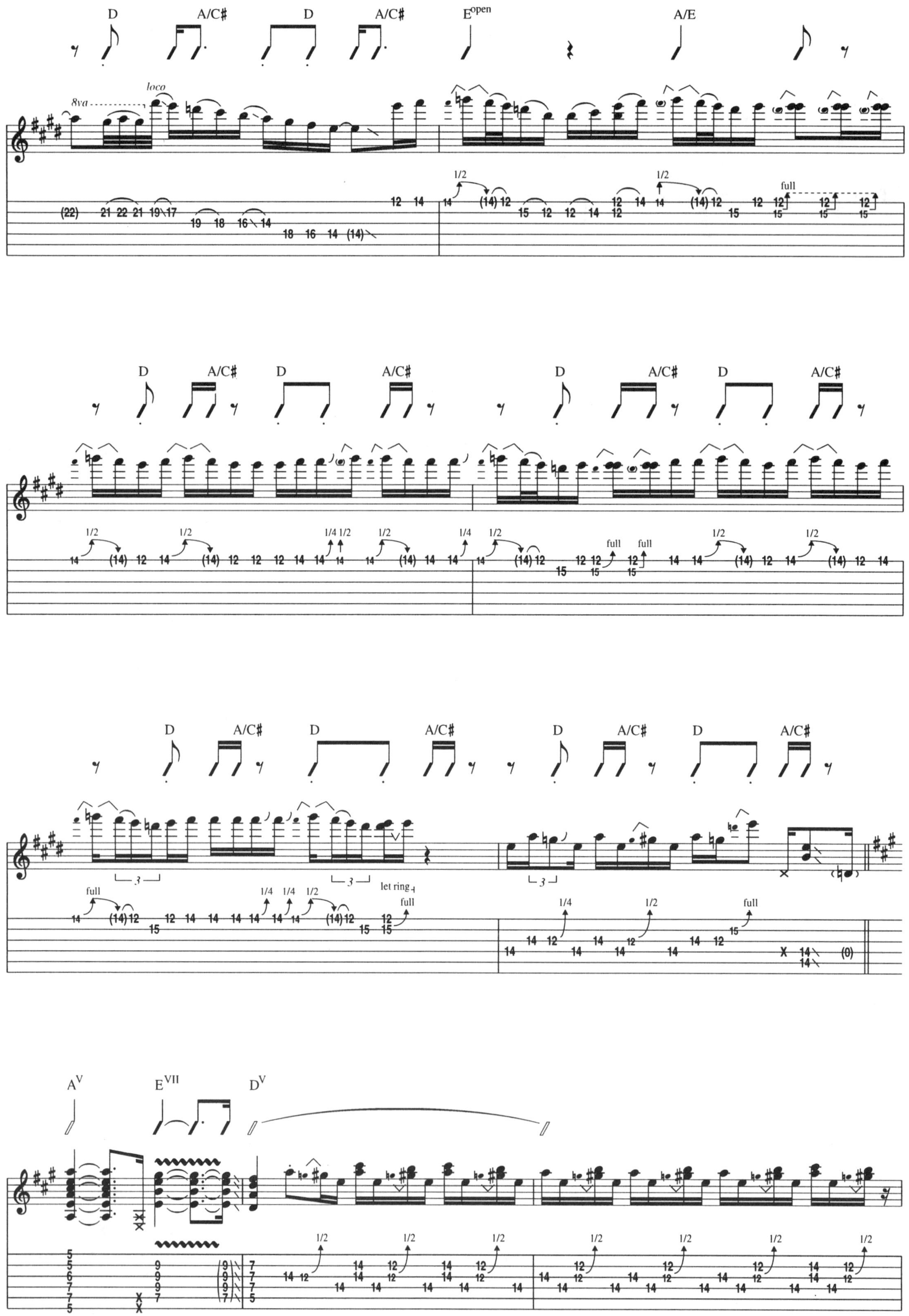
D A/C# D A/C# E open A/E
8va
loco
D A/C# D A/C# D A/C# D A/C#
D A/C# D A/C# D A/C# D A/C#
let ring
A V E VII D V

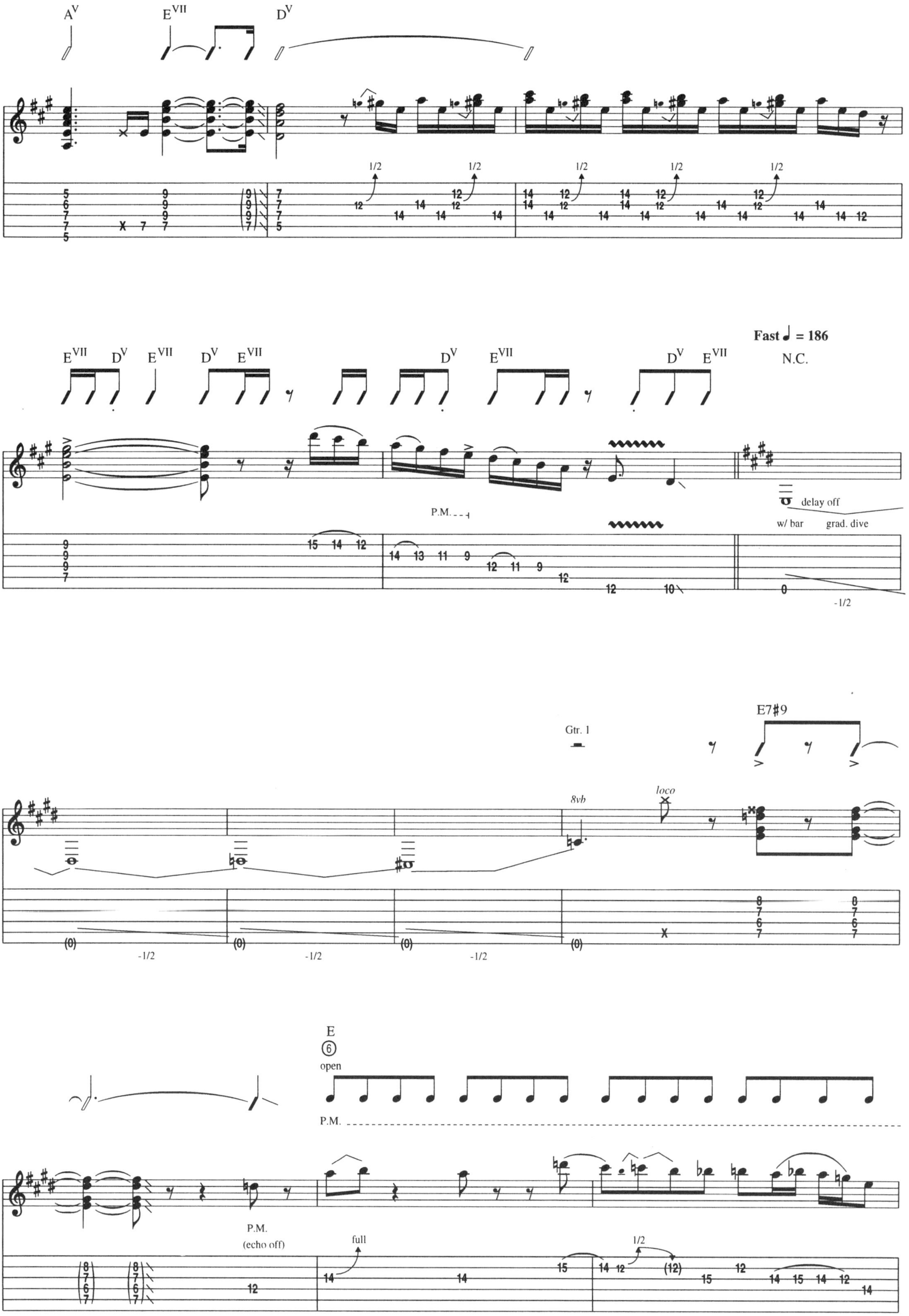
A V
E VII
D V
1/2
Fast ♩ = 186
N.C.
P.M.
delay off
w/ bar
grad. dive
-1/2
Gtr. 1
E7#9
8vb
loco
E
open
(echo off)
full

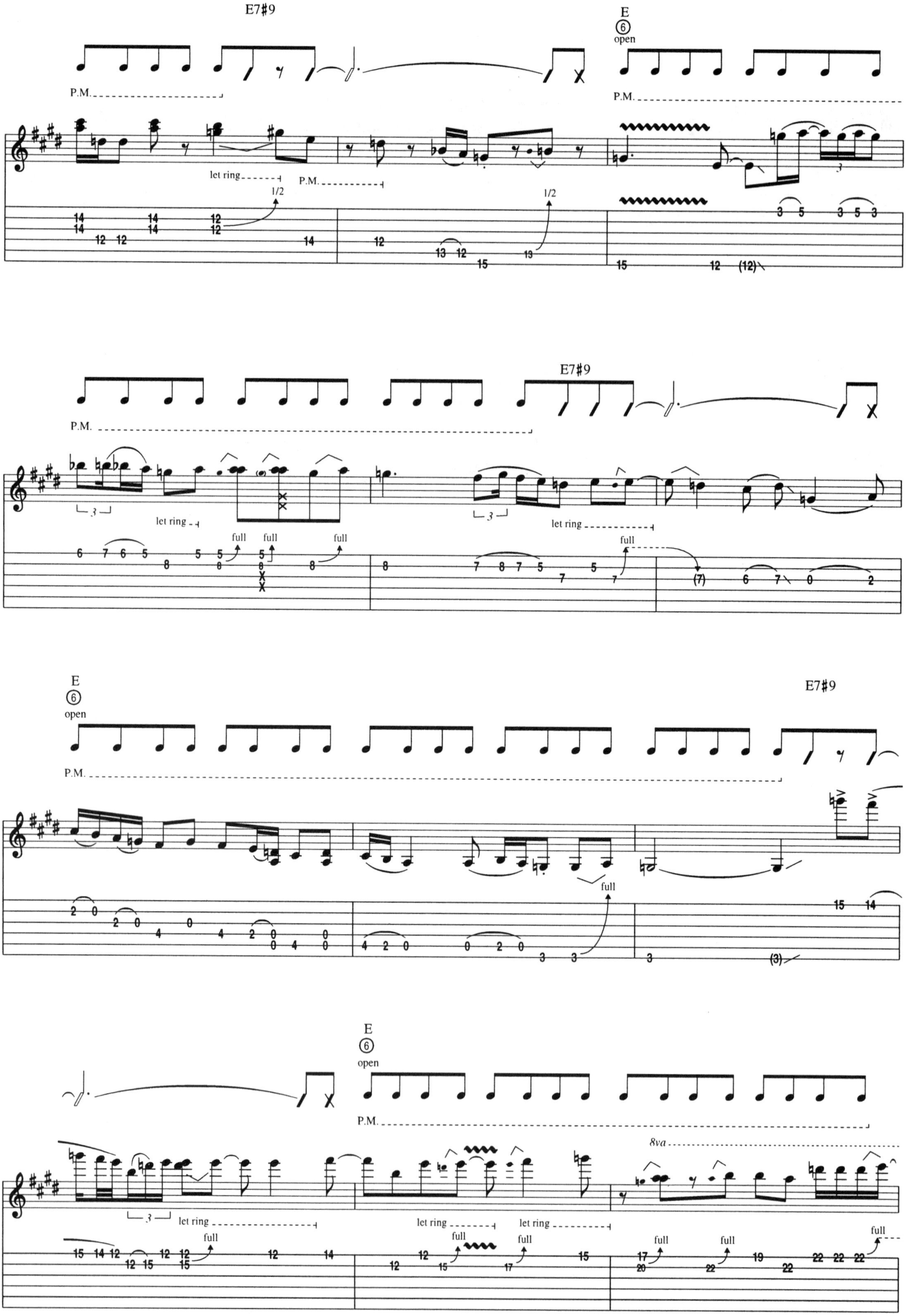

E7#9
E
6
open
P.M.
let ring
1/2
full
8va

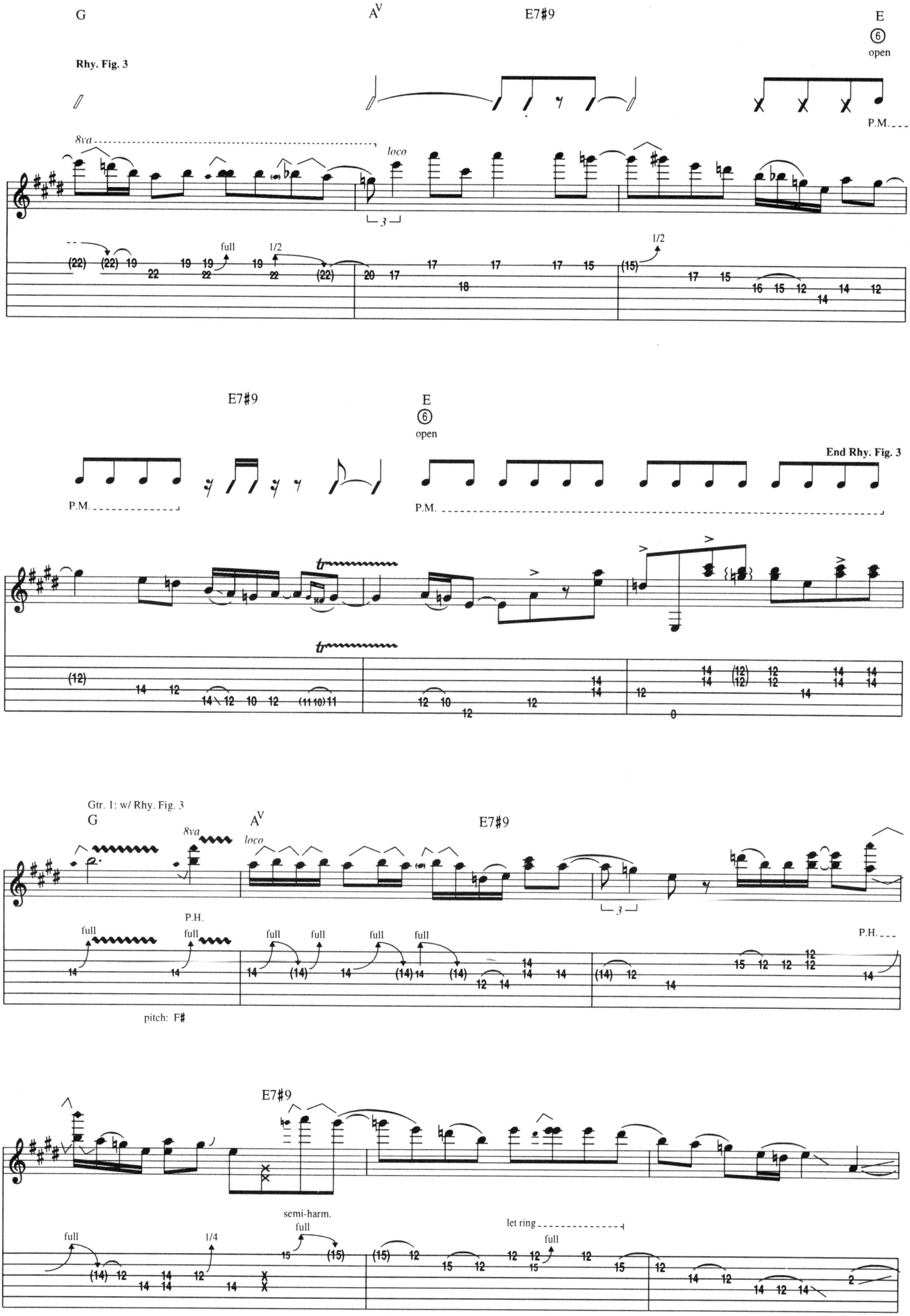
G
A^V
E7#9
E
⑥ open
Rhy. Fig. 3
P.M.
8va
loco
full
1/2
E7#9
E
⑥ open
End Rhy. Fig. 3
P.M.
tr
Gtr. 1: w/ Rhy. Fig. 3
G
8va
A^V
loco
E7#9
P.H.
full
pitch: F#
E7#9
semi-harm.
full
1/4
let ring

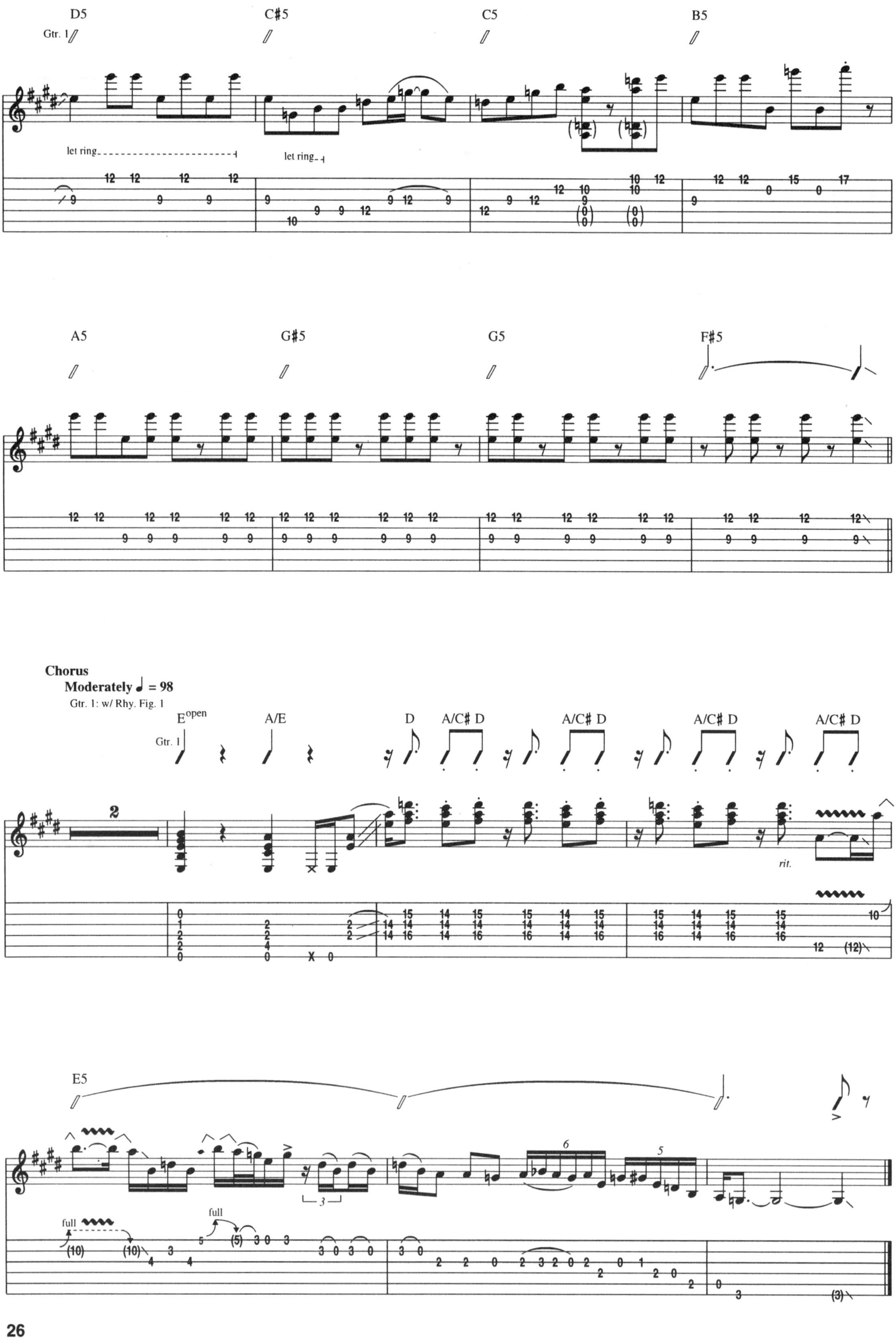
D5
C#5
C5
B5
Gtr. 1
let ring
A5
G#5
G5
F#5
Chorus
Moderately ♩ = 98
Gtr. 1: w/ Rhy. Fig. 1
E^open
A/E
D
A/C# D
rit.
E5
full

M.E. 262

Words and Music by Samuel Pearlman, Donald Roeser and Eric Bloom

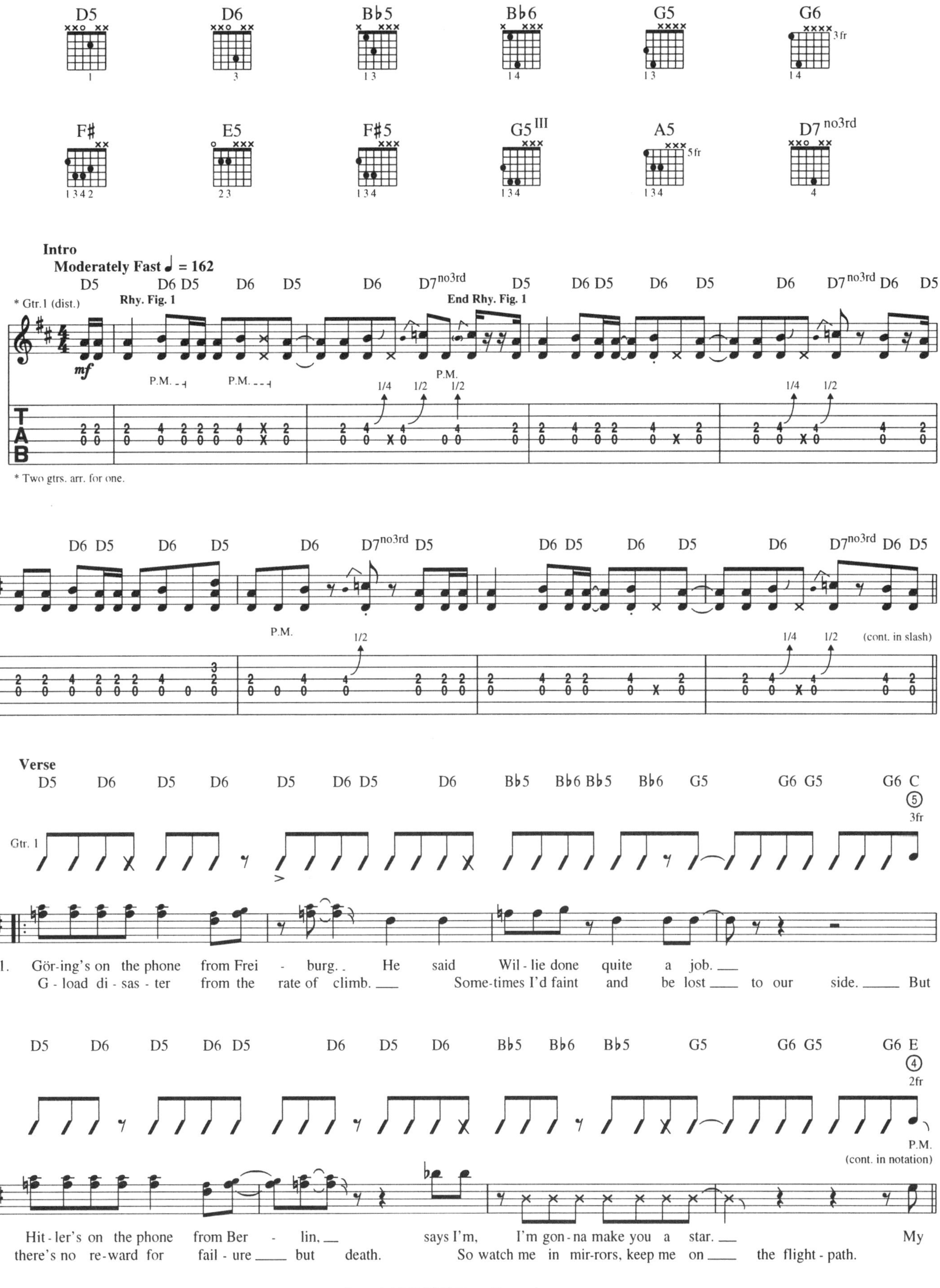

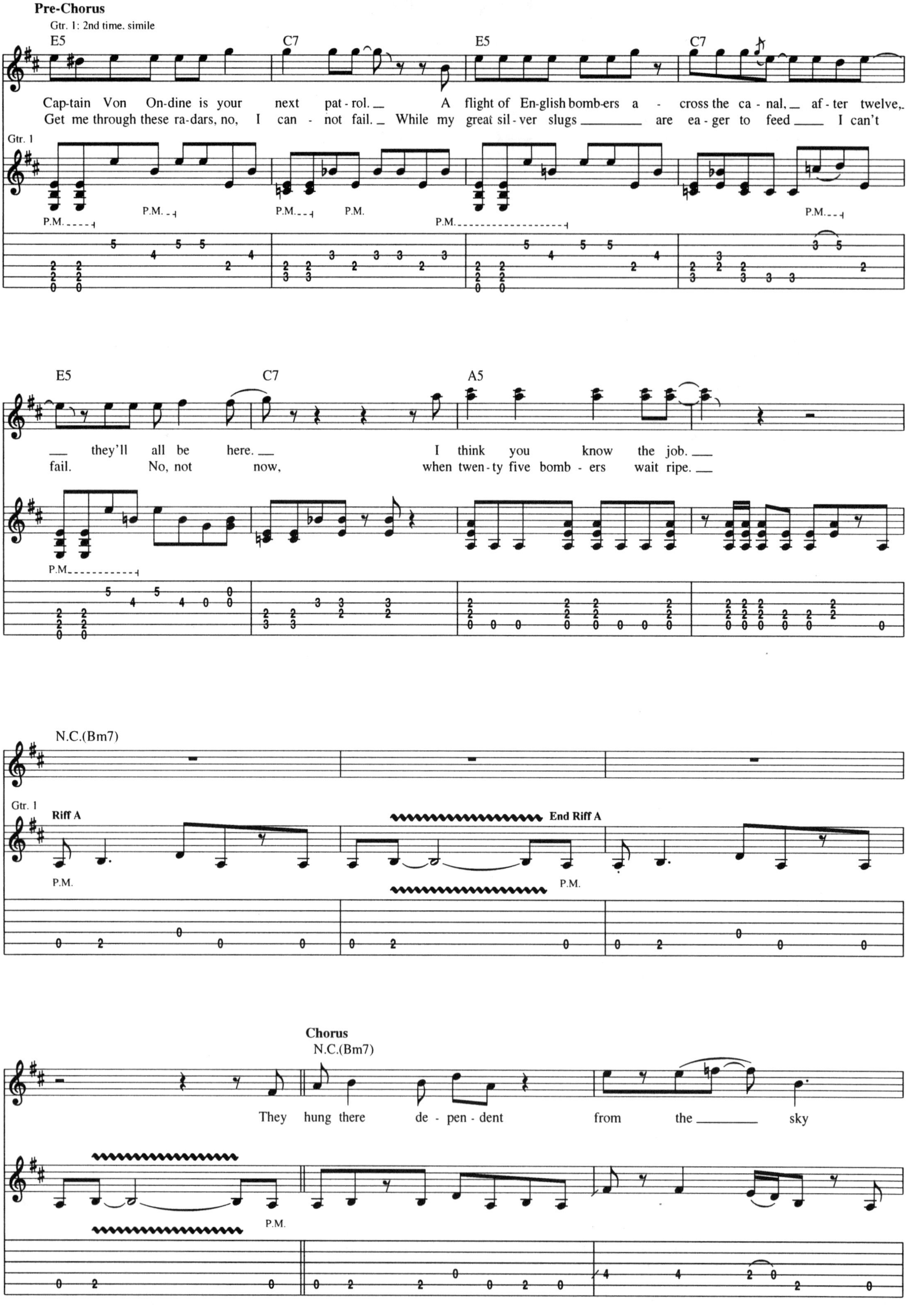
Pre-Chorus
Gtr. 1: 2nd time, simile
E5 C7 E5 C7
Cap-tain Von On-dine is your next pat-rol. A flight of En-glish bomb-ers a - cross the ca - nal, af - ter twelve,
Get me through these ra-dars, no, I can - not fail. While my great sil - ver slugs are ea - ger to feed I can't
Gtr. 1
P.M.
E5 C7 A5
they'll all be here. I think you know the job.
fail. No, not now, when twen-ty five bomb - ers wait ripe.
P.M.
N.C.(Bm7)
Gtr. 1
Riff A
End Riff A
P.M.
Chorus
N.C.(Bm7)
They hung there de - pen - dent from the sky
P.M.

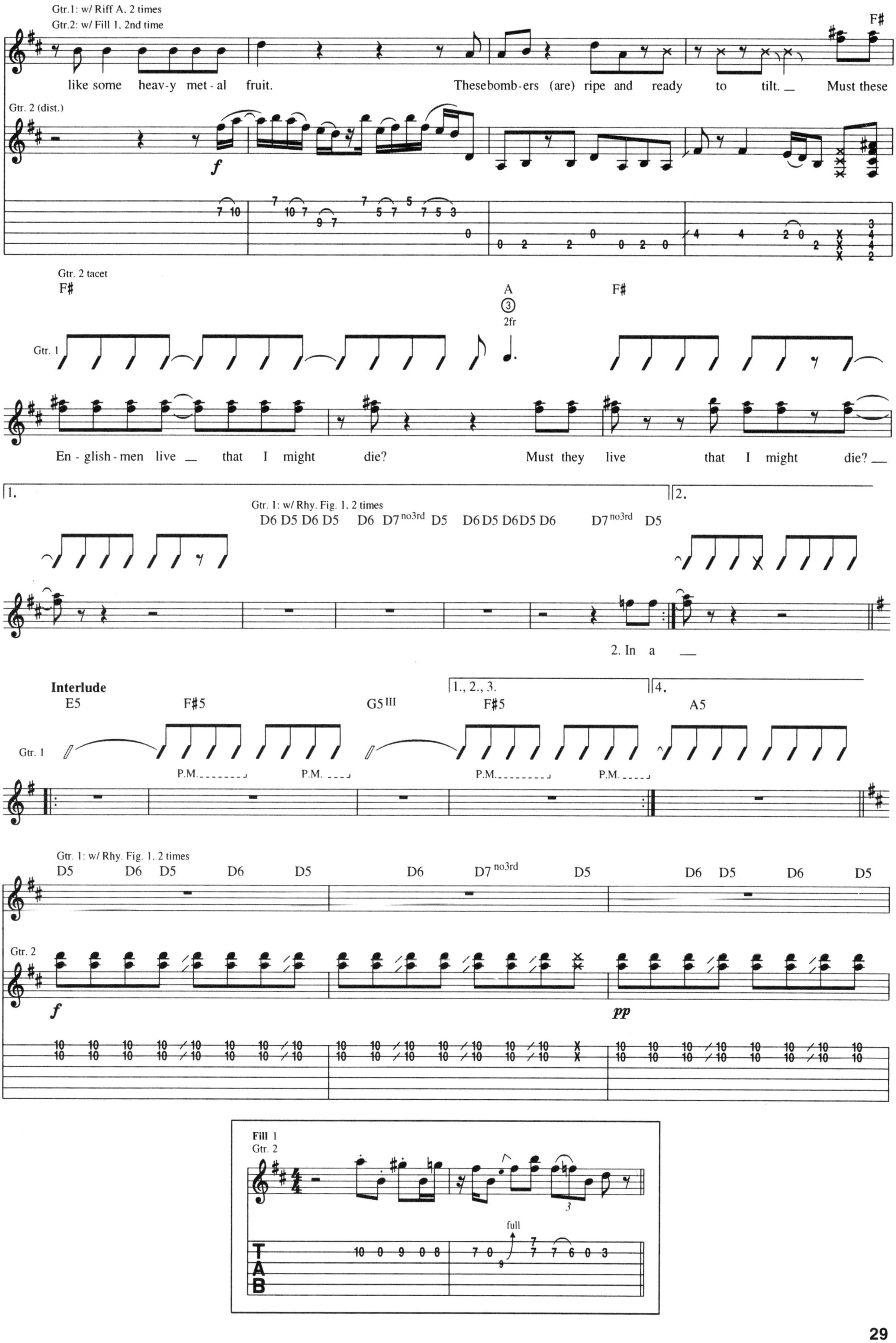
Gtr. 1: w/ Riff A, 2 times
Gtr. 2: w/ Fill 1, 2nd time
F♯
like some heav-y met-al fruit. These bomb-ers (are) ripe and ready to tilt. Must these
Gtr. 2 (dist.)
Gtr. 2 tacet
F♯
A
2fr
F♯
Gtr. 1
En-glish-men live that I might die? Must they live that I might die?
1.
Gtr. 1: w/ Rhy. Fig. 1, 2 times
D6 D5 D6 D5 D6 D7no3rd D5 D6 D5 D6 D5 D6 D7no3rd D5
2.
2. In a
Interlude
E5 F♯5 G5 III F♯5 A5
1., 2., 3.
4.
Gtr. 1
P.M.
Gtr. 1: w/ Rhy. Fig. 1, 2 times
D5 D6 D5 D6 D5 D6 D7no3rd D5 D6 D5 D6 D5
Gtr. 2
Fill 1
Gtr. 2
full
TAB

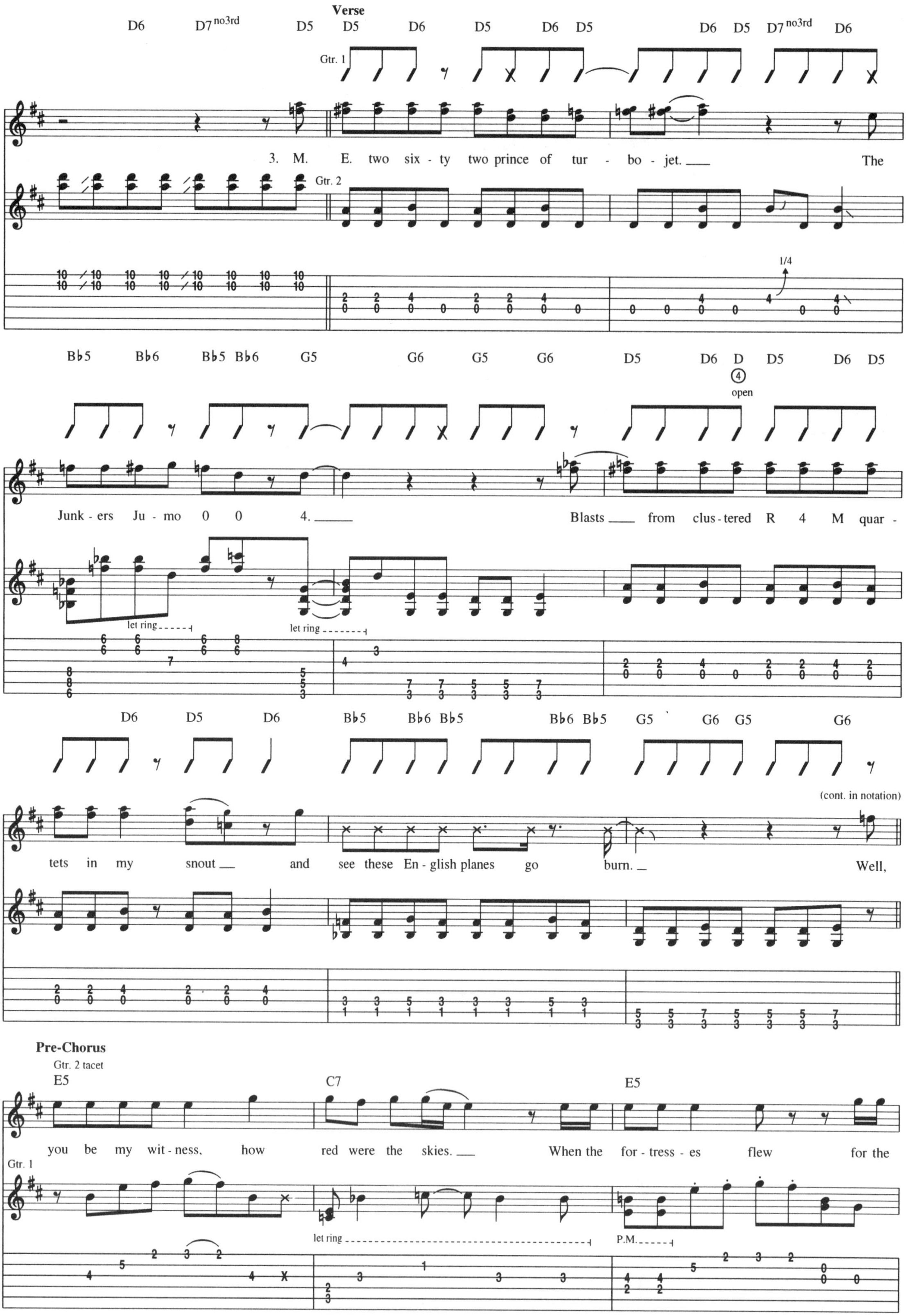
Verse
D6 D7no3rd D5 D5 D6 D5 D6 D5 D6 D5 D7no3rd D6
Gtr. 1
3. M. E. two six - ty two prince of tur - bo - jet. The
Gtr. 2
1/4
Bb5 Bb6 Bb5 Bb6 G5 G6 G5 G6 D5 D6 D D5 D6 D5
open
Junk - ers Ju - mo 0 0 4. Blasts from clus - tered R 4 M quar -
let ring
let ring
D6 D5 D6 Bb5 Bb6 Bb5 Bb6 Bb5 G5 G6 G5 G6
(cont. in notation)
tets in my snout and see these En - glish planes go burn. Well,
Pre-Chorus
Gtr. 2 tacet
E5 C7 E5
you be my wit - ness, how red were the skies. When the for - tress - es flew for the
Gtr. 1
let ring
P.M.

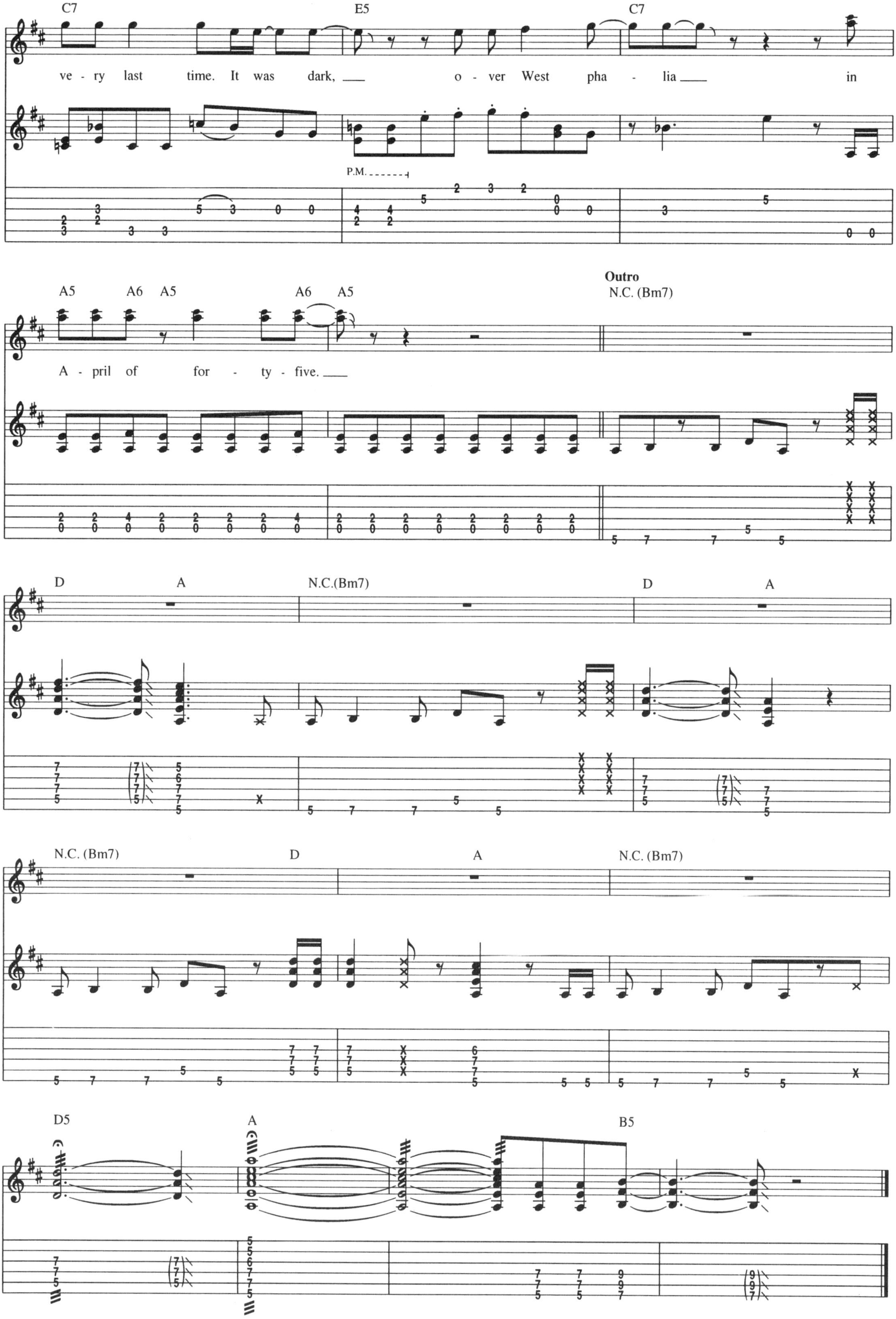
C7
E5
C7
very last time. It was dark, over West phalia in
P.M.
A5 A6 A5 A6 A5
A - pril of for - ty - five.
Outro
N.C. (Bm7)
D A
N.C.(Bm7)
D A
N.C. (Bm7)
D A
N.C. (Bm7)
D5
A
B5

This Ain't the Summer of Love

Words and Music by Donald Roeser, D. Waller and M. Krugman

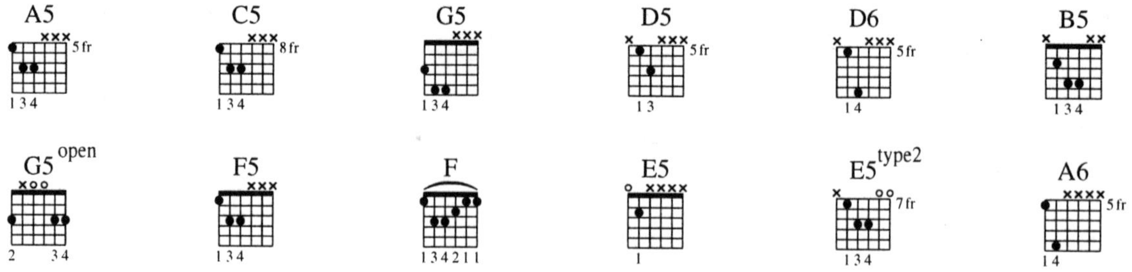

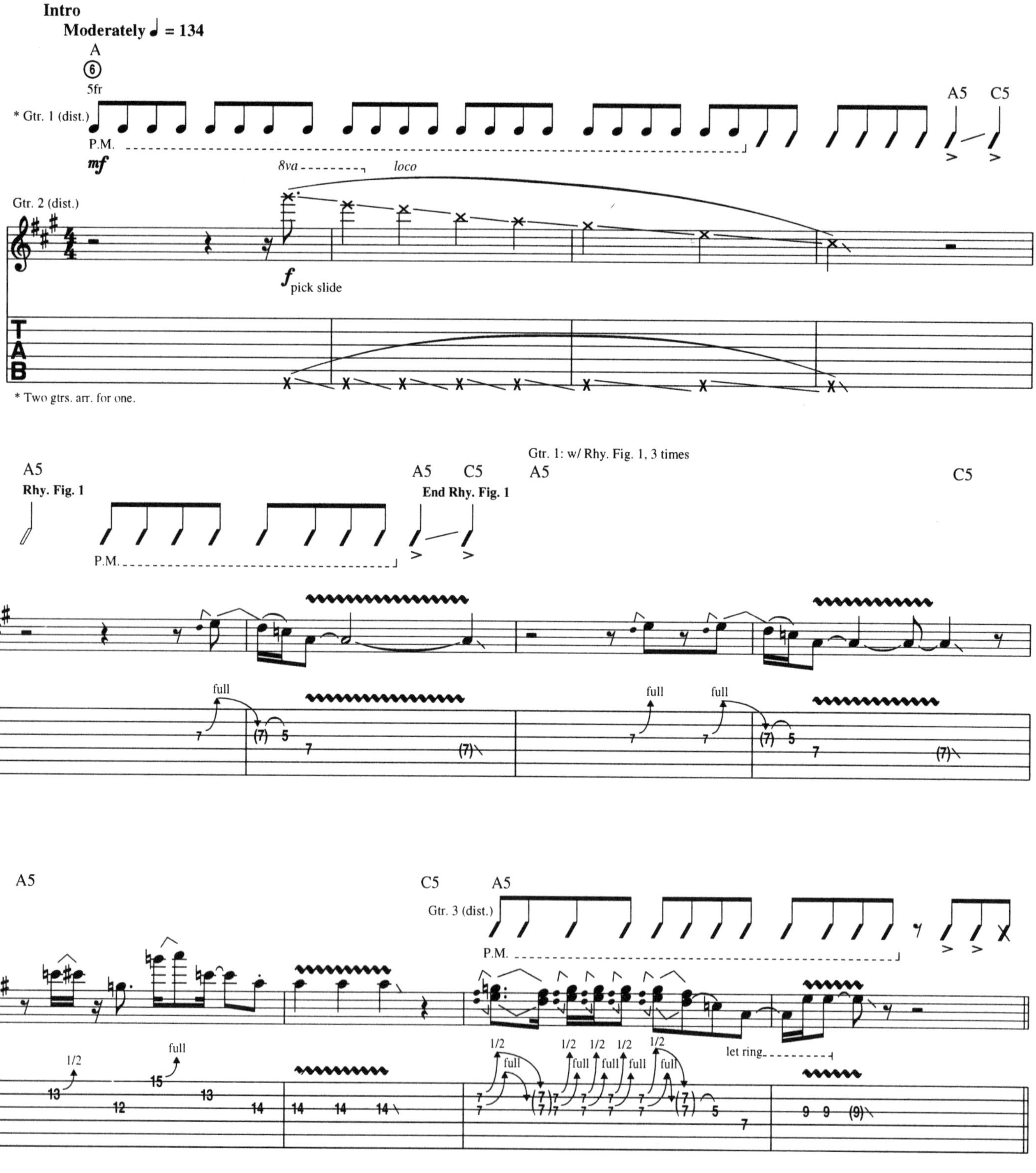

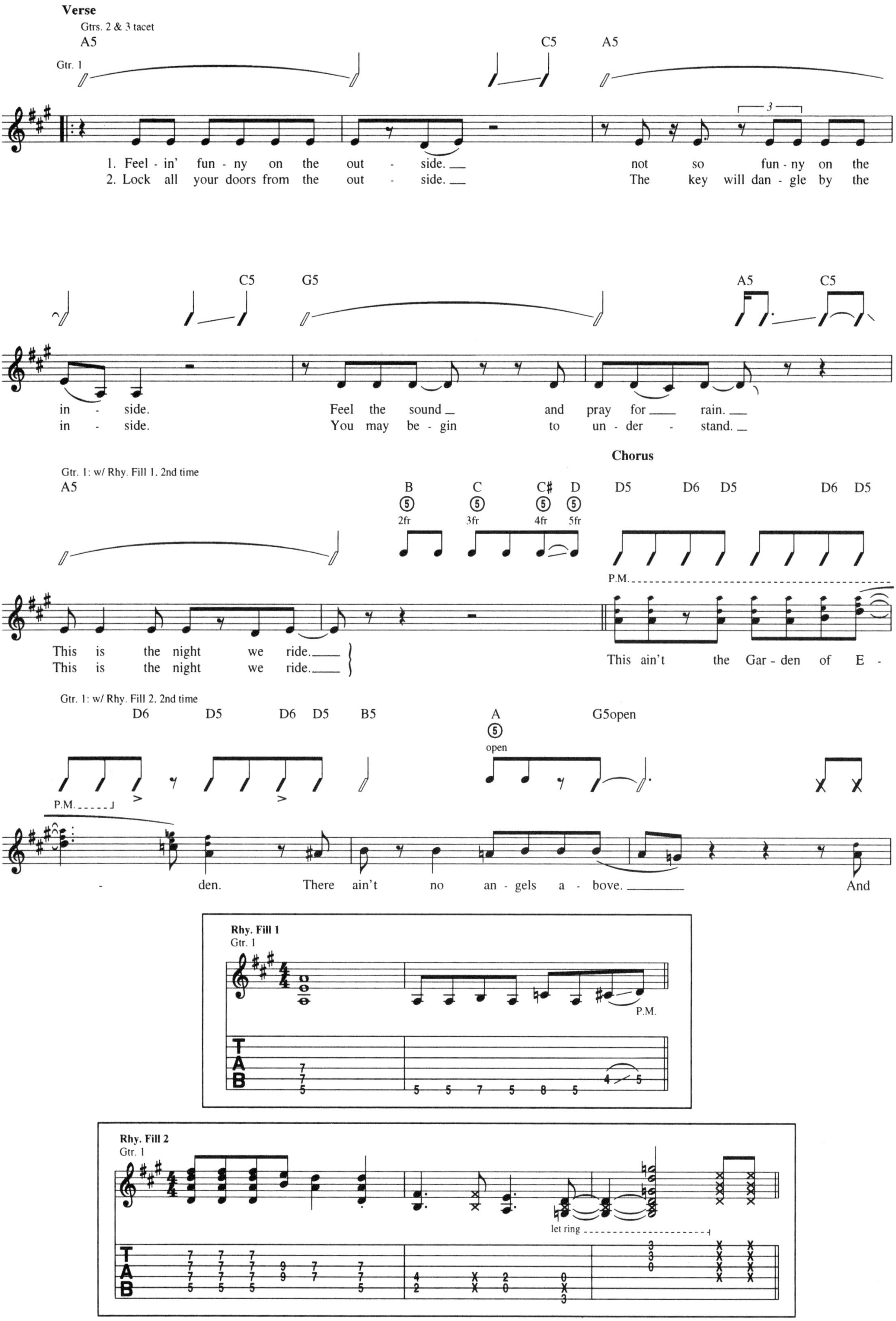
Verse
Gtrs. 2 & 3 tacet
A5 C5 A5
Gtr. 1
1. Feel - in' fun - ny on the out - side. not so fun - ny on the
2. Lock all your doors from the out - side. The key will dan - gle by the
C5 G5 A5 C5
in - side. Feel the sound and pray for rain.
in - side. You may be - gin to un - der - stand.
Gtr. 1: w/ Rhy. Fill 1, 2nd time
A5 B C C♯ D
2fr 3fr 4fr 5fr
This is the night we ride.
This is the night we ride.
Chorus
D5 D6 D5 D6 D5
P.M.
This ain't the Gar - den of E -
Gtr. 1: w/ Rhy. Fill 2, 2nd time
D6 D5 D6 D5 B5 A G5open
open
P.M.
- den. There ain't no an - gels a - bove. And
Rhy. Fill 1
Gtr. 1
P.M.
Rhy. Fill 2
Gtr. 1
let ring

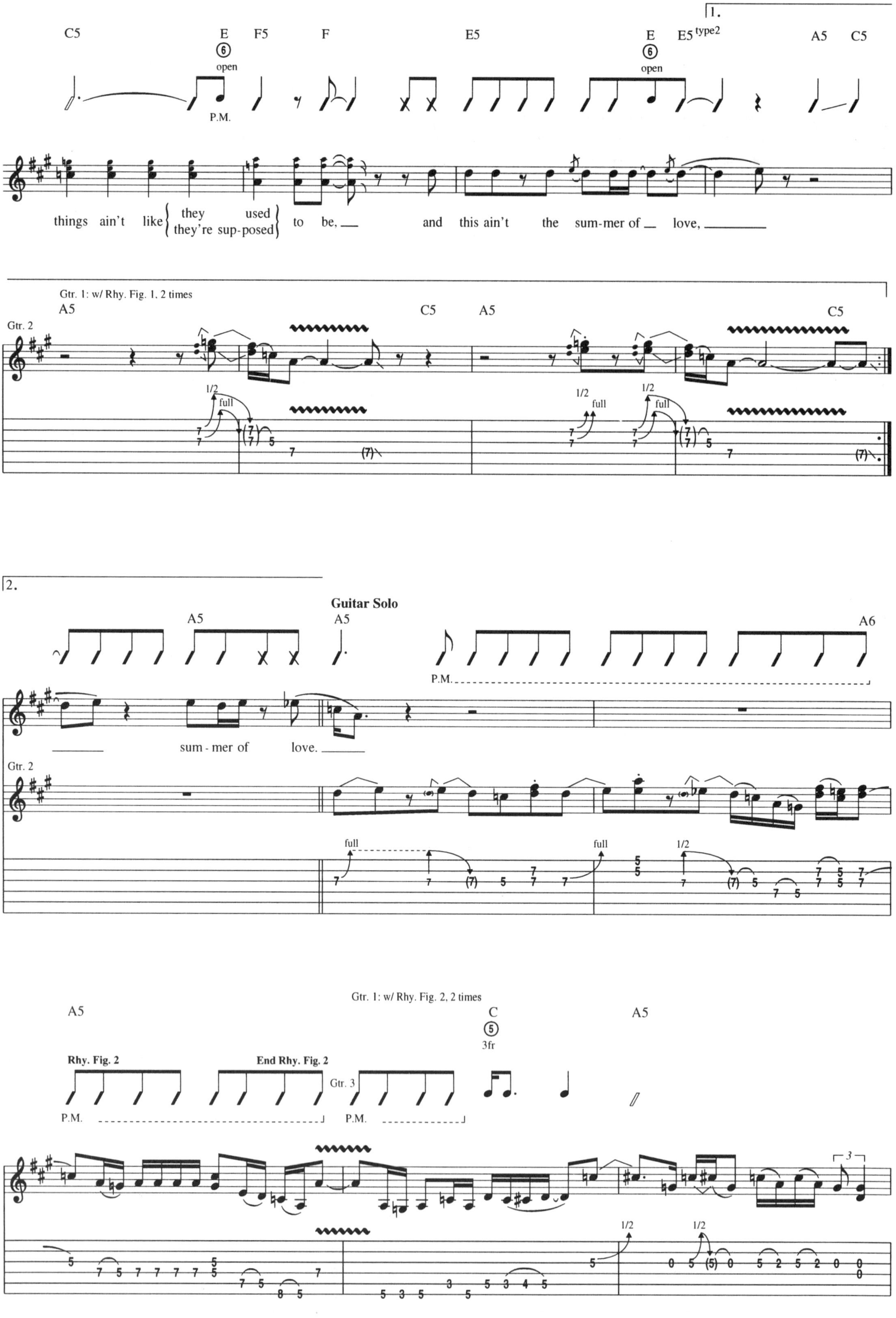

1.
C5
E
open
F5
F
E5
E5 type2
A5
P.M.
things ain't like they used to be, and this ain't the summer of love,
they're sup-posed
Gtr. 1: w/ Rhy. Fig. 1, 2 times
Gtr. 2
1/2
full
2.
Guitar Solo
A6
summer of love.
Rhy. Fig. 2
End Rhy. Fig. 2
Gtr. 3
Gtr. 1: w/ Rhy. Fig. 2, 2 times
C
3fr

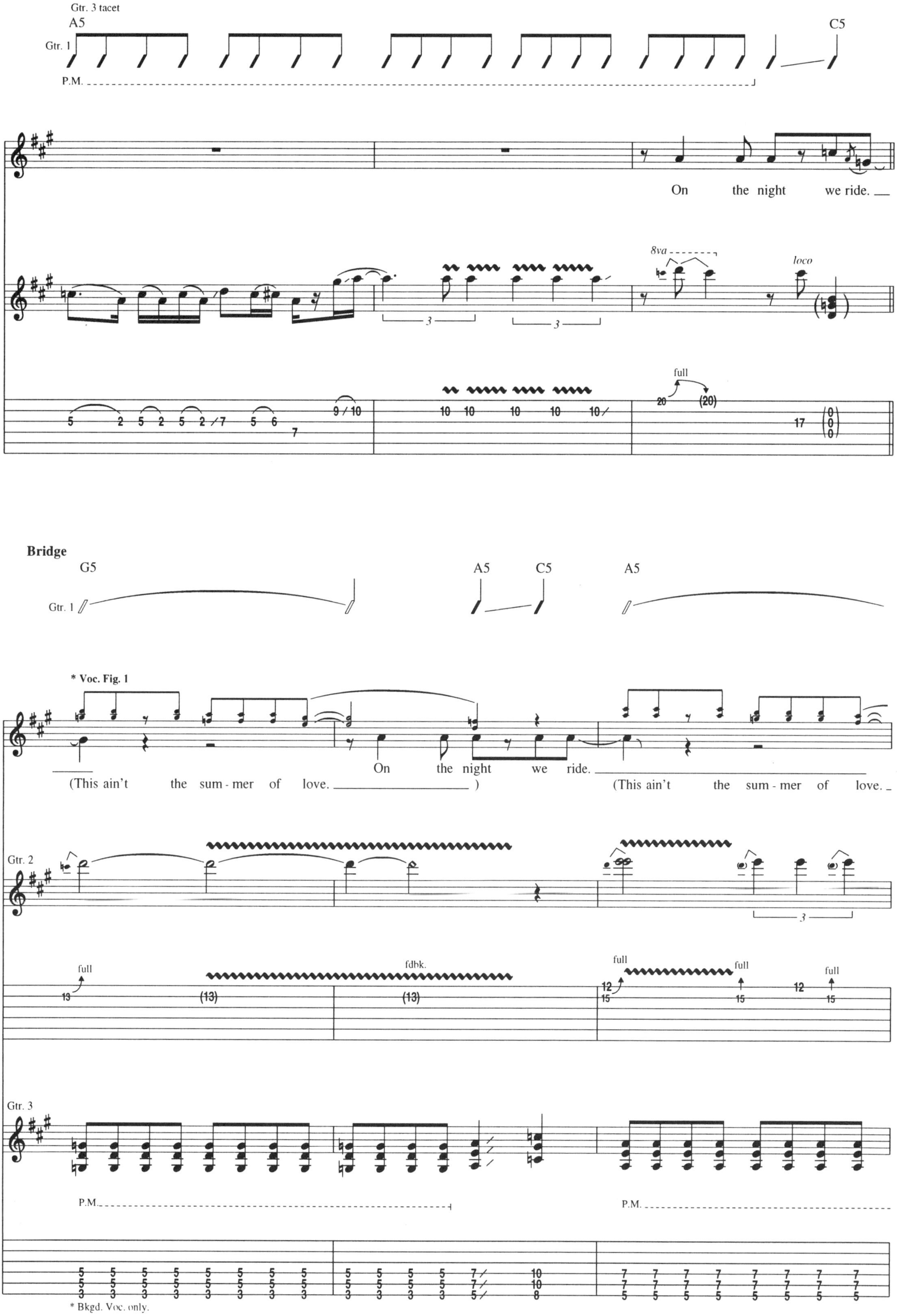

Gtr. 3 tacet
A5
C5
Gtr. 1
P.M.
On the night we ride.
8va
loco
full
Bridge
G5
A5
C5
A5
Gtr. 1
* Voc. Fig. 1
On the night we ride.
(This ain't the sum - mer of love.)
(This ain't the sum - mer of love.
Gtr. 2
full
fdbk.
full
full
full
Gtr. 3
P.M.
P.M.
* Bkgd. Voc. only.

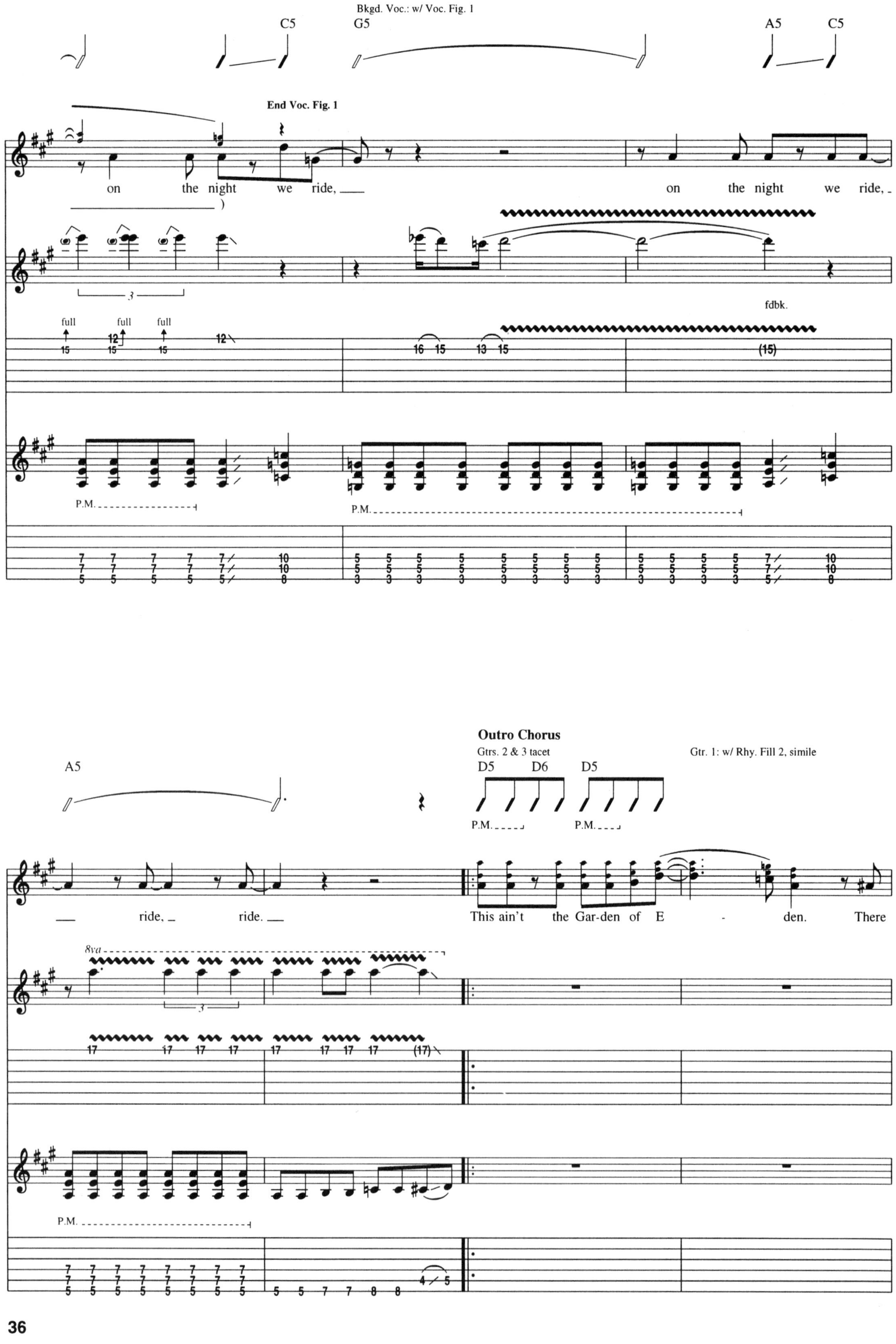
Bkgd. Voc.: w/ Voc. Fig. 1
C5 G5 A5 C5
End Voc. Fig. 1
on the night we ride, on the night we ride,
full full full
fdbk.
P.M.
A5
Outro Chorus
Gtrs. 2 & 3 tacet
Gtr. 1: w/ Rhy. Fill 2, simile
D5 D6 D5
ride, ride.
This ain't the Gar-den of E - den. There
8va

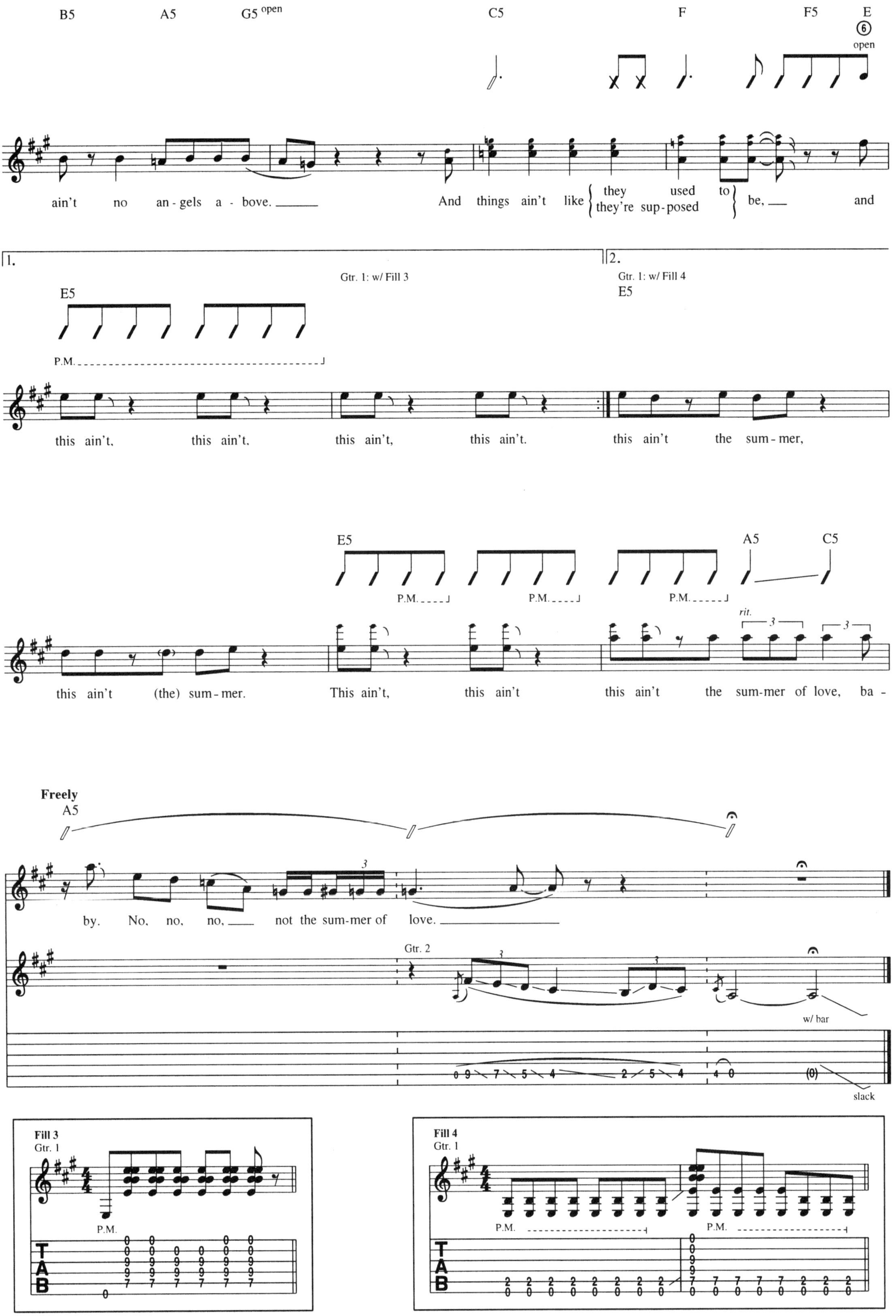
B5 A5 G5 open C5 F F5 E
6 open
ain't no an-gels a-bove.
And things ain't like they used to / they're sup-posed be, and
1.
Gtr. 1: w/ Fill 3
E5
P.M.
this ain't, this ain't, this ain't, this ain't.
2.
Gtr. 1: w/ Fill 4
E5
this ain't the sum-mer,
this ain't (the) sum-mer.
E5
P.M. P.M. P.M.
This ain't, this ain't
A5 C5
rit.
this ain't the sum-mer of love, ba-
Freely
A5
by. No, no, no, not the sum-mer of love.
Gtr. 2
w/ bar
slack
Fill 3
Gtr. 1
P.M.
Fill 4
Gtr. 1
P.M.
P.M.

Burning For You

Words and Music by Donald Roeser and R. Meltzer

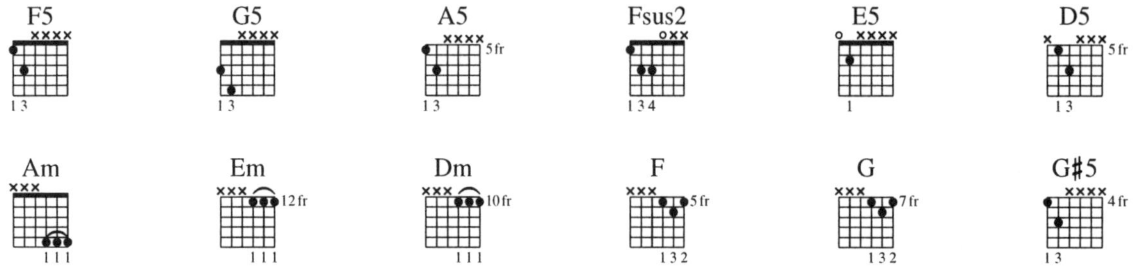

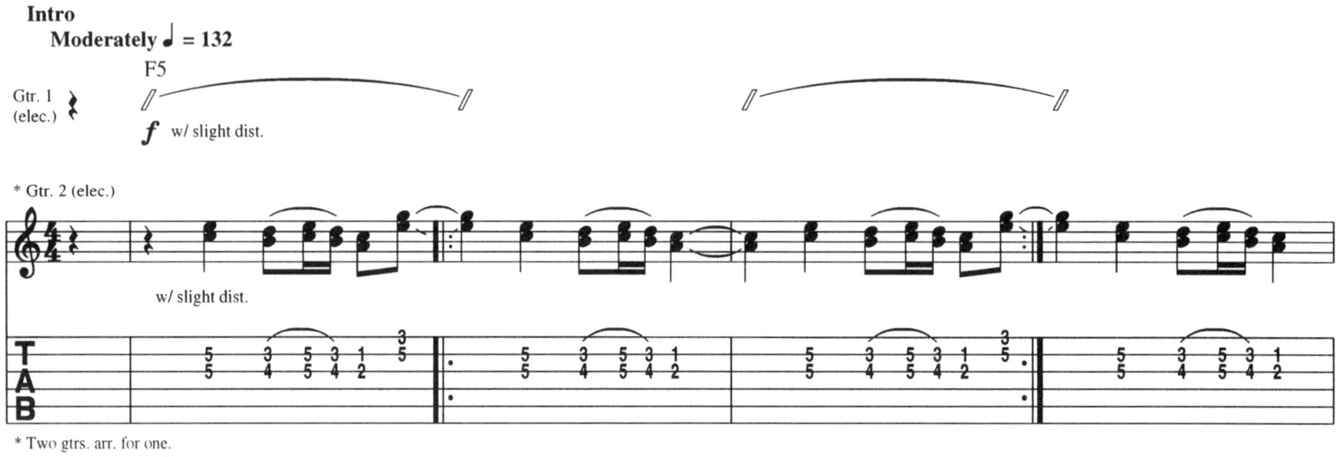

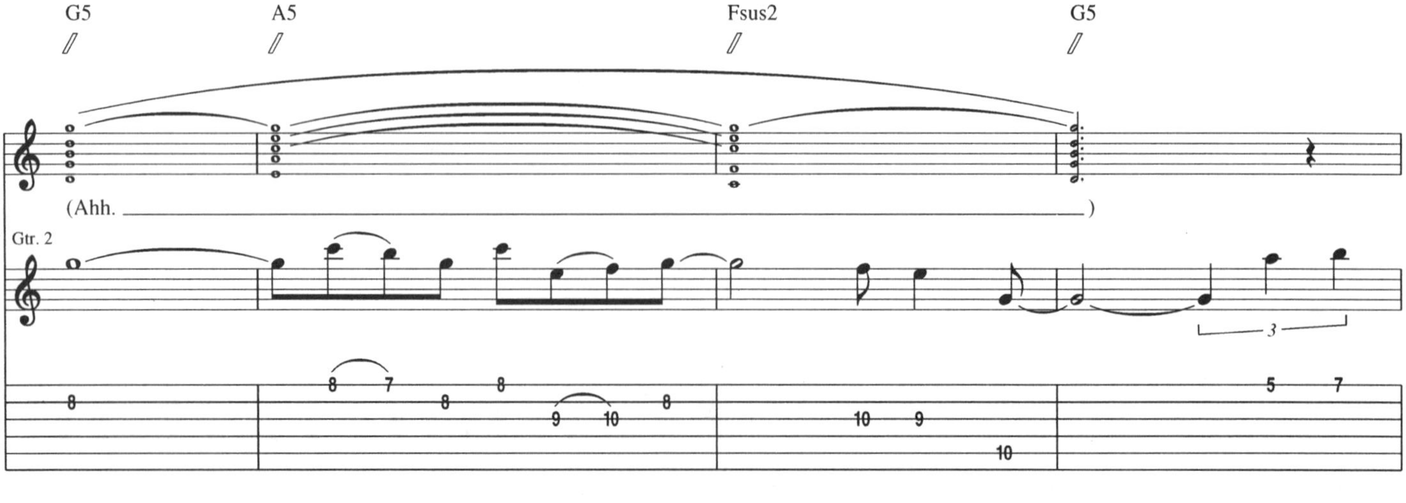

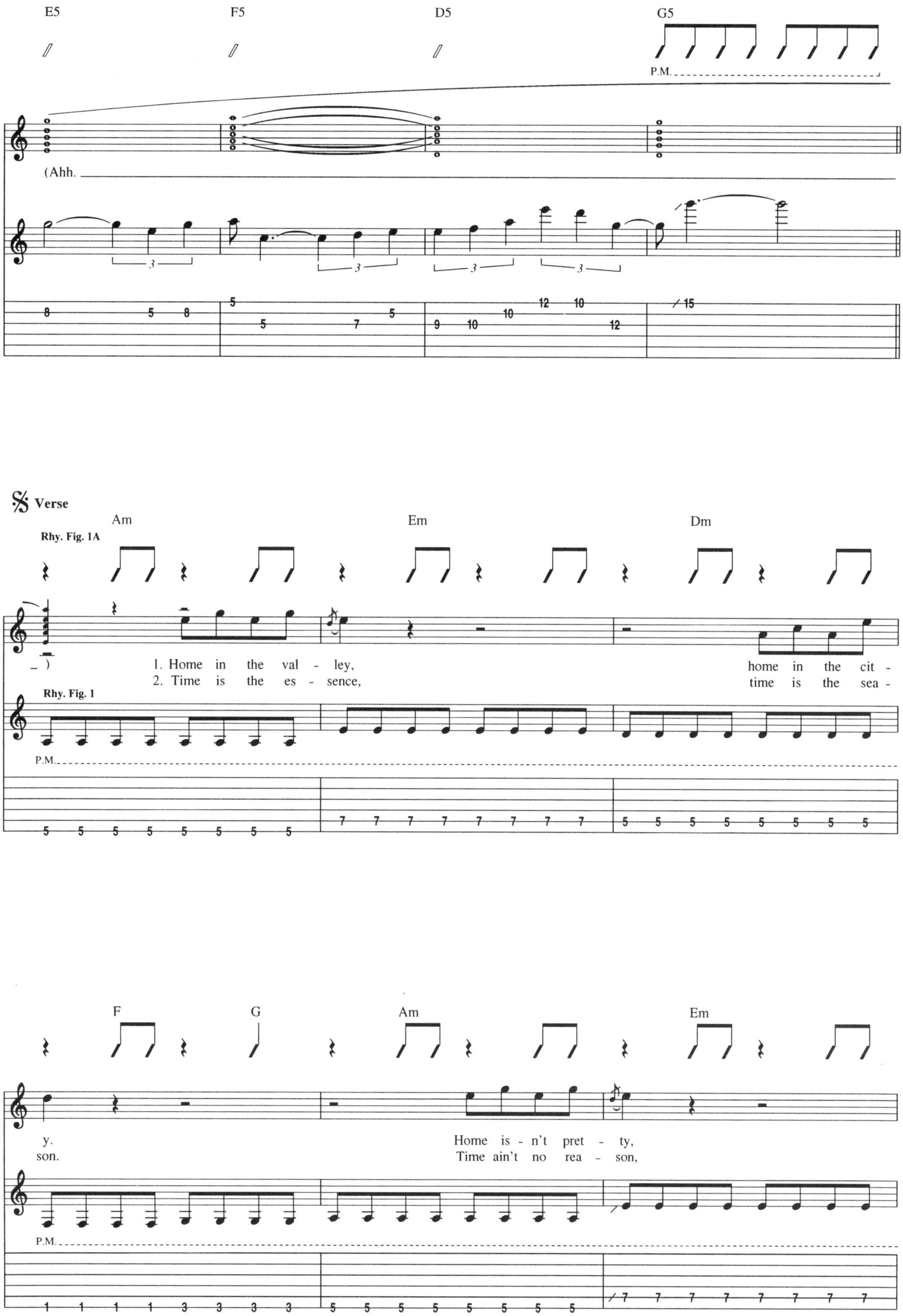
E5 F5 D5 G5
P.M.
(Ahh.
Verse
Am Em Dm
Rhy. Fig. 1A
)
1. Home in the val - ley,
2. Time is the es - sence,
home in the cit -
time is the sea -
Rhy. Fig. 1
P.M.
F G Am Em
y.
son.
Home is - n't pret - ty,
Time ain't no rea - son,
P.M.

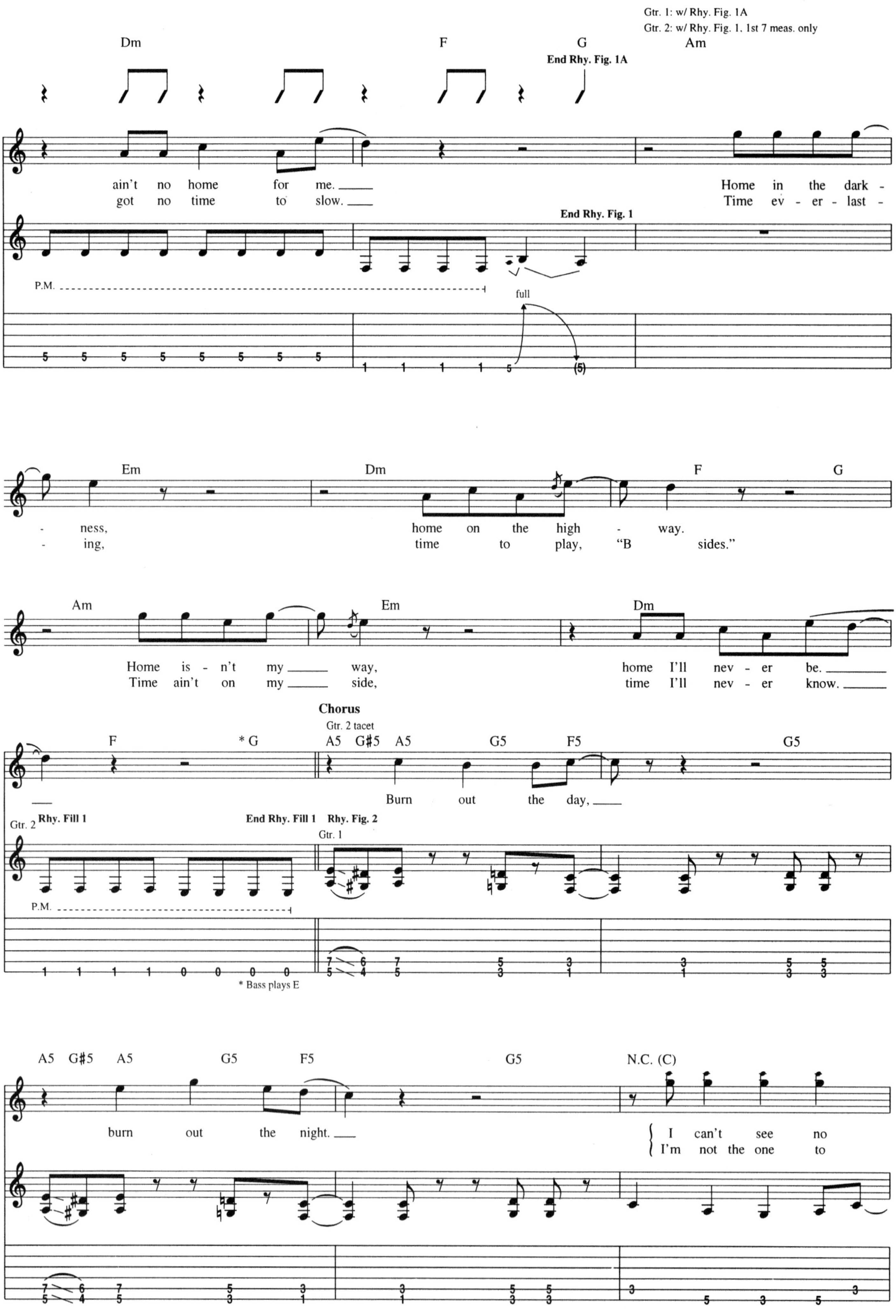
Gtr. 1: w/ Rhy. Fig. 1A
Gtr. 2: w/ Rhy. Fig. 1, 1st 7 meas. only
Dm F G Am
End Rhy. Fig. 1A
ain't no home for me.
got no time to slow.
Home in the dark-
Time ev - er - last -
End Rhy. Fig. 1
P.M.
full
Em Dm F G
- ness, home on the high - way.
- ing, time to play, "B sides."
Am Em Dm
Home is - n't my way, home I'll nev - er be.
Time ain't on my side, time I'll nev - er know.
Chorus
Gtr. 2 tacet
F *G A5 G#5 A5 G5 F5 G5
Burn out the day,
Gtr. 2 Rhy. Fill 1
End Rhy. Fill 1 Rhy. Fig. 2
Gtr. 1
P.M.
* Bass plays E
A5 G#5 A5 G5 F5 G5 N.C. (C)
burn out the night.
I can't see no
I'm not the one to

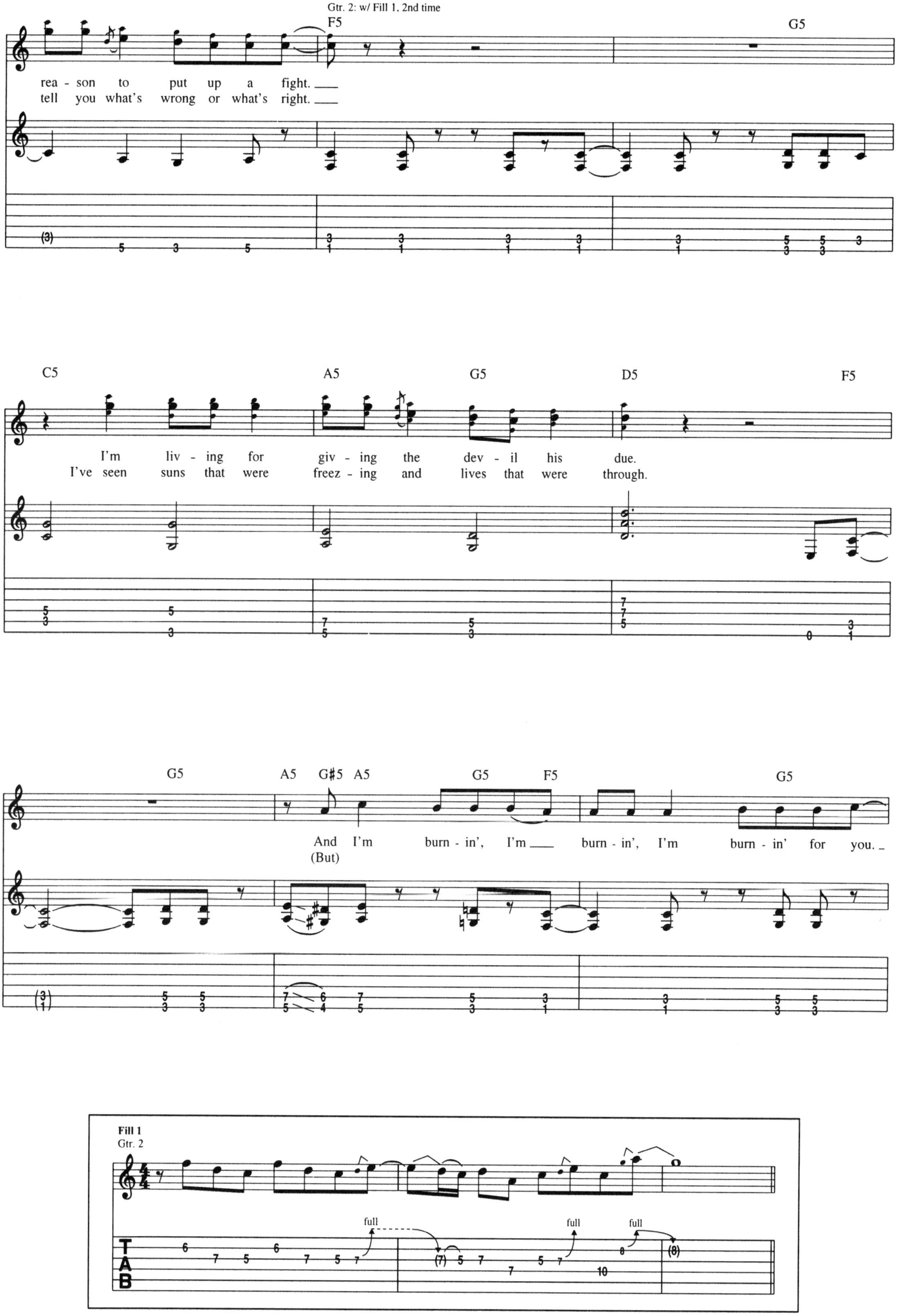
Gtr. 2: w/ Fill 1, 2nd time
F5
G5
rea - son to put up a fight.
tell you what's wrong or what's right.
C5
A5
G5
D5
F5
I'm liv - ing for giv - ing the dev - il his due.
I've seen suns that were freez - ing and lives that were through.
G5
A5 G#5 A5
G5
F5
G5
And I'm burn - in', I'm burn - in', I'm burn - in' for you.
(But)
Fill 1
Gtr. 2
full
full
full

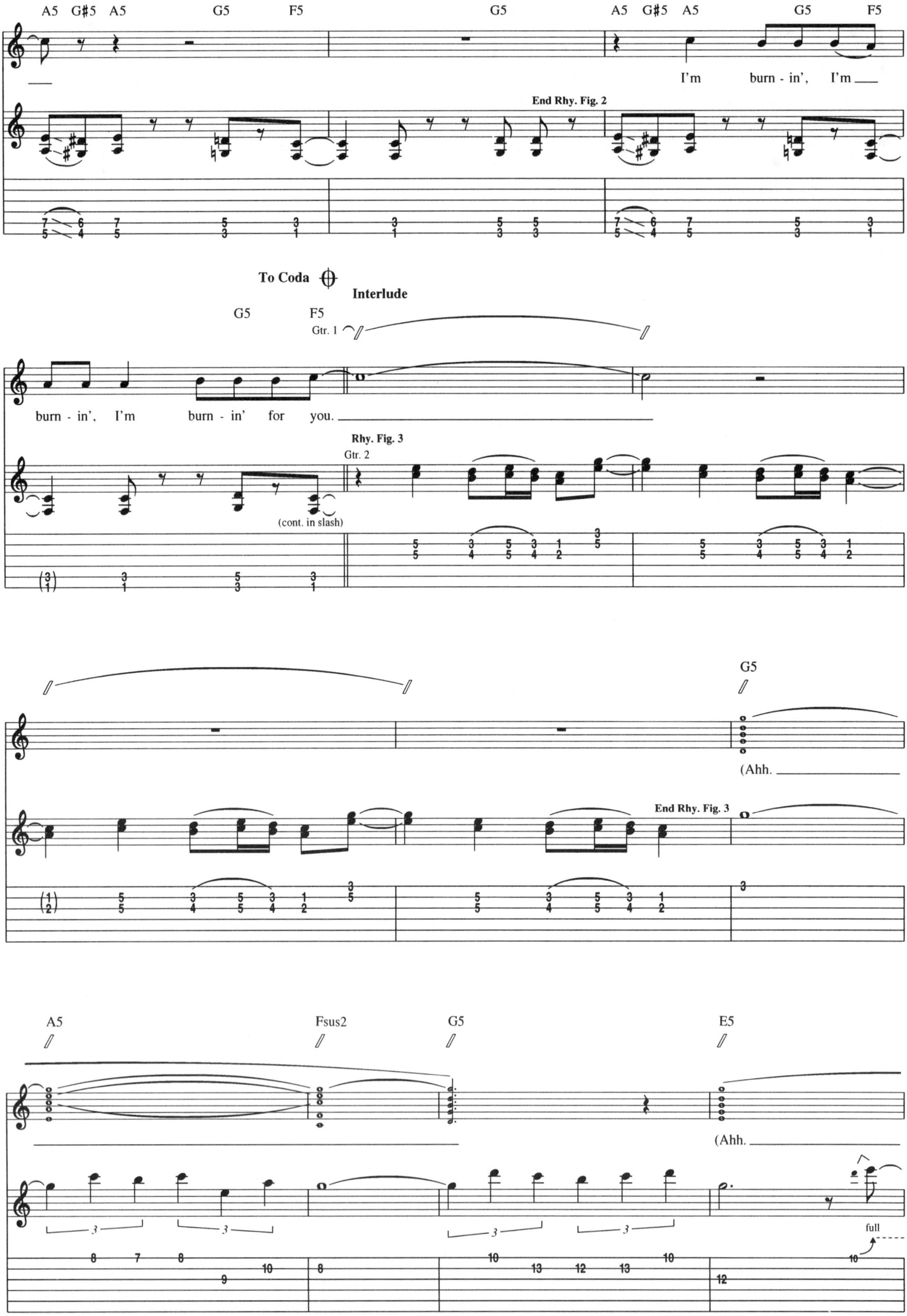
A5 G#5 A5 G5 F5 G5 A5 G#5 A5 G5 F5
I'm burn - in', I'm
End Rhy. Fig. 2
To Coda
Interlude
G5 F5
Gtr. 1
burn - in', I'm burn - in' for you.
Rhy. Fig. 3
Gtr. 2
(cont. in slash)
G5
(Ahh.
End Rhy. Fig. 3
A5 Fsus2 G5 E5
(Ahh.
full

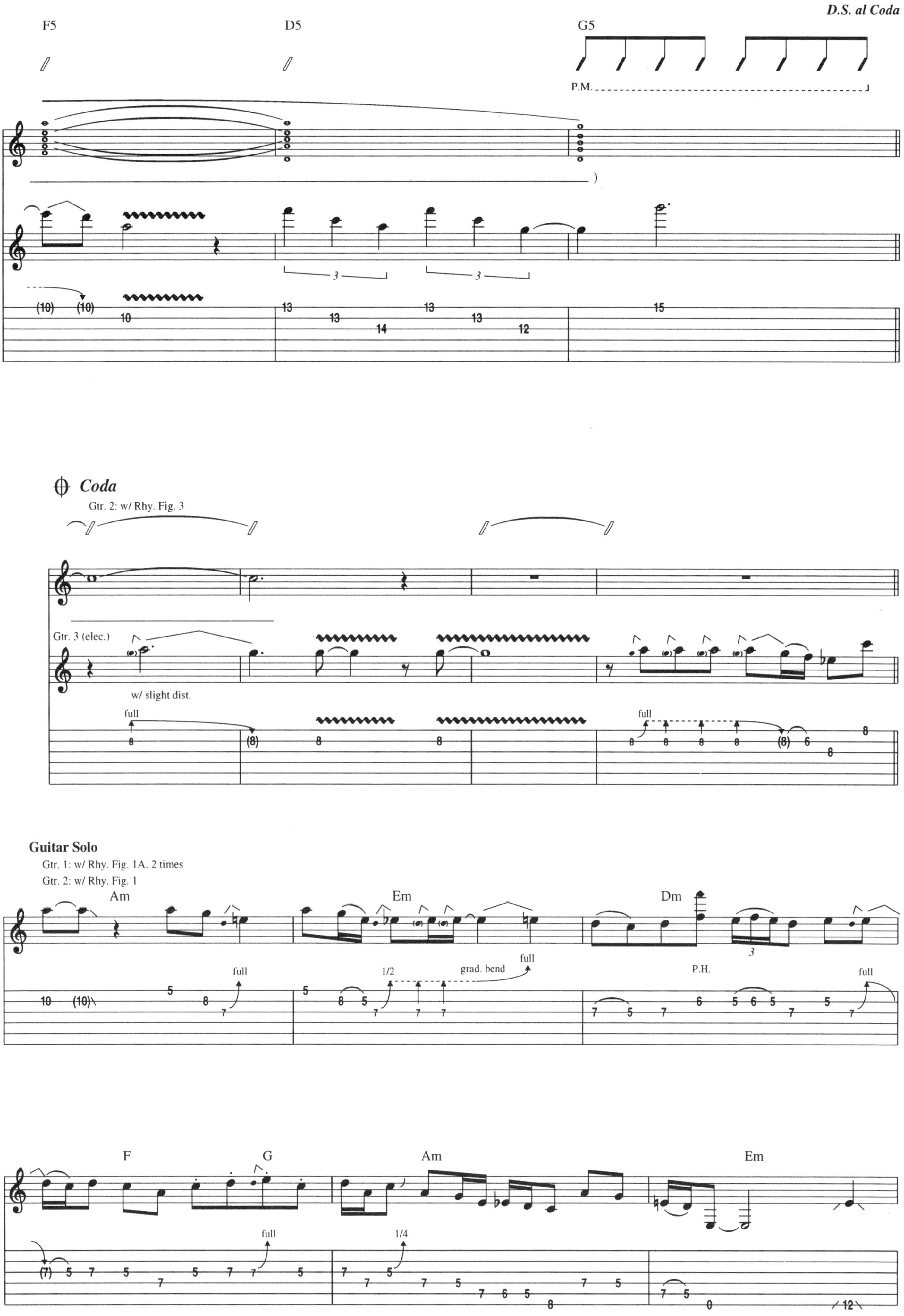
D.S. al Coda
F5
D5
G5
P.M.
Coda
Gtr. 2: w/ Rhy. Fig. 3
Gtr. 3 (elec.)
w/ slight dist.
full
Guitar Solo
Gtr. 1: w/ Rhy. Fig. 1A, 2 times
Gtr. 2: w/ Rhy. Fig. 1
Am
Em
Dm
1/2
grad. bend
P.H.
F
G
1/4

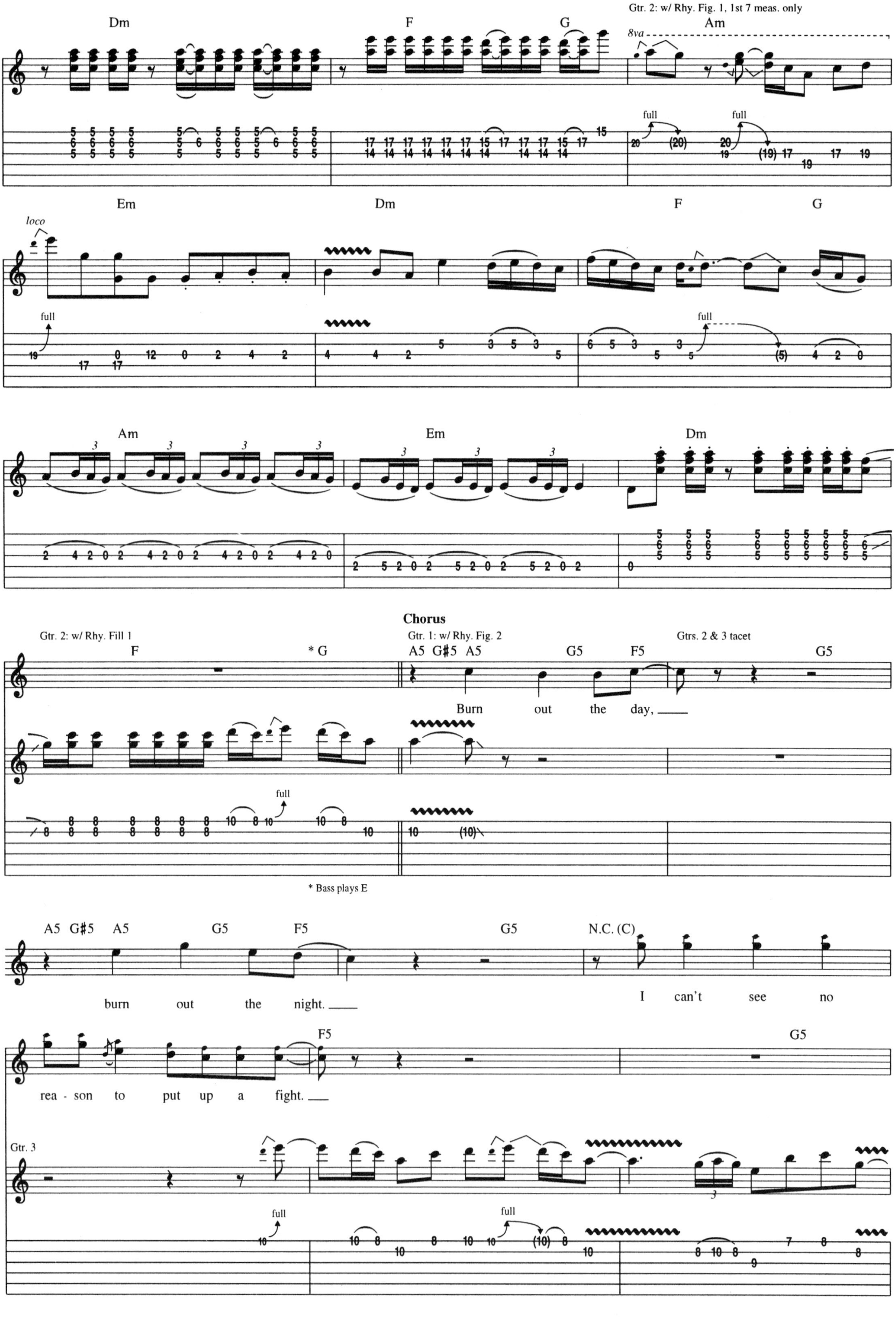
Gtr. 2: w/ Rhy. Fig. 1, 1st 7 meas. only
Dm
F
G
Am
8va
full
full
Em
Dm
F
G
loco
full
full
Am
Em
Dm
Chorus
Gtr. 2: w/ Rhy. Fill 1
F
*G
Gtr. 1: w/ Rhy. Fig. 2
A5 G#5 A5
G5
F5
Gtrs. 2 & 3 tacet
G5
Burn out the day,
full
* Bass plays E
A5 G#5 A5
G5
F5
G5
N.C. (C)
burn out the night.
I can't see no
F5
G5
rea - son to put up a fight.
Gtr. 3
full
full

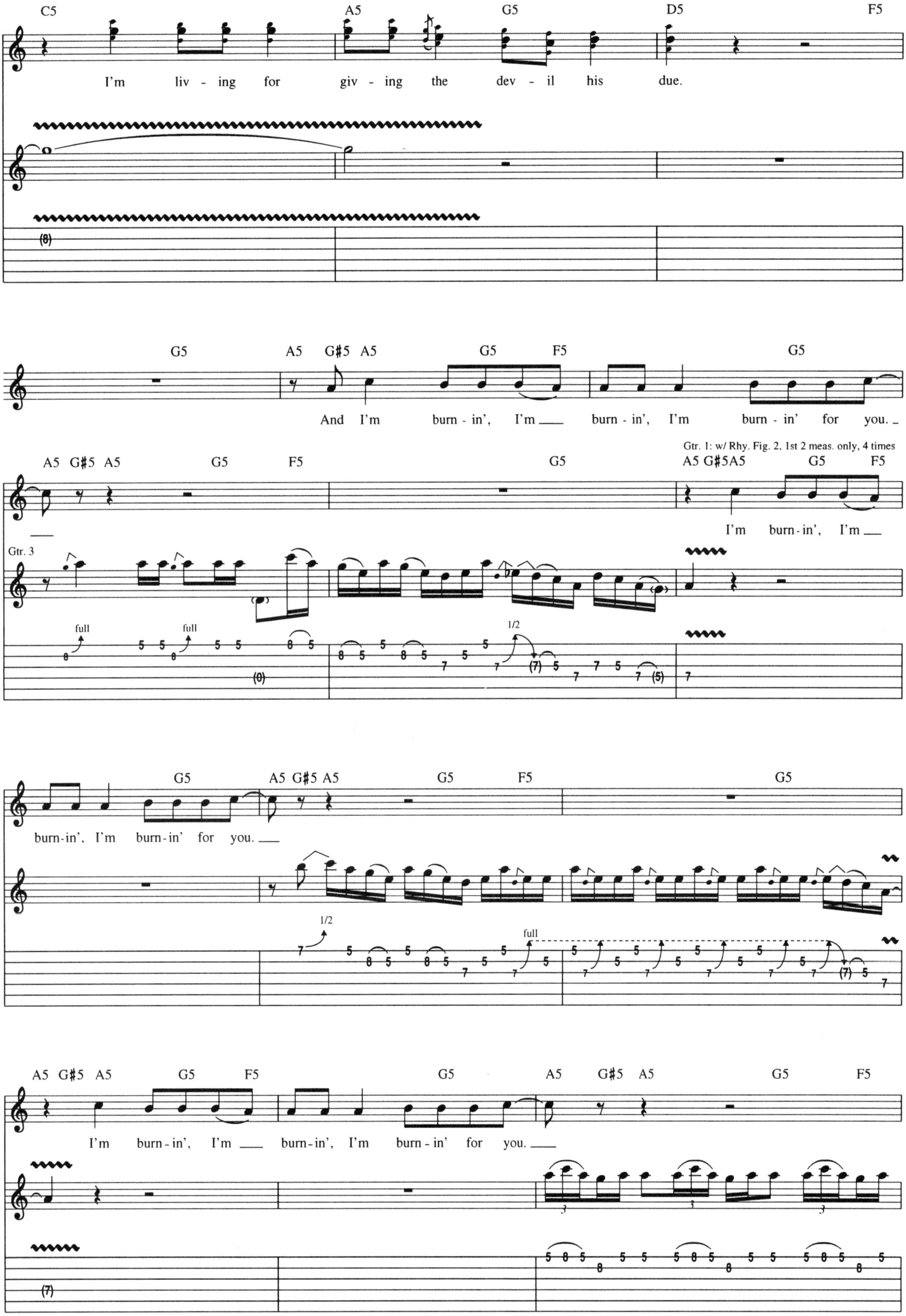
C5 A5 G5 D5 F5
I'm liv - ing for giv - ing the dev - il his due.
G5 A5 G#5 A5 G5 F5 G5
And I'm burn - in', I'm burn - in', I'm burn - in' for you.
A5 G#5 A5 G5 F5 G5 A5 G#5A5 G5 F5
Gtr. 1: w/ Rhy. Fig. 2, 1st 2 meas. only, 4 times
I'm burn - in', I'm
Gtr. 3
full
1/2
G5 A5 G#5 A5 G5 F5 G5
burn-in', I'm burn-in' for you.
A5 G#5 A5 G5 F5 G5 A5 G#5 A5 G5 F5
I'm burn - in', I'm burn-in', I'm burn-in' for you.

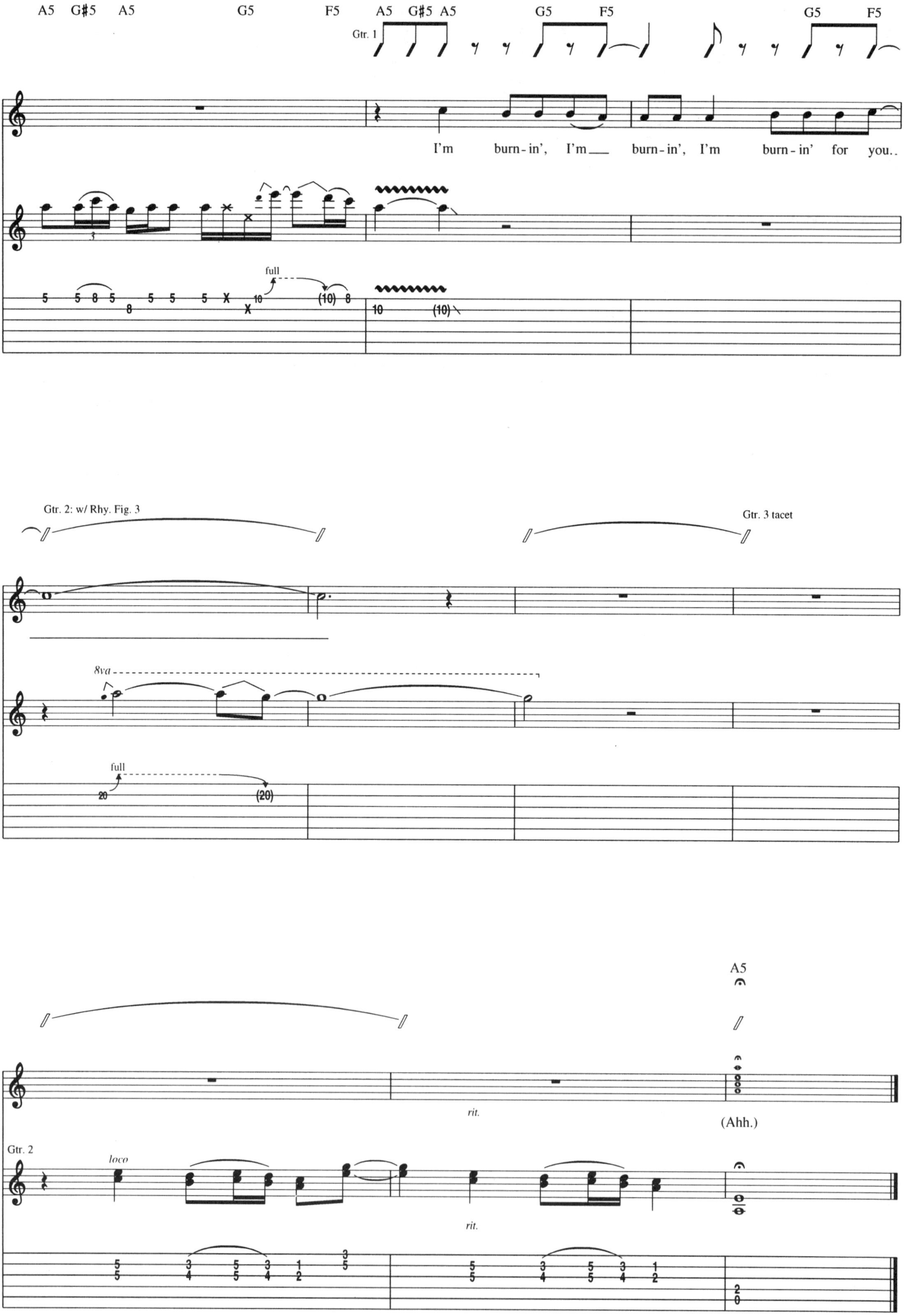
A5 G♯5 A5 G5 F5 A5 G♯5 A5 G5 F5 G5 F5
Gtr. 1
I'm burn-in', I'm burn-in', I'm burn-in' for you..
full
Gtr. 2: w/ Rhy. Fig. 3
Gtr. 3 tacet
8va
full
A5
rit.
(Ahh.)
Gtr. 2
loco
rit.

O.D.'d On Life Itself

Words and Music by Samuel Pearlman, Donald Roeser, Albert Bouchard and Eric Bloom

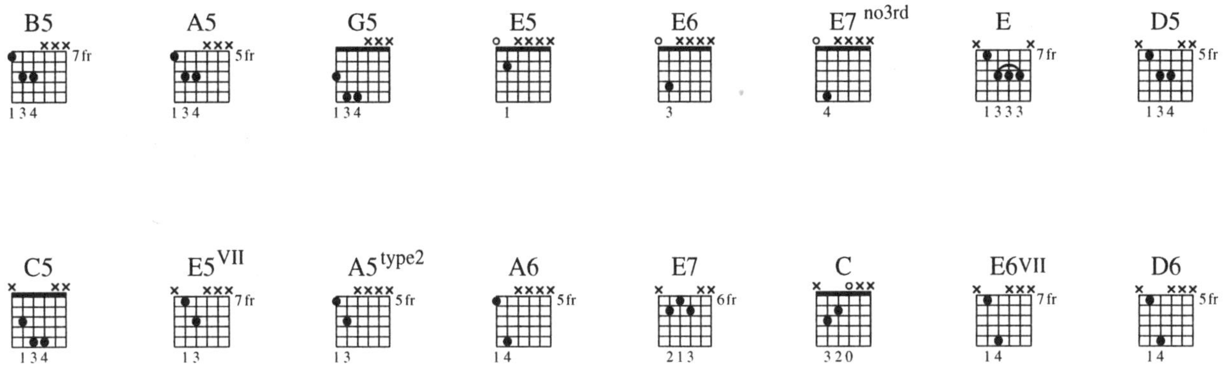

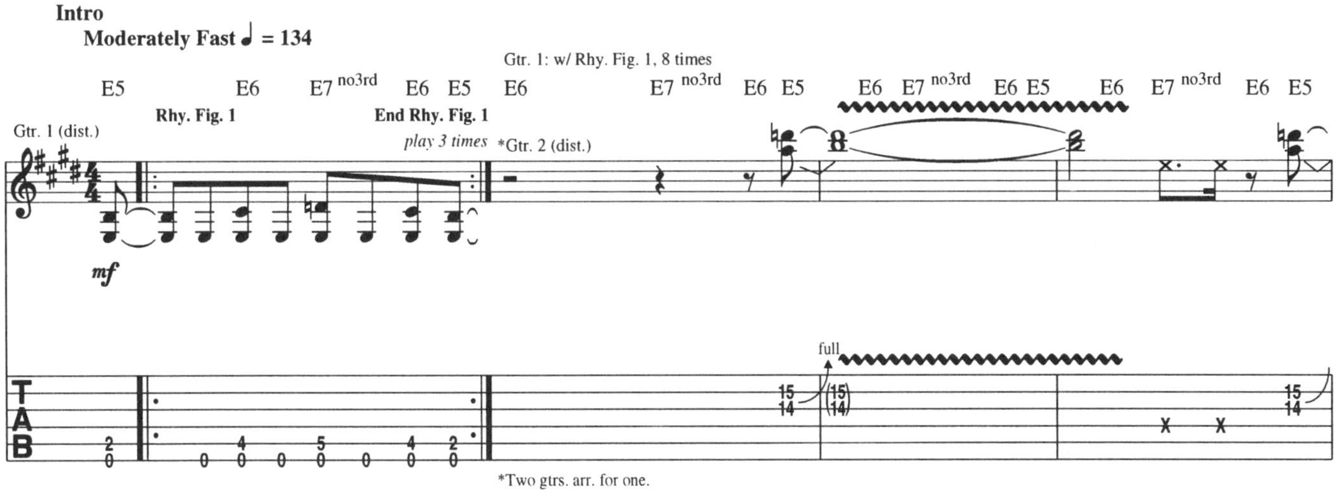

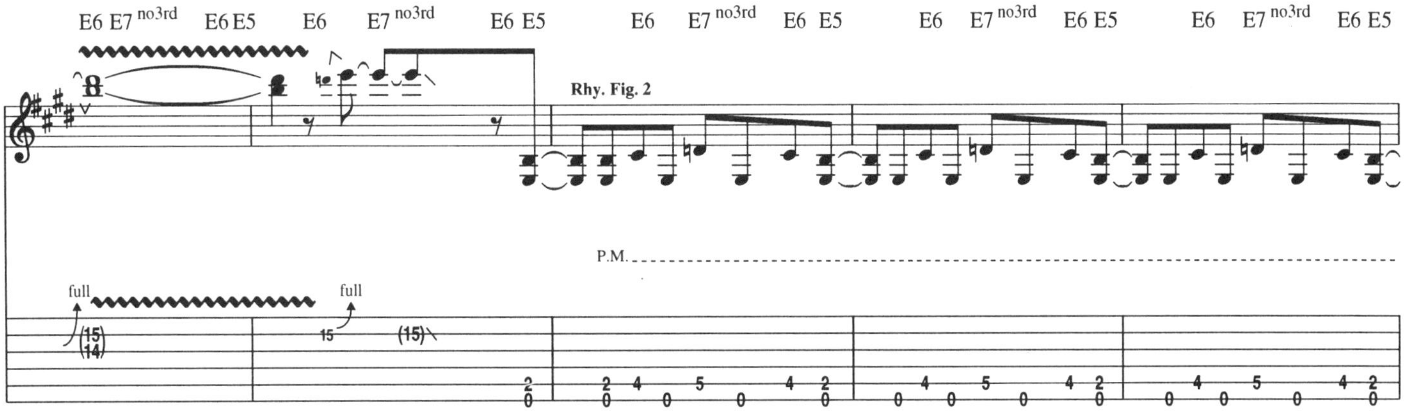

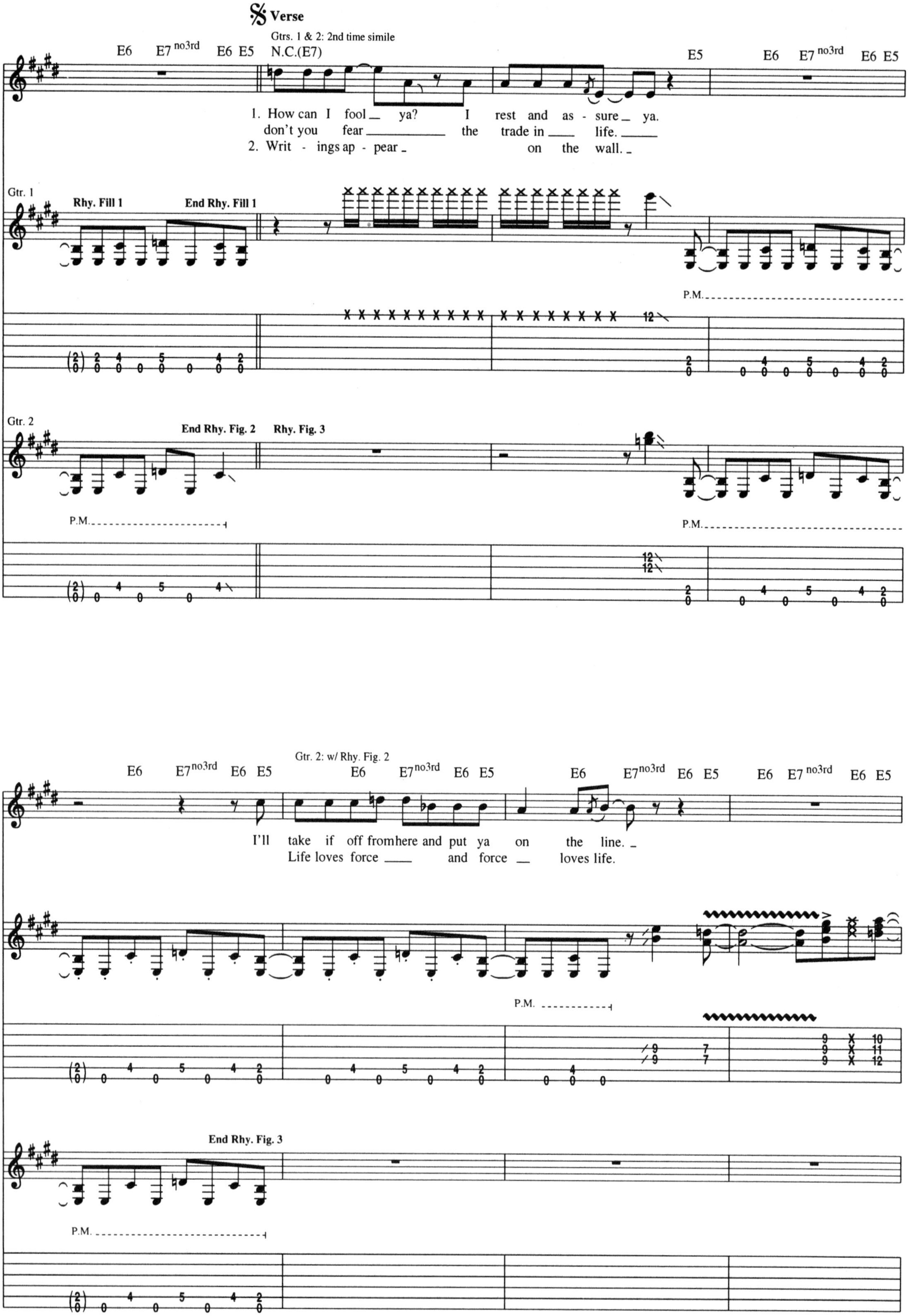

Verse
Gtrs. 1 & 2: 2nd time simile
E6 E7no3rd E6 E5 N.C.(E7) E5 E6 E7no3rd E6 E5
1. How can I fool ya? I rest and as - sure ya.
don't you fear the trade in life.
2. Writ - ings ap - pear on the wall.
Gtr. 1
Rhy. Fill 1
End Rhy. Fill 1
P.M.
Gtr. 2
End Rhy. Fig. 2
Rhy. Fig. 3
P.M.
E6 E7no3rd E6 E5
Gtr. 2: w/ Rhy. Fig. 2
E6 E7no3rd E6 E5 E6 E7no3rd E6 E5 E6 E7no3rd E6 E5
I'll take if off from here and put ya on the line.
Life loves force and force loves life.
P.M.
End Rhy. Fig. 3
P.M.

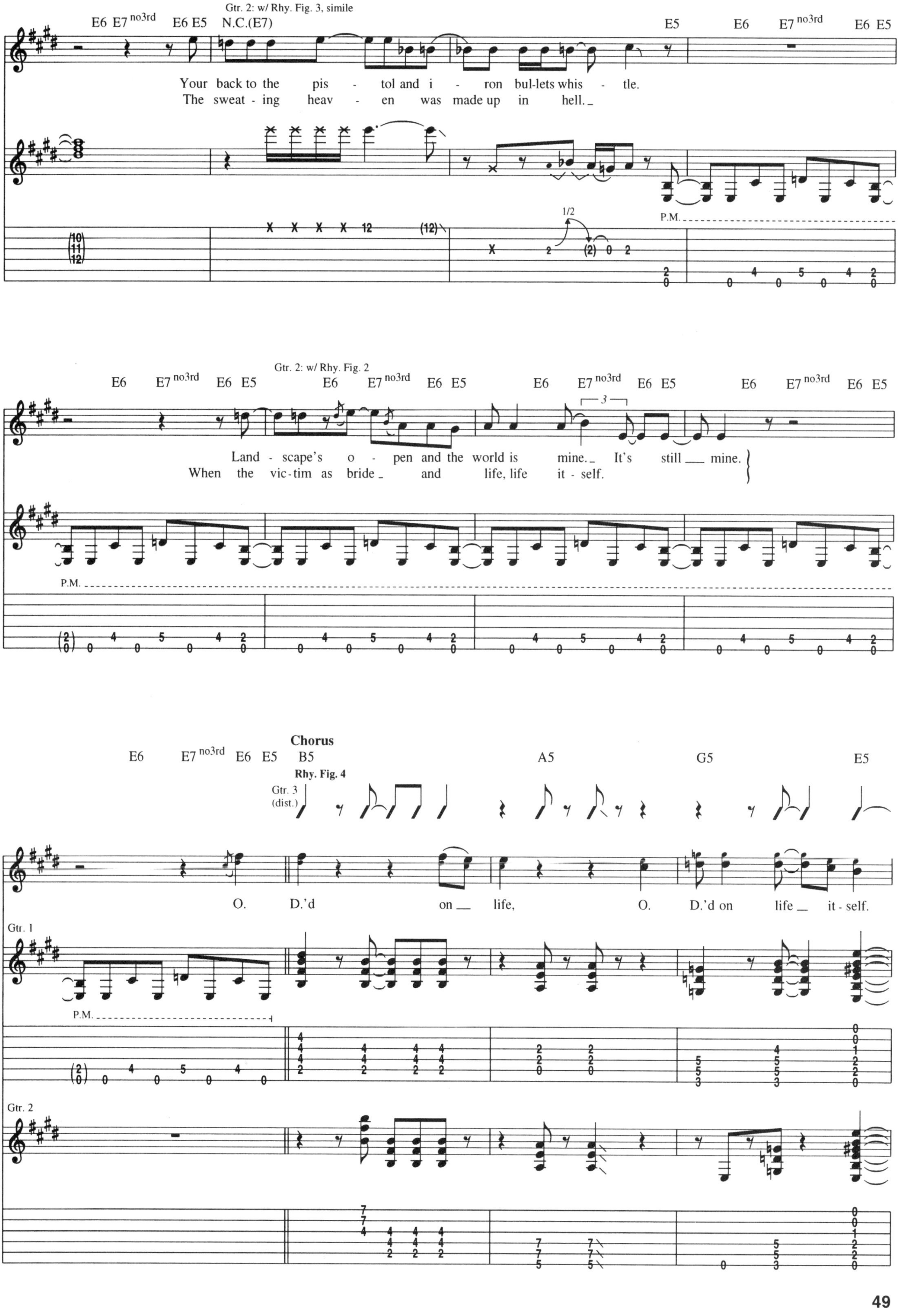
Gtr. 2: w/ Rhy. Fig. 3, simile
E6 E7 no3rd E6 E5 N.C.(E7) E5 E6 E7 no3rd E6 E5
Your back to the pis - tol and i - ron bul-lets whis - tle.
The sweat - ing heav - en was made up in hell.
1/2
P.M.
Gtr. 2: w/ Rhy. Fig. 2
E6 E7 no3rd E6 E5 E6 E7 no3rd E6 E5 E6 E7 no3rd E6 E5 E6 E7 no3rd E6 E5
Land - scape's o - pen and the world is mine. It's still mine.
When the vic - tim as bride and life, life it - self.
P.M.
Chorus
E6 E7 no3rd E6 E5 B5 A5 G5 E5
Rhy. Fig. 4
Gtr. 3 (dist.)
O. D.'d on life, O. D.'d on life it - self.
Gtr. 1
P.M.
Gtr. 2

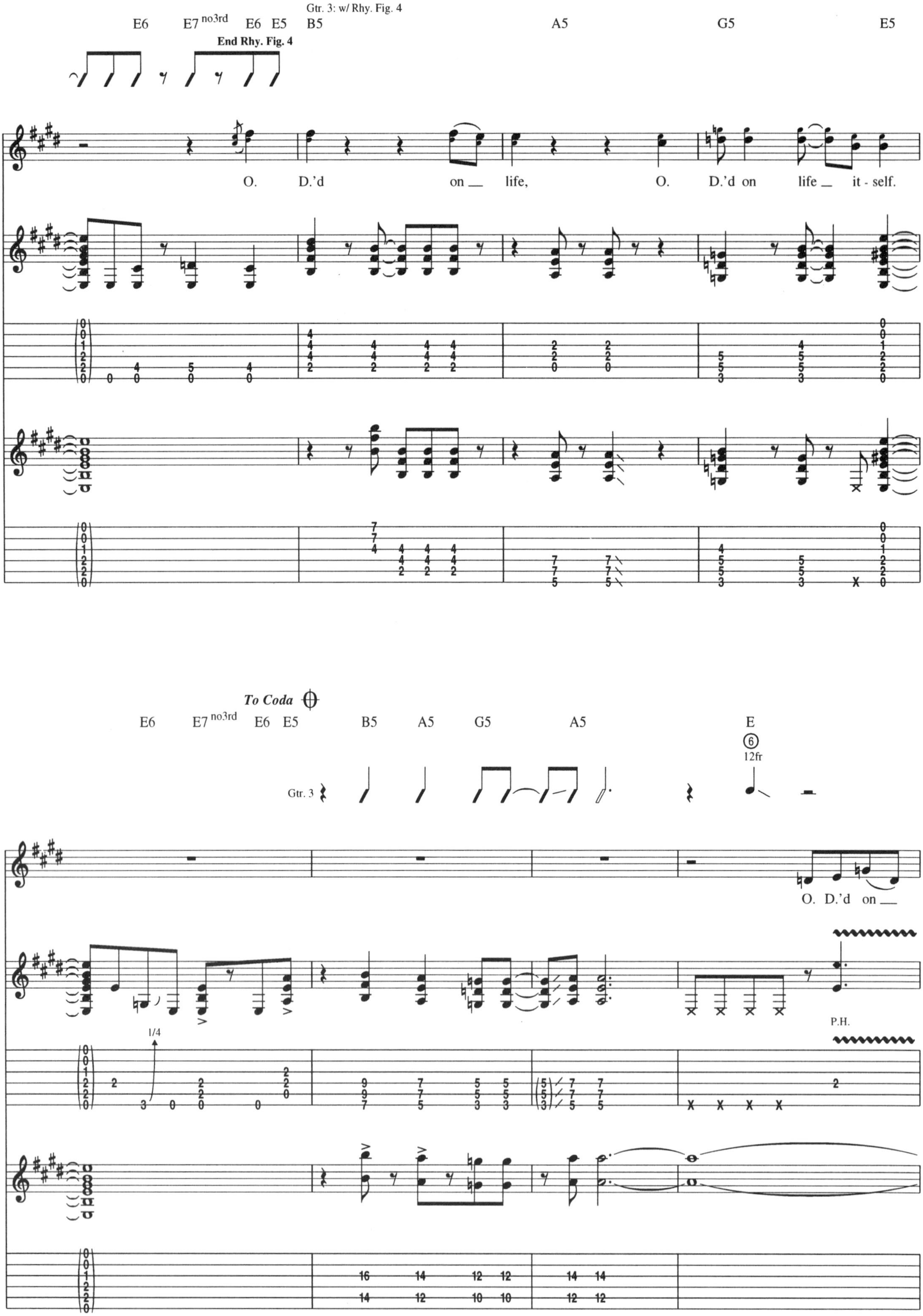
Gtr. 3: w/ Rhy. Fig. 4
E6 E7no3rd E6 E5 B5 A5 G5 E5
End Rhy. Fig. 4
O. D.'d on life, O. D.'d on life it - self.
To Coda
E6 E7no3rd E6 E5 B5 A5 G5 A5 E
12fr
Gtr. 3
O. D.'d on
1/4
P.H.

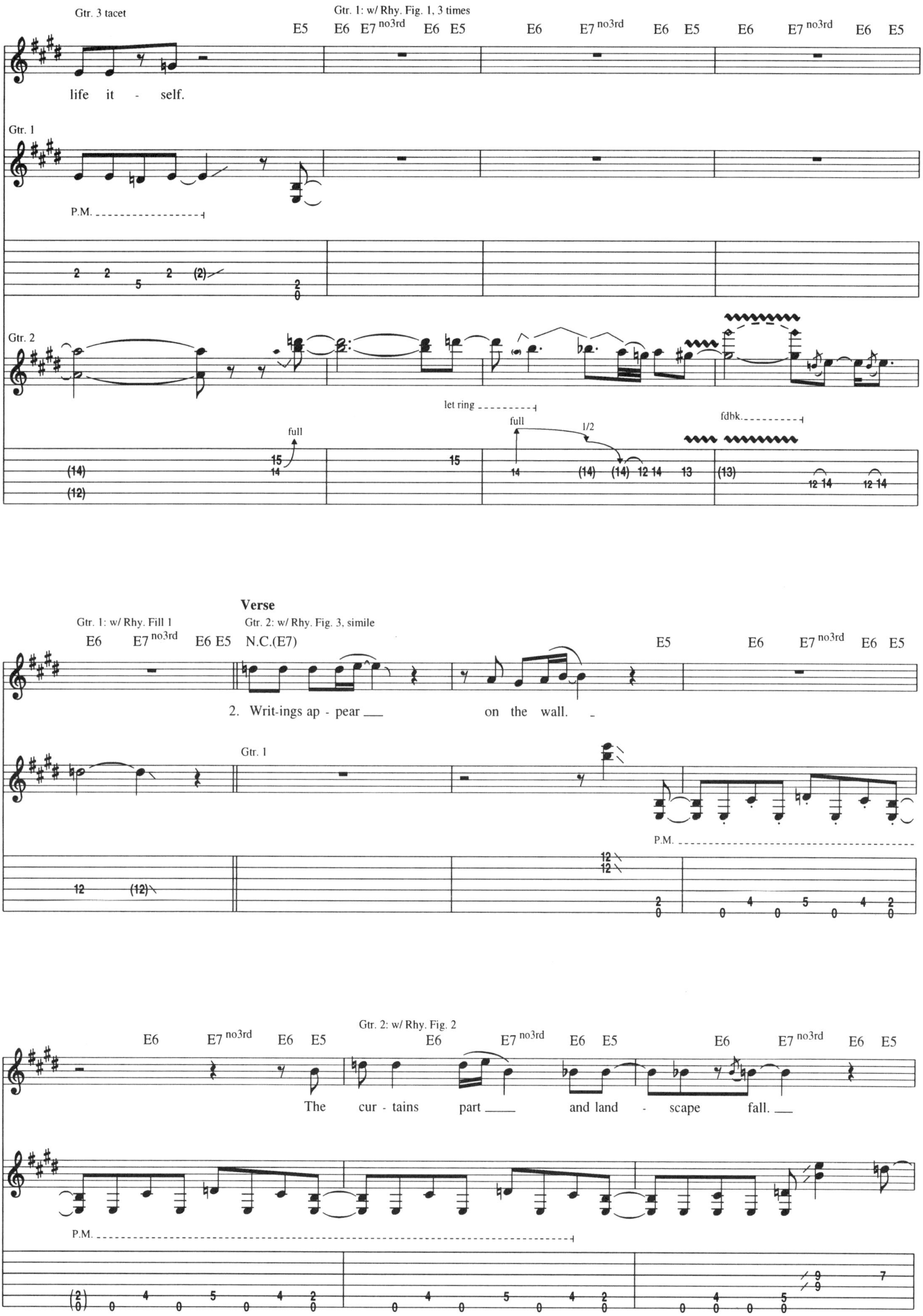
Gtr. 3 tacet
Gtr. 1: w/ Rhy. Fig. 1, 3 times
E5 E6 E7no3rd E6 E5 E6 E7no3rd E6 E5 E6 E7no3rd E6 E5
life it - self.
Gtr. 1
P.M.
Gtr. 2
let ring
full
full
1/2
fdbk.
Verse
Gtr. 1: w/ Rhy. Fill 1
Gtr. 2: w/ Rhy. Fig. 3, simile
E6 E7no3rd E6 E5 N.C.(E7) E5 E6 E7no3rd E6 E5
2. Writ-ings ap - pear on the wall.
Gtr. 1
P.M.
Gtr. 2: w/ Rhy. Fig. 2
E6 E7no3rd E6 E5 E6 E7no3rd E6 E5 E6 E7no3rd E6 E5
The cur - tains part and land - scape fall.
P.M.

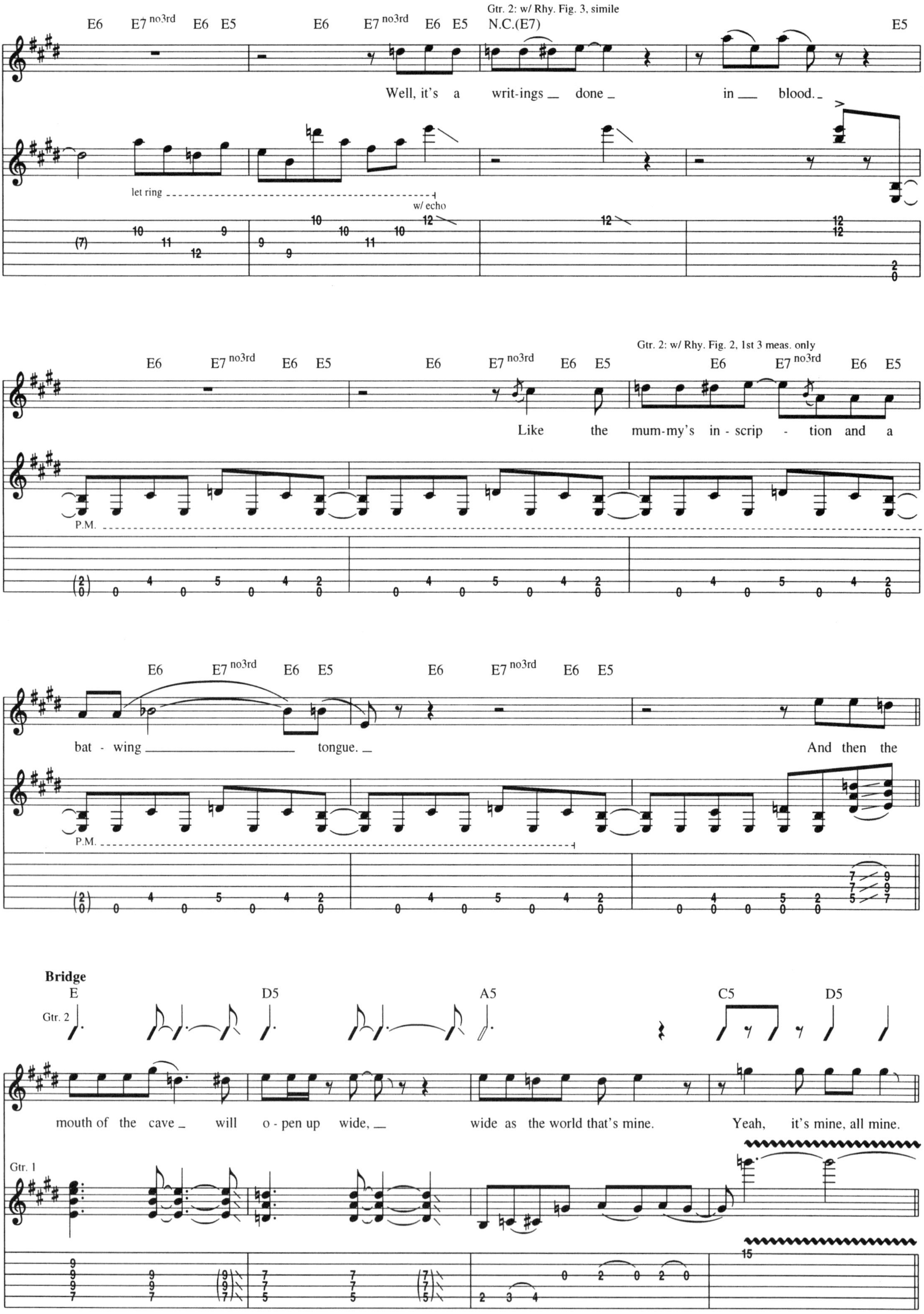
Gtr. 2: w/ Rhy. Fig. 3, simile
E6 E7 no3rd E6 E5 E6 E7 no3rd E6 E5 N.C.(E7) E5
Well, it's a writ-ings done in blood.
let ring
w/ echo
Gtr. 2: w/ Rhy. Fig. 2, 1st 3 meas. only
E6 E7 no3rd E6 E5 E6 E7 no3rd E6 E5 E6 E7 no3rd E6 E5
Like the mum-my's in-scrip-tion and a
P.M.
E6 E7 no3rd E6 E5 E6 E7 no3rd E6 E5
bat-wing tongue. And then the
P.M.
Bridge
E D5 A5 C5 D5
Gtr. 2
mouth of the cave will o-pen up wide, wide as the world that's mine. Yeah, it's mine, all mine.
Gtr. 1

Guitar Solo

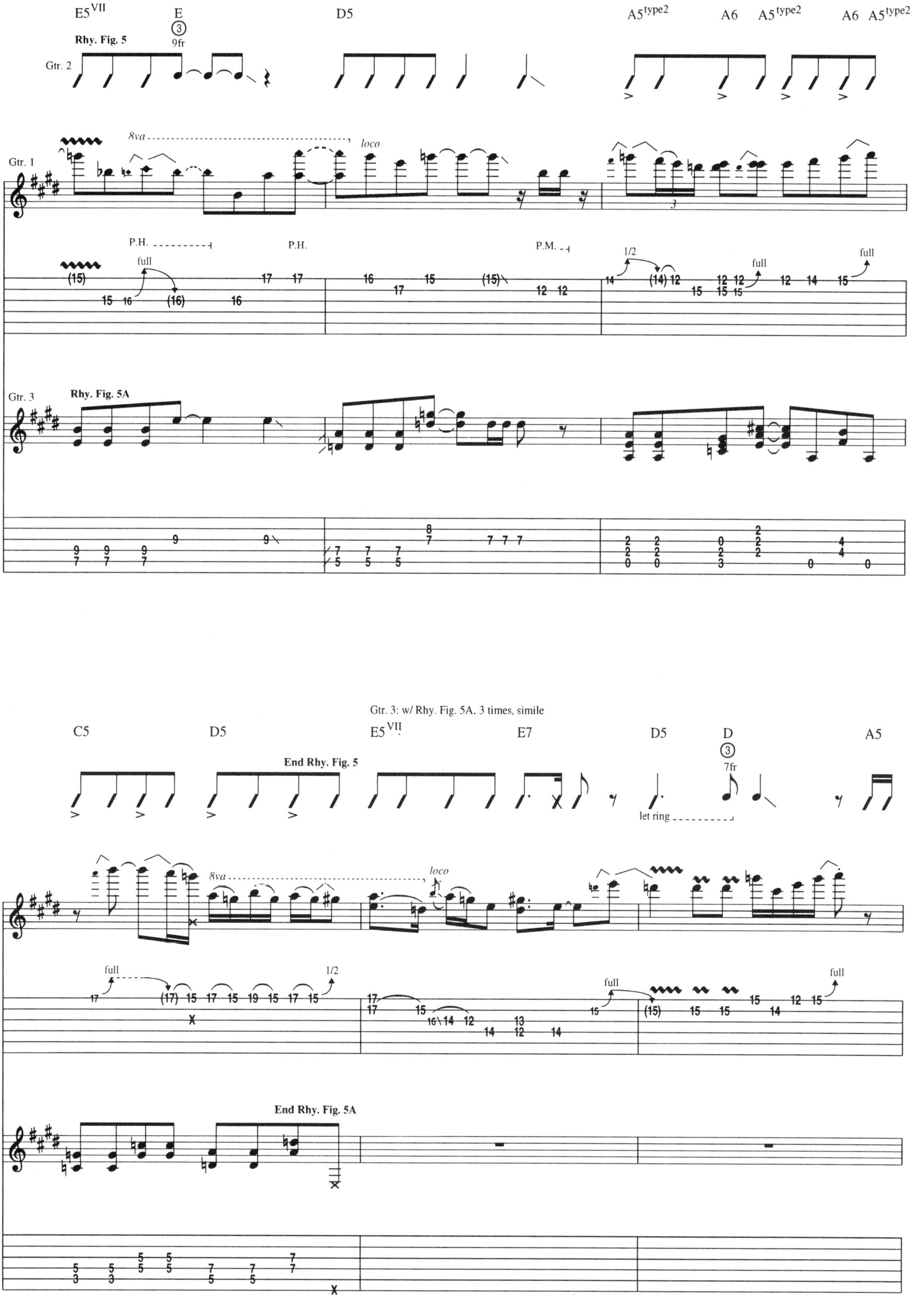
E5VII
E
9fr
D5
A5type2
A6
Rhy. Fig. 5
Gtr. 2
Gtr. 1
8va
loco
P.H.
full
P.M.
1/2
Gtr. 3
Rhy. Fig. 5A
Gtr. 3: w/ Rhy. Fig. 5A, 3 times, simile
C5
E7
D
7fr
A5
End Rhy. Fig. 5
let ring
End Rhy. Fig. 5A

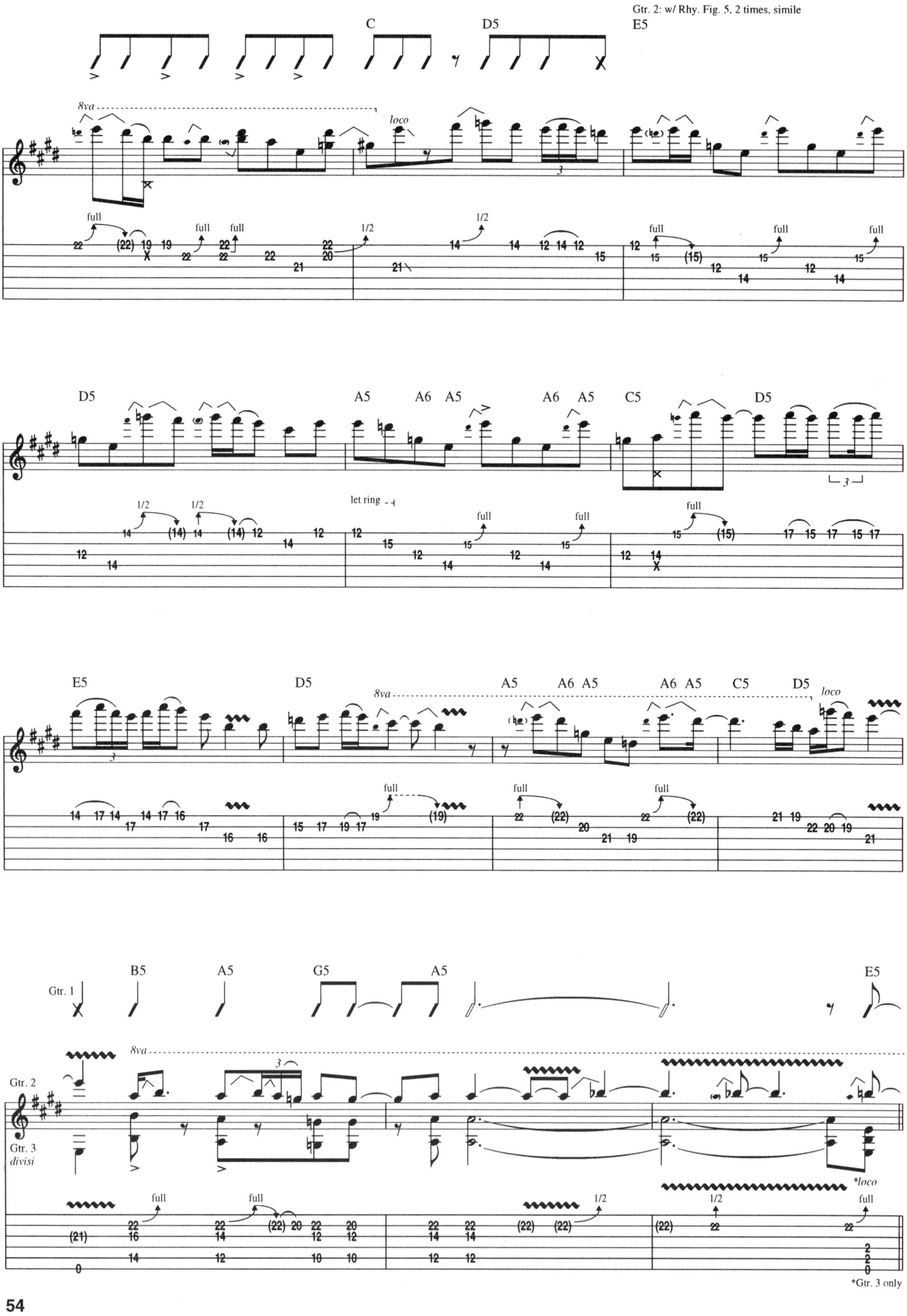
Gtr. 2: w/ Rhy. Fig. 5, 2 times, simile
C
D5
E5
8va
loco
full
1/2
D5
A5 A6 A5 A6 A5
C5
D5
let ring
E5
D5
8va
A5 A6 A5 A6 A5 C5 D5
loco
Gtr. 1
B5 A5 G5 A5
E5
Gtr. 2
Gtr. 3
divisi
*loco
*Gtr. 3 only

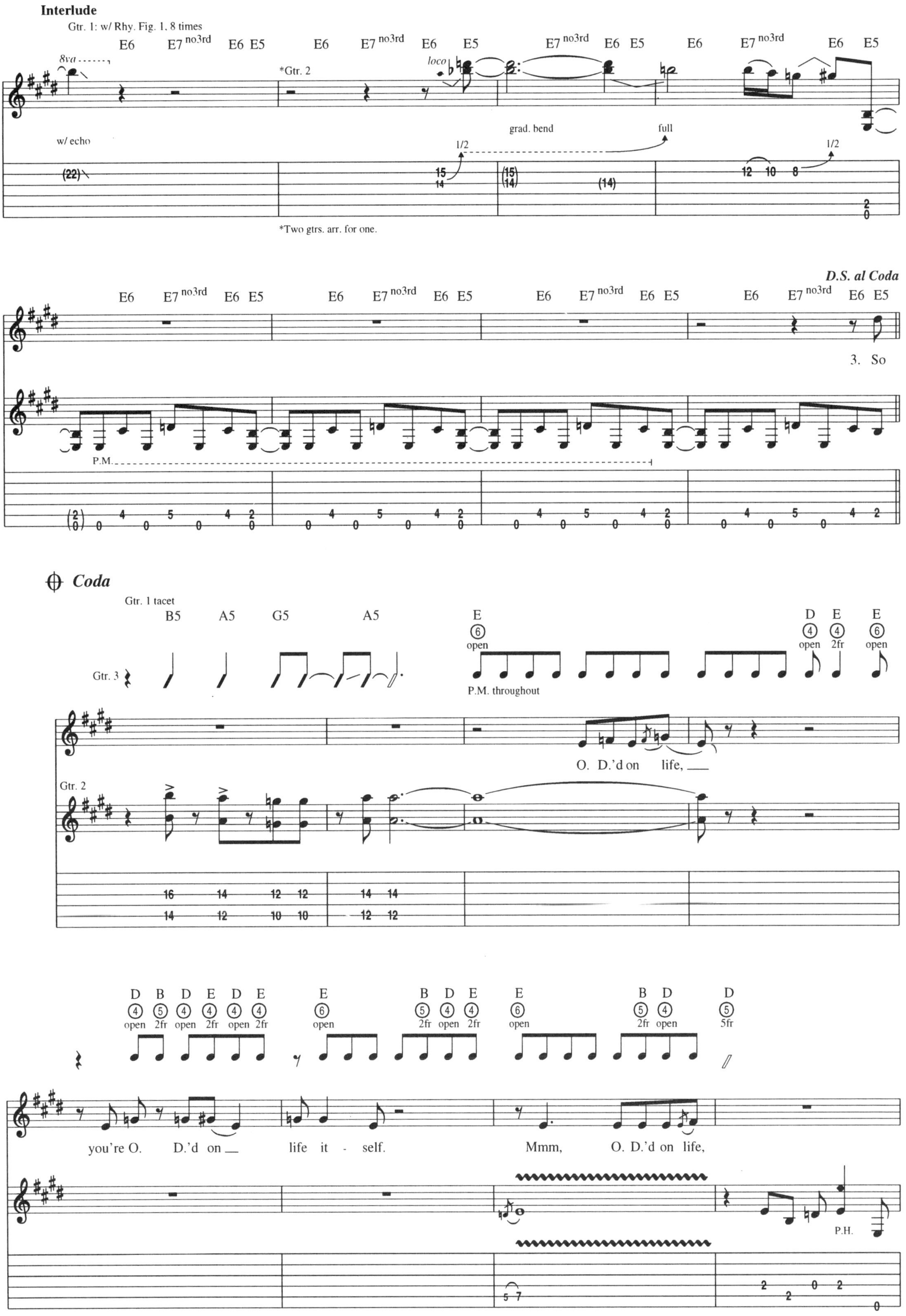
Interlude
Gtr. 1: w/ Rhy. Fig. 1, 8 times
E6 E7 no3rd E6 E5
8va
loco
*Gtr. 2
w/ echo
grad. bend
full
1/2
*Two gtrs. arr. for one.
D.S. al Coda
3. So
P.M.
Coda
Gtr. 1 tacet
B5 A5 G5 A5
E D E E
open 2fr
Gtr. 3
P.M. throughout
O. D.'d on life,
Gtr. 2
D B D E D E
you're O. D.'d on life it - self.
Mmm, O. D.'d on life,
5fr
P.H.

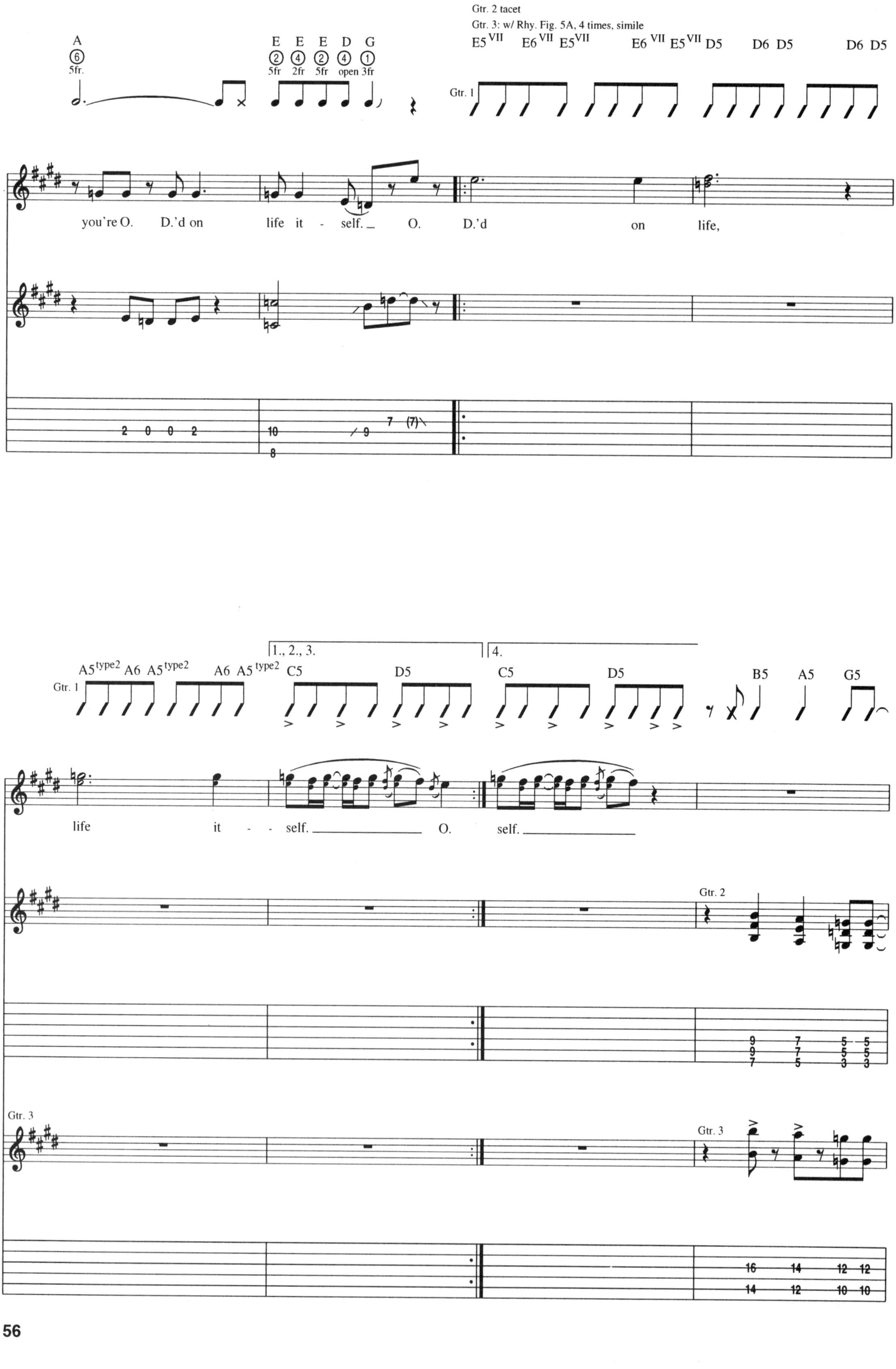
Gtr. 2 tacet
Gtr. 3: w/ Rhy. Fig. 5A, 4 times, simile
A
5fr.
E E E D G
5fr 2fr 5fr open 3fr
E5VII E6VII E5VII E6VII E5VII D5 D6 D5 D6 D5
Gtr. 1
you're O. D.'d on life it - self. O. D.'d on life,
A5type2 A6 A5type2 A6 A5type2
1., 2., 3.
4.
C5 D5 C5 D5 B5 A5 G5
life it - - self. O. self.
Gtr. 2
Gtr. 3

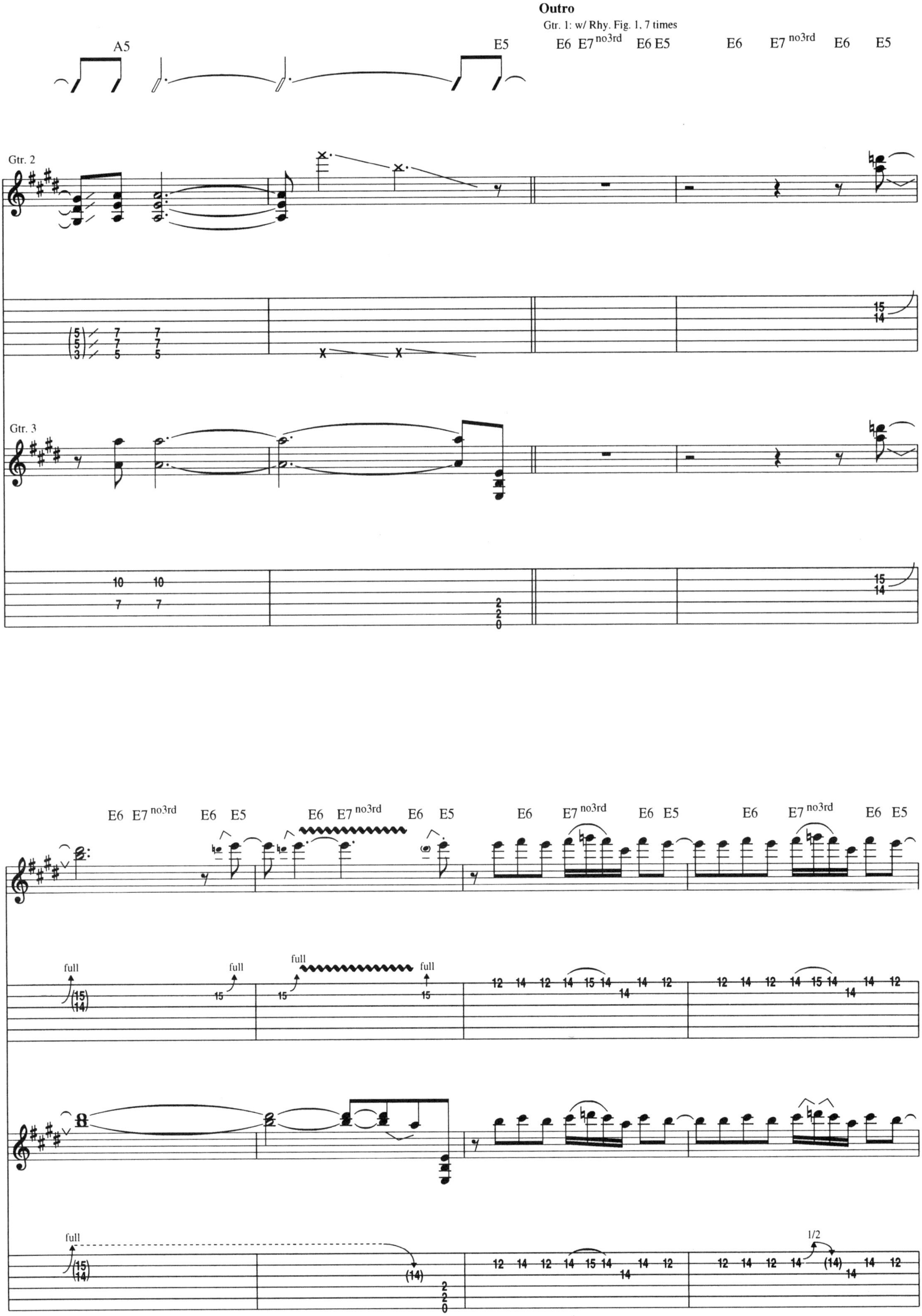
Outro
Gtr. 1: w/ Rhy. Fig. 1, 7 times
A5
E5
E6 E7no3rd E6 E5
E6 E7no3rd E6 E5
Gtr. 2
Gtr. 3
E6 E7no3rd E6 E5
E6 E7no3rd E6 E5
E6 E7no3rd E6 E5
E6 E7no3rd E6 E5
full
1/2

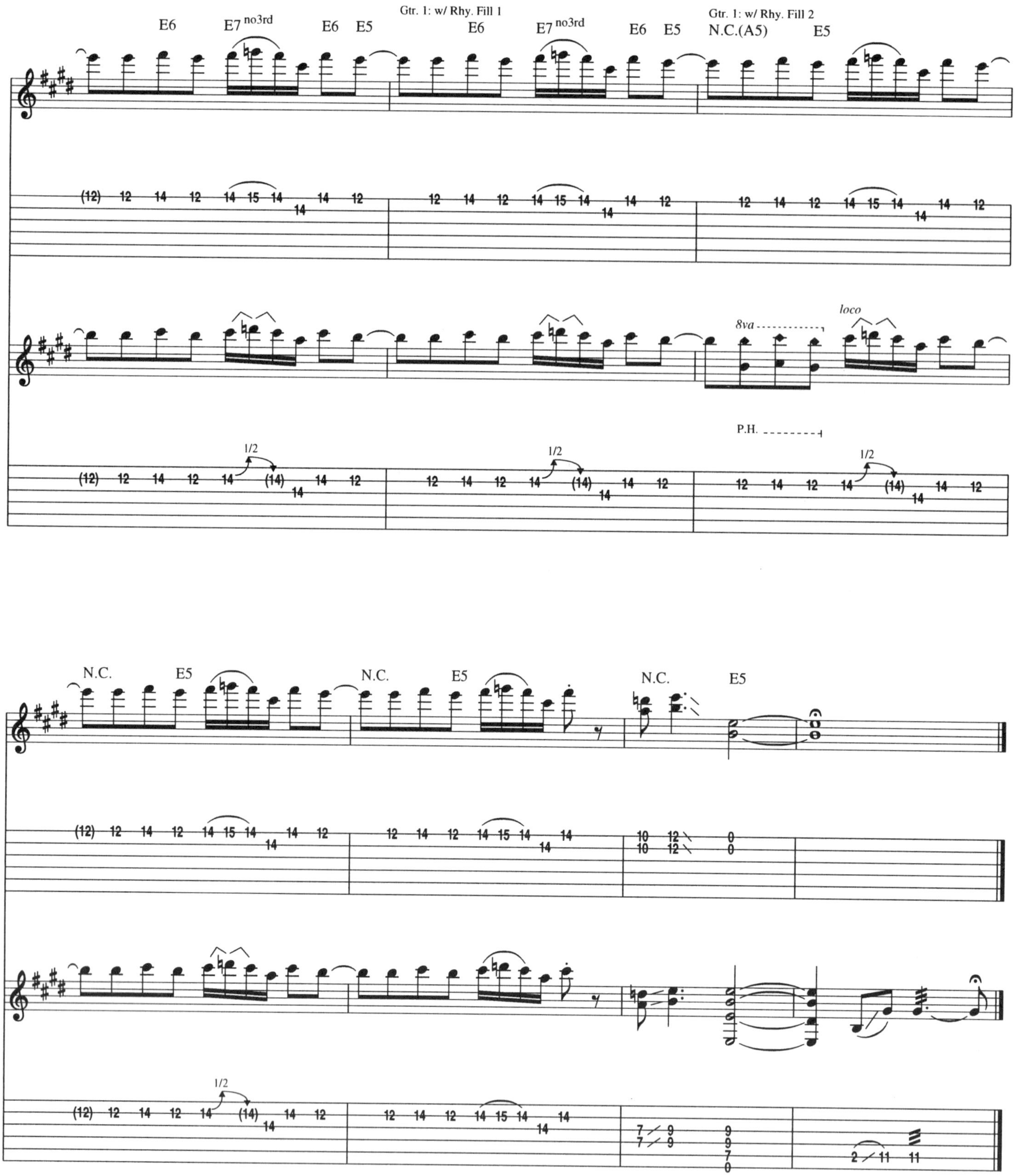
Gtr. 1: w/ Rhy. Fill 1
Gtr. 1: w/ Rhy. Fill 2
E6
E7 no3rd
E6 E5
E6
E7 no3rd
E6 E5
N.C.(A5)
E5
8va
loco
P.H.
1/2
N.C.
E5
N.C.
E5
N.C.
E5

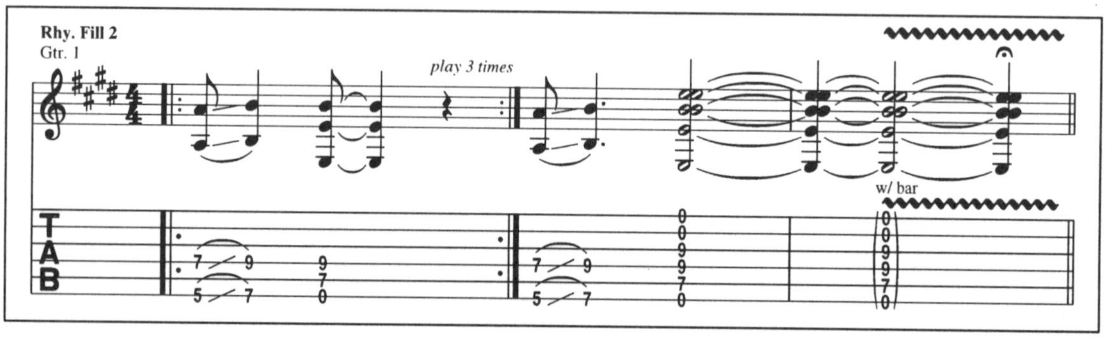
Rhy. Fill 2
Gtr. 1
play 3 times
w/ bar

Flaming Telepaths

Words and Music by Samuel Pearlman, Donald Roeser and Albert Bouchard

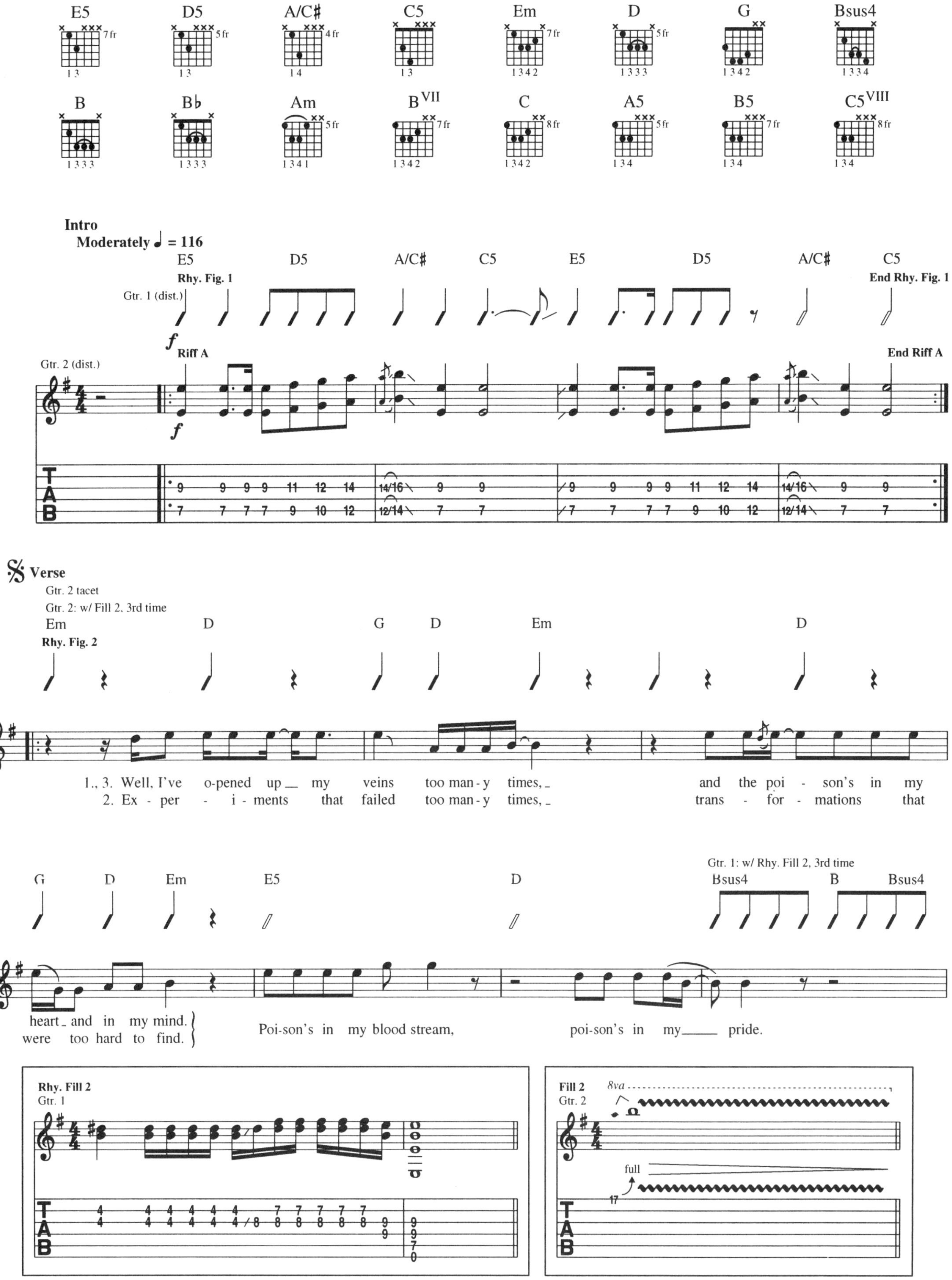

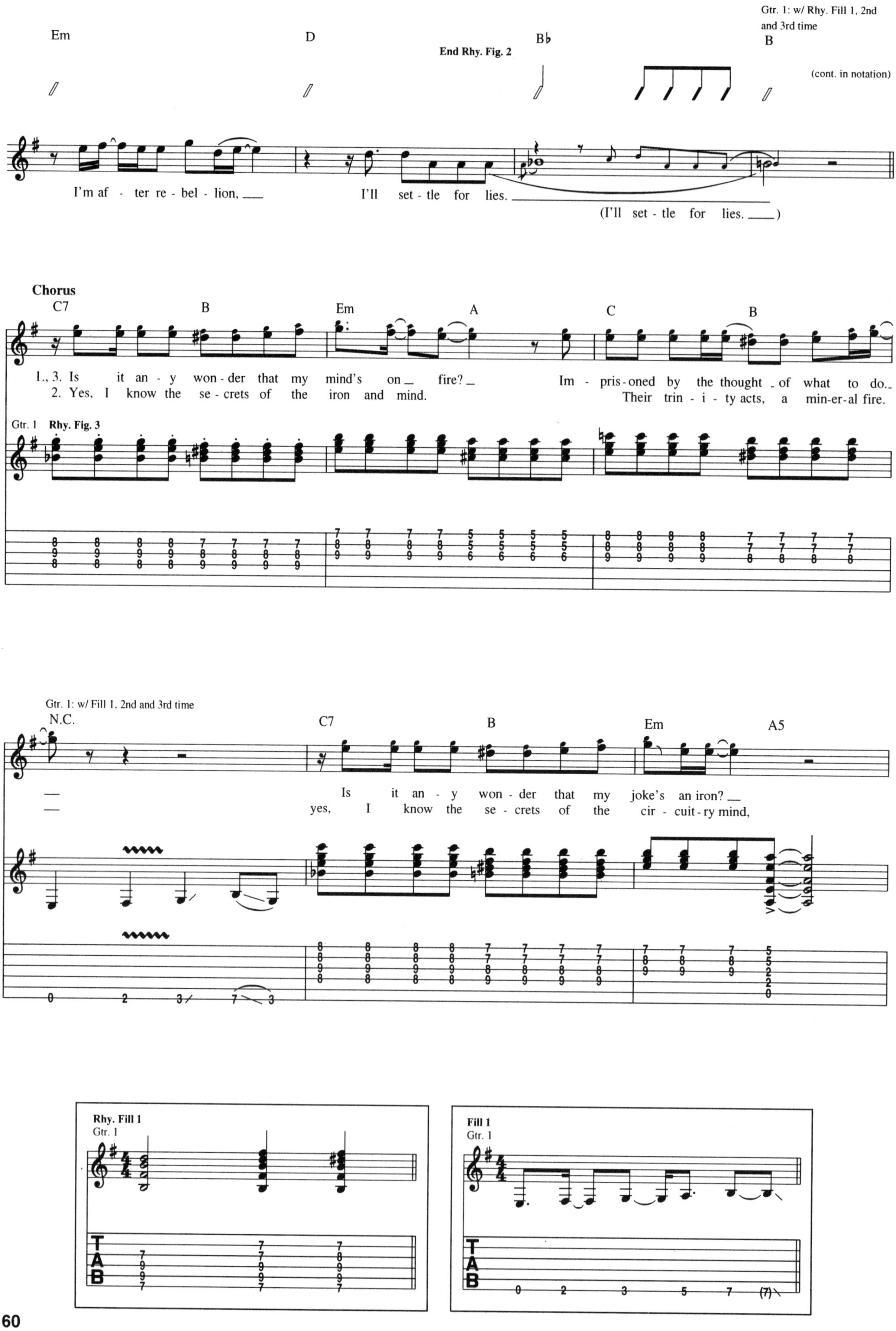
Gtr. 1: w/ Rhy. Fill 1, 2nd and 3rd time
Em
D
End Rhy. Fig. 2
B♭
B
(cont. in notation)
I'm af - ter re - bel - lion, __ I'll set - tle for lies. __
(I'll set - tle for lies. __)
Chorus
C7 B Em A C B
1., 3. Is it an - y won - der that my mind's on __ fire? __ Im - pris - oned by the thought - of what to do. _
2. Yes, I know the se - crets of the iron and mind. Their trin - i - ty acts, a min - er - al fire.
Gtr. 1 Rhy. Fig. 3
Gtr. 1: w/ Fill 1, 2nd and 3rd time
N.C.
C7 B Em A5
Is it an - y won - der that my joke's an iron? __
yes, I know the se - crets of the cir - cuit - ry mind,
Rhy. Fill 1
Gtr. 1
Fill 1
Gtr. 1
TAB

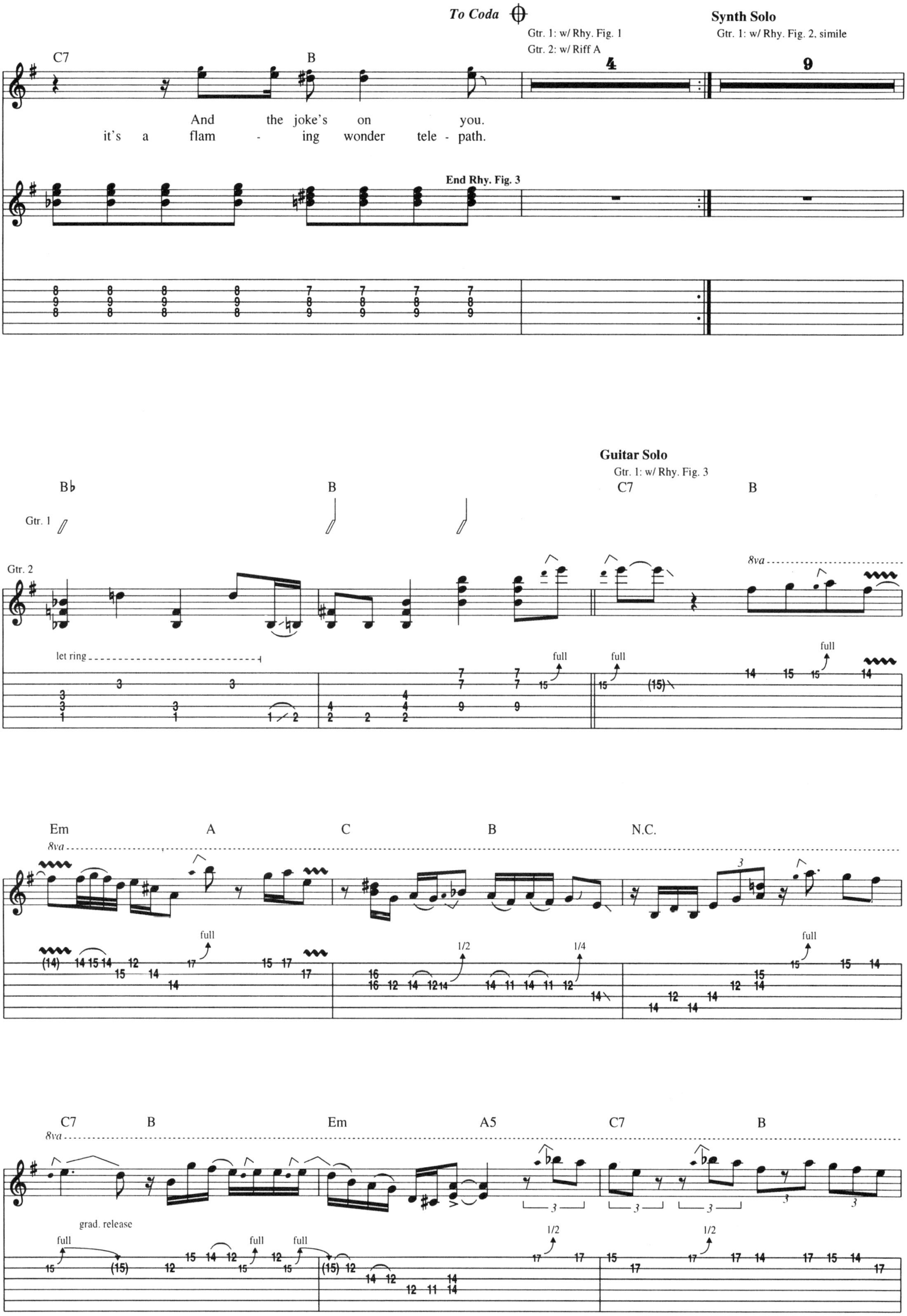
To Coda
Synth Solo
Gtr. 1: w/ Rhy. Fig. 1
Gtr. 2: w/ Riff A
Gtr. 1: w/ Rhy. Fig. 2, simile
C7
B
And the joke's on you.
it's a flam - ing wonder tele - path.
End Rhy. Fig. 3
Guitar Solo
Gtr. 1: w/ Rhy. Fig. 3
Bb
B
C7
B
Gtr. 1
Gtr. 2
8va
let ring
full
Em
A
C
B
N.C.
8va
full
1/2
1/4
full
C7
B
Em
A5
C7
B
8va
grad. release
full
full
full
1/2
1/2

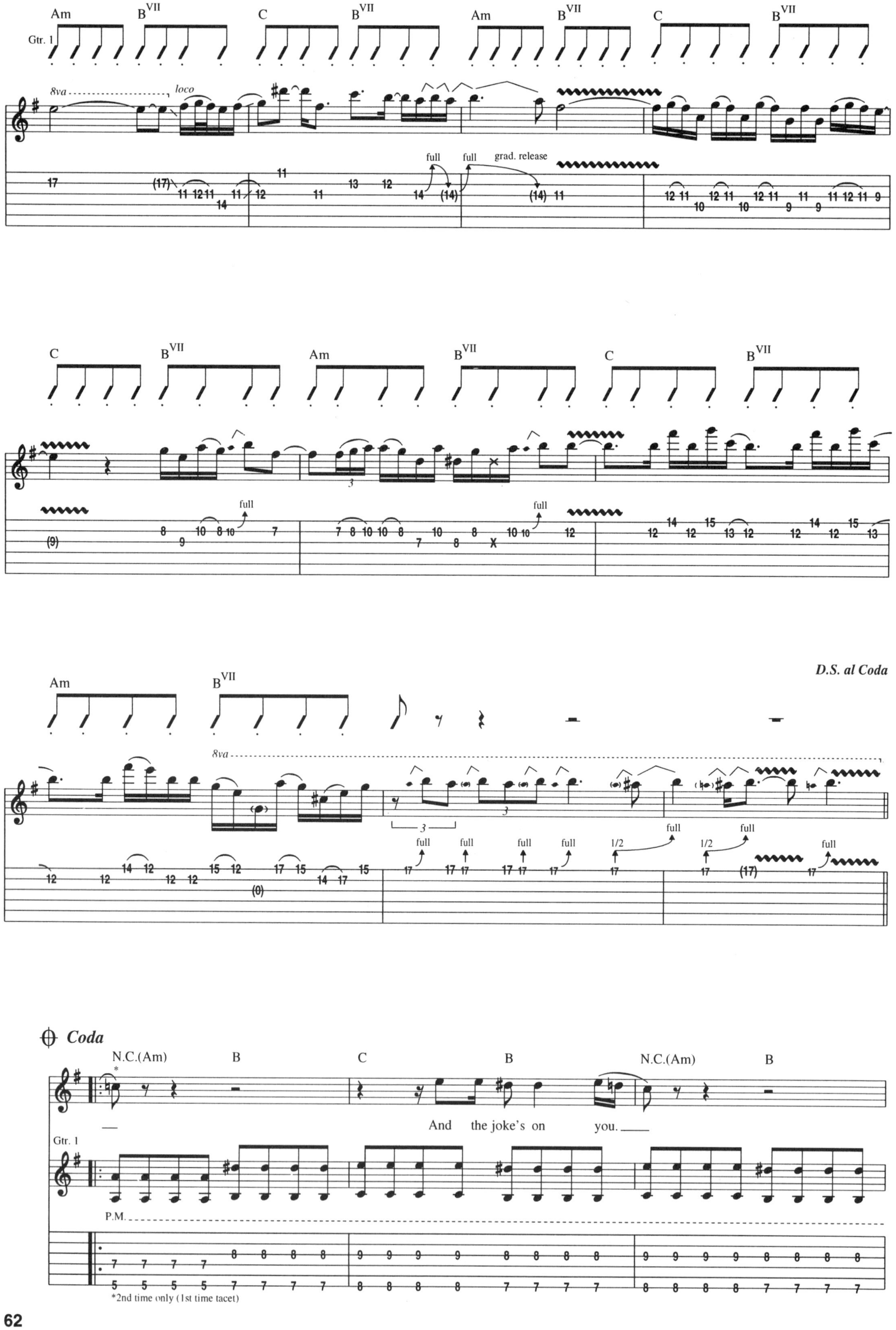
Am B^VII C B^VII Am B^VII C B^VII
Gtr. 1
8va loco
full full grad. release
C B^VII Am B^VII C B^VII
full full
Am B^VII
D.S. al Coda
8va
full full full full 1/2 full 1/2 full full
Coda
N.C.(Am) B C B N.C.(Am) B
And the joke's on you.
Gtr. 1
P.M.
*2nd time only (1st time tacet)

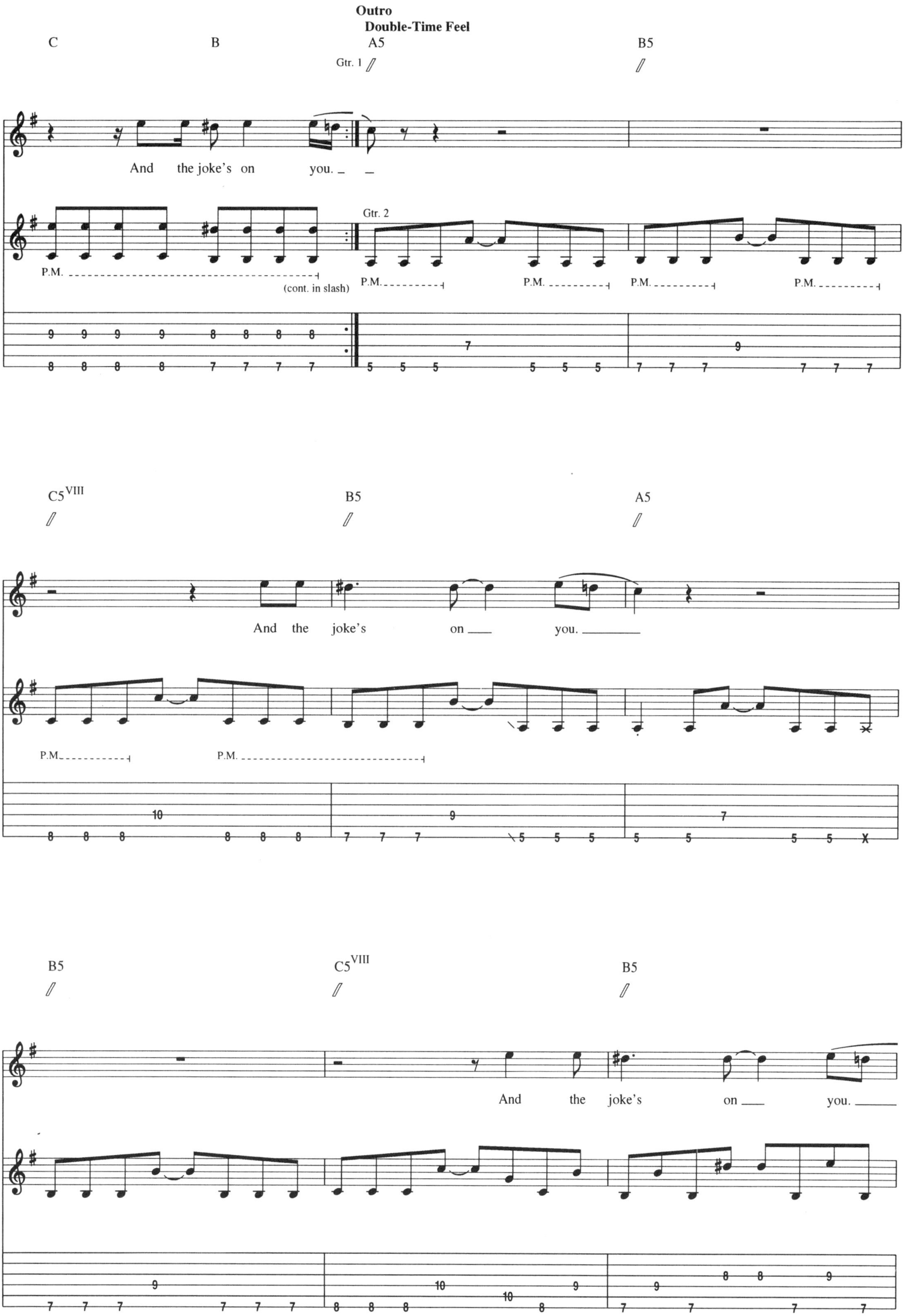
Outro
Double-Time Feel
C B A5 B5
Gtr. 1
And the joke's on you.
Gtr. 2
P.M.
(cont. in slash)
C5VIII B5 A5
And the joke's on you.
B5 C5VIII B5
And the joke's on you.

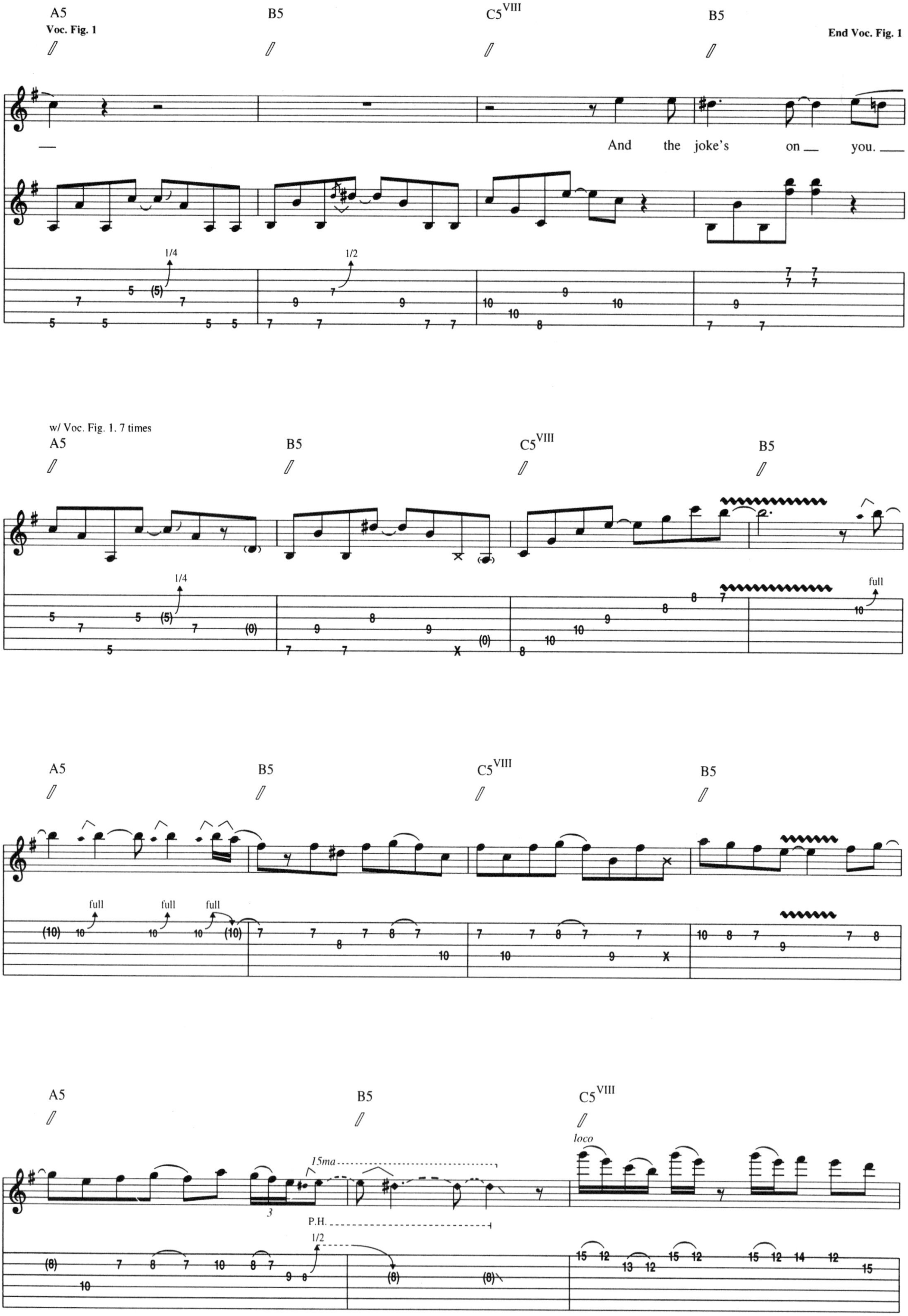
A5
B5
C5VIII
B5
Voc. Fig. 1
End Voc. Fig. 1
And the joke's on you.
1/4
1/2
w/ Voc. Fig. 1. 7 times
full
15ma
P.H.
loco

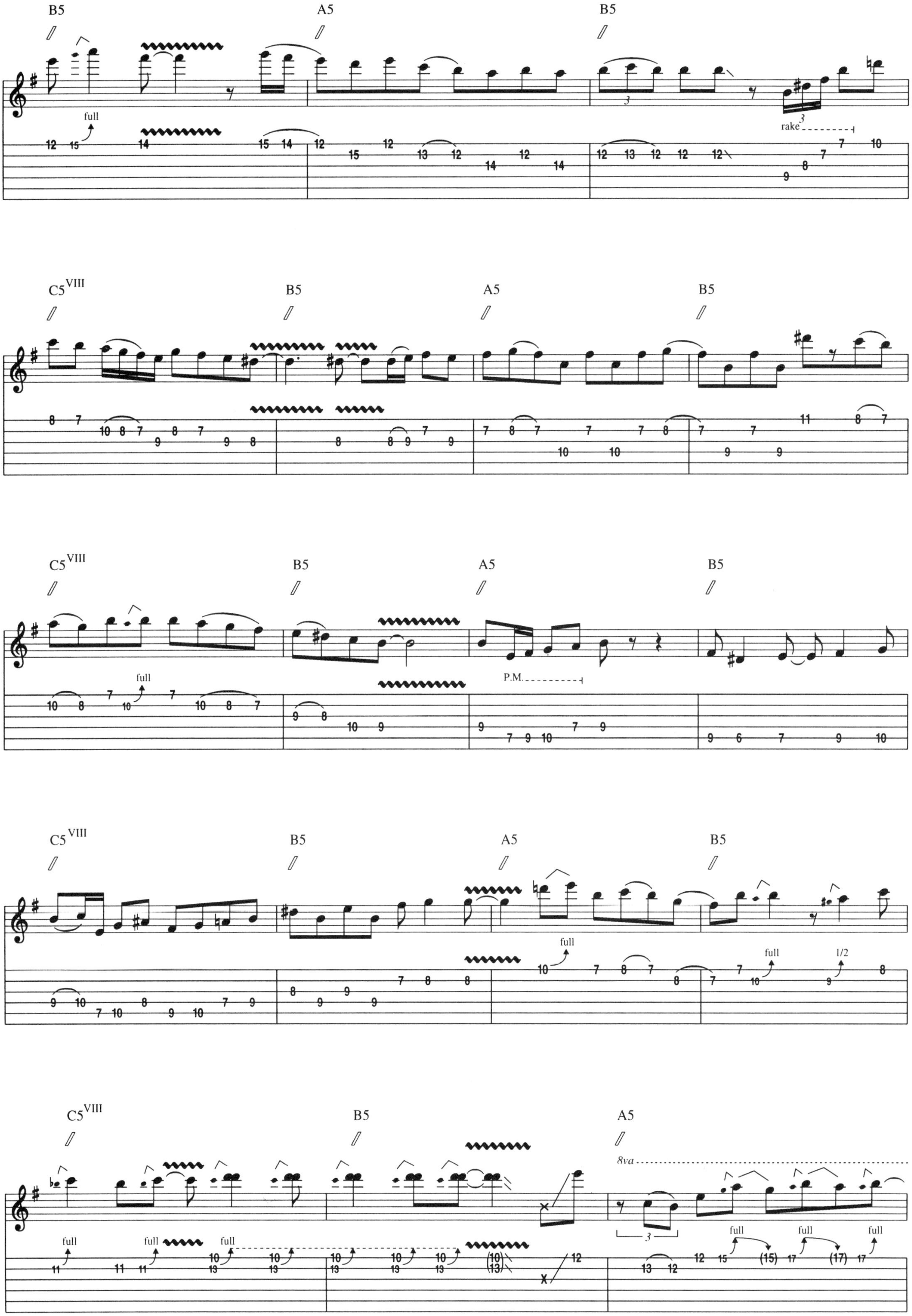

B5
A5
B5
full
rake
C5 VIII
B5
A5
B5
C5 VIII
B5
A5
B5
full
P.M.
C5 VIII
B5
A5
B5
full
full
1/2
C5 VIII
B5
A5
8va
full
full
full
full
full
full

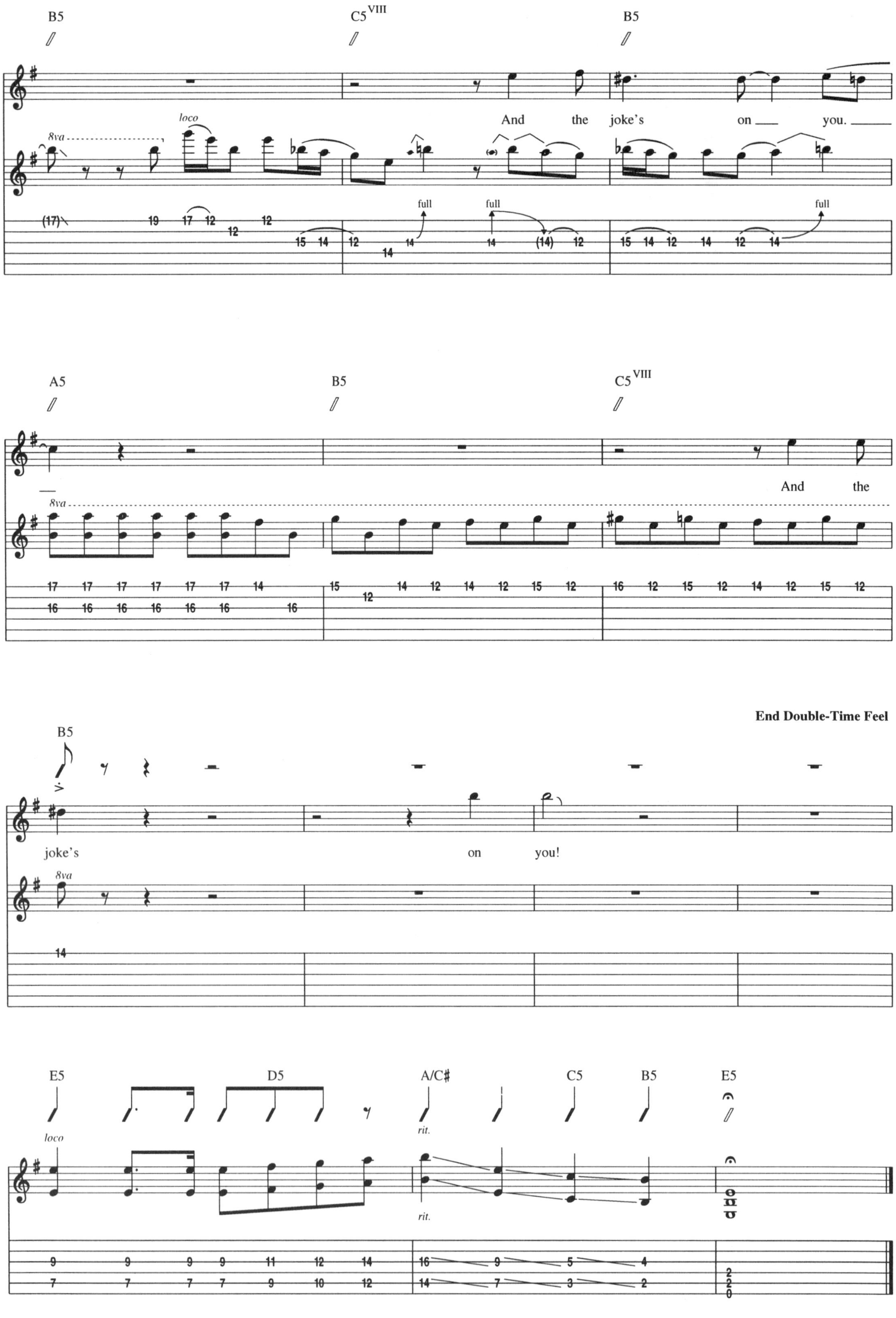
B5
C5 VIII
B5
And the joke's on you.
8va
loco
full
A5
B5
C5 VIII
And the
B5
End Double-Time Feel
joke's on you!
E5
D5
A/C♯
C5
B5
E5
loco
rit.

Godzilla

Words and Music by Donald Roeser

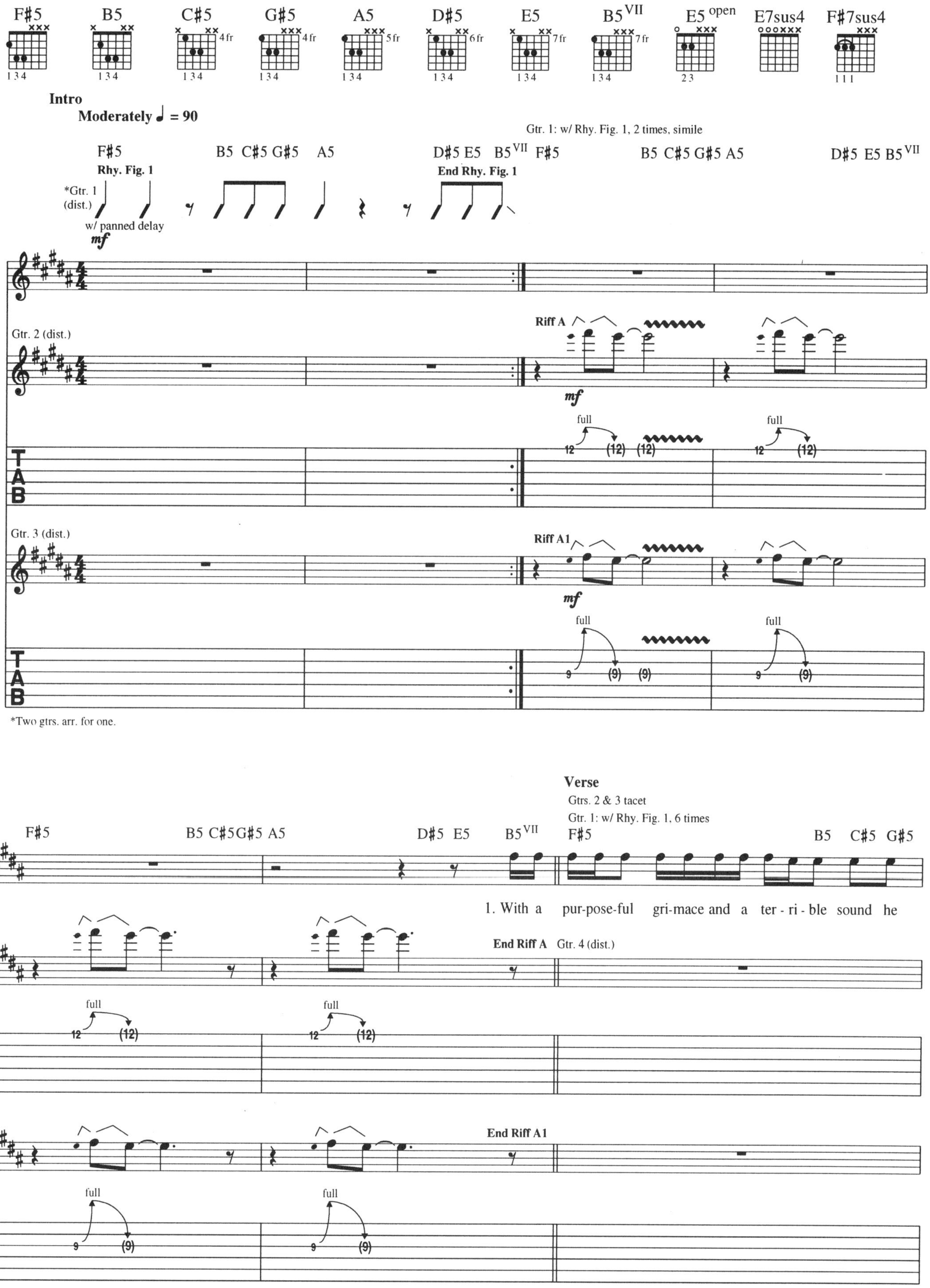

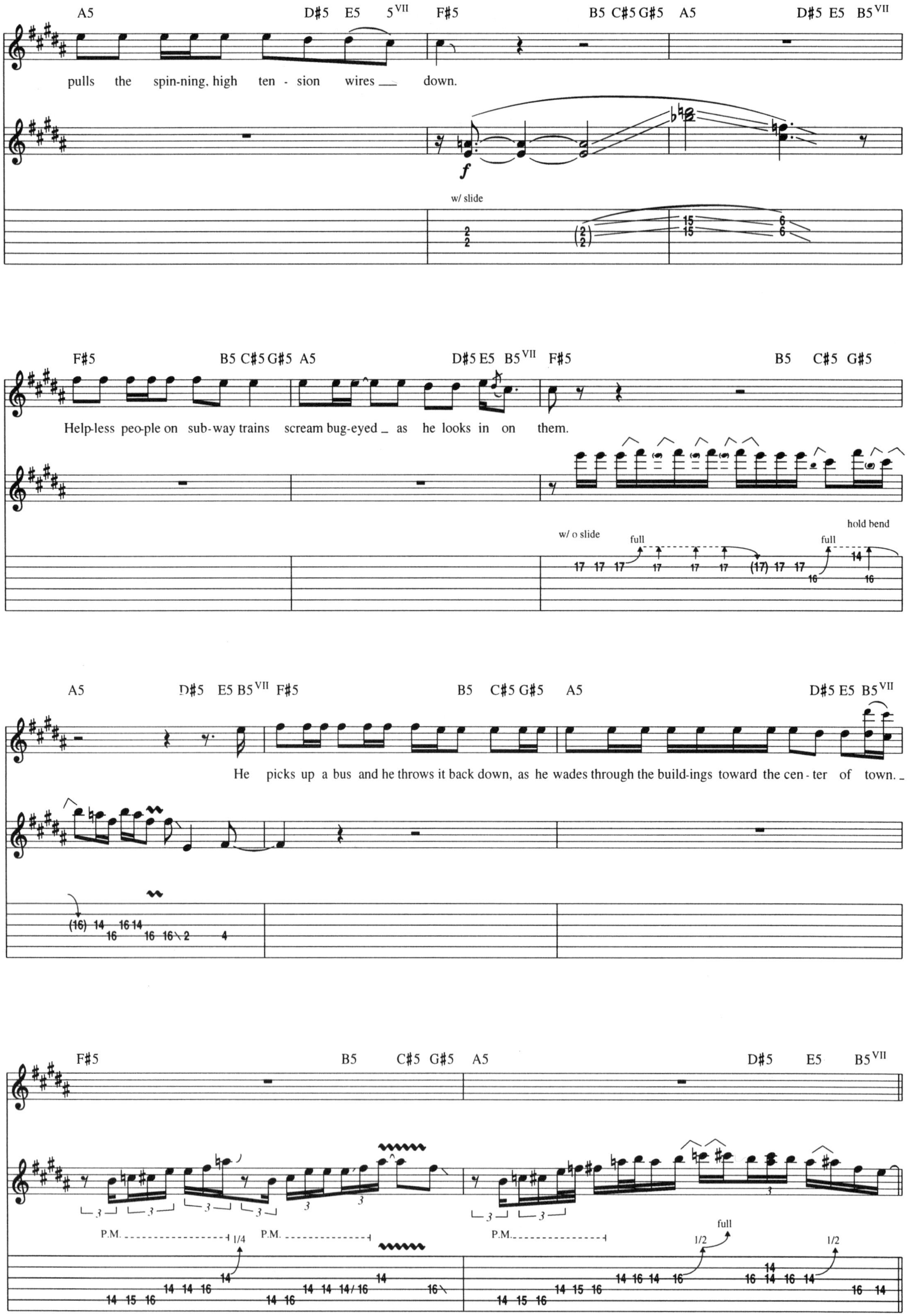
A5 D#5 E5 5VII F#5 B5 C#5 G#5 A5 D#5 E5 B5VII
pulls the spin-ning, high ten - sion wires down.
w/ slide
F#5 B5 C#5 G#5 A5 D#5 E5 B5VII F#5 B5 C#5 G#5
Help-less peo-ple on sub-way trains scream bug-eyed as he looks in on them.
w/ o slide
full
hold bend
A5 D#5 E5 B5VII F#5 B5 C#5 G#5 A5 D#5 E5 B5VII
He picks up a bus and he throws it back down, as he wades through the build-ings toward the cen - ter of town.
F#5 B5 C#5 G#5 A5 D#5 E5 B5VII
P.M.
1/4
1/2
full

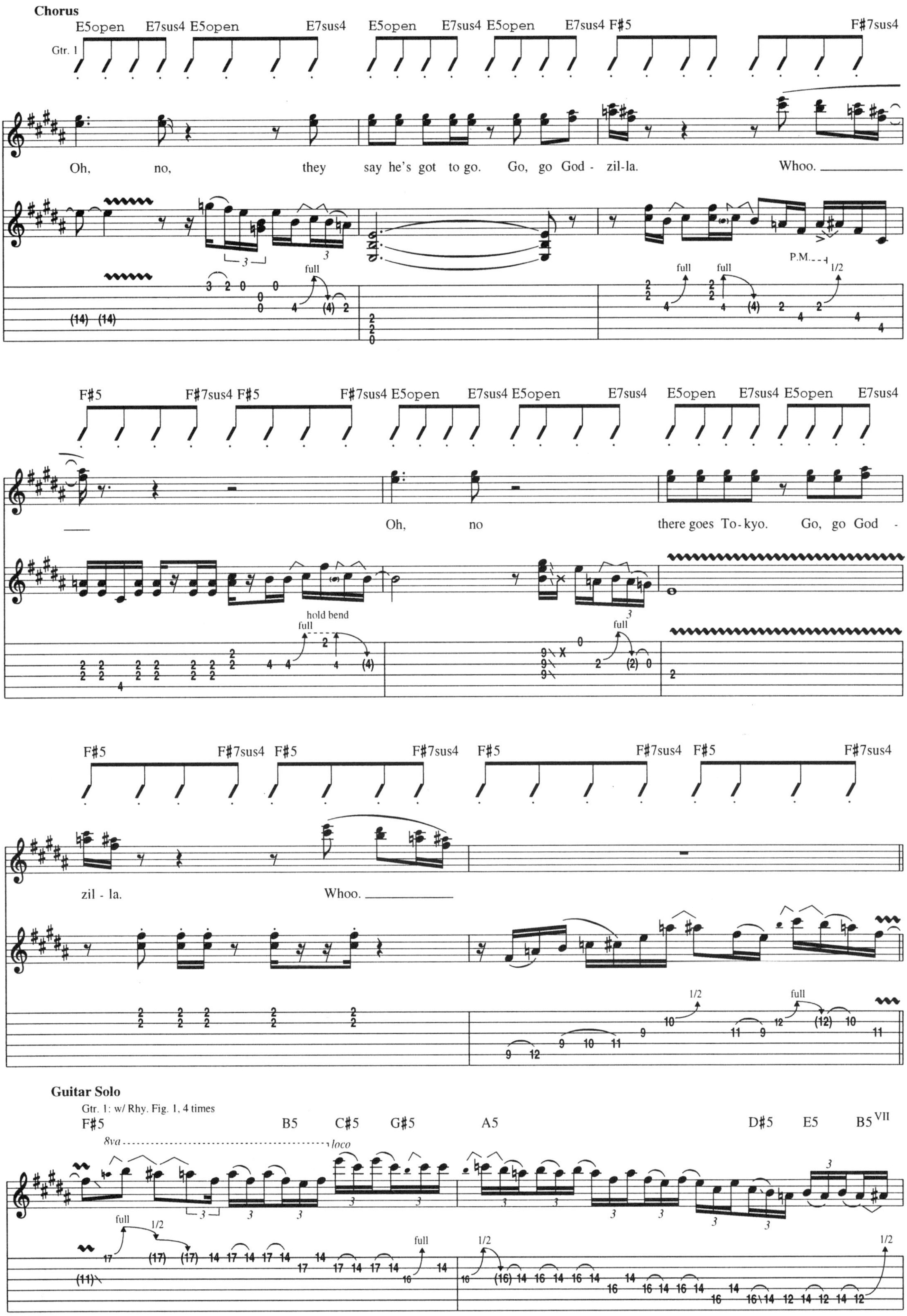
Chorus
E5open E7sus4 E5open E7sus4 E5open E7sus4 E5open E7sus4 F#5 F#7sus4
Gtr. 1
Oh, no, they say he's got to go. Go, go God - zil-la. Whoo.
full
P.M.
1/2
F#5 F#7sus4 F#5 F#7sus4 E5open E7sus4 E5open E7sus4 E5open E7sus4 E5open E7sus4
Oh, no there goes To-kyo. Go, go God -
hold bend
F#5 F#7sus4 F#5 F#7sus4 F#5 F#7sus4 F#5 F#7sus4
zil - la. Whoo.
Guitar Solo
Gtr. 1: w/ Rhy. Fig. 1, 4 times
F#5 B5 C#5 G#5 A5 D#5 E5 B5 VII
8va
loco

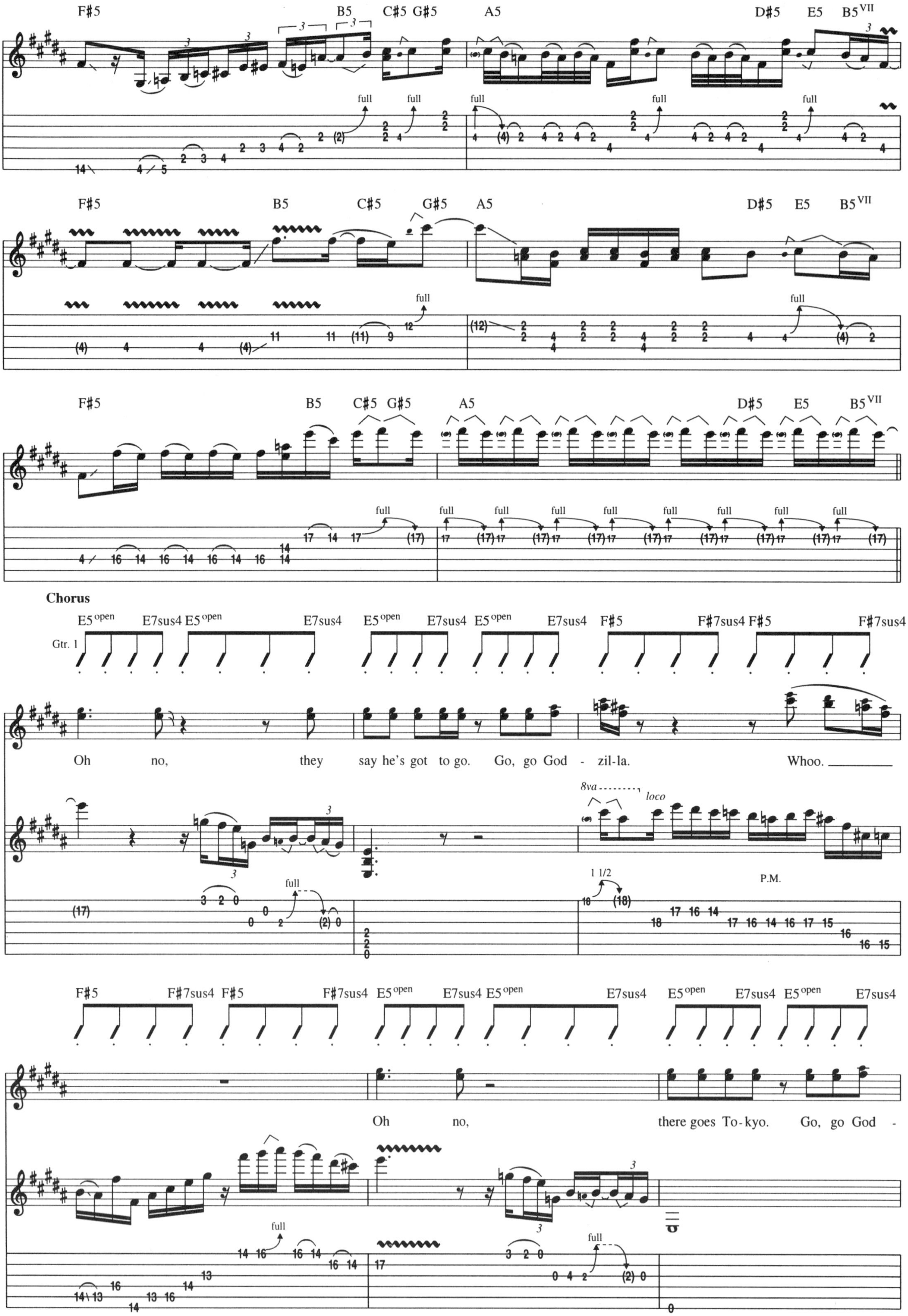
F#5 B5 C#5 G#5 A5 D#5 E5 B5VII
full
F#5 B5 C#5 G#5 A5 D#5 E5 B5VII
full
F#5 B5 C#5 G#5 A5 D#5 E5 B5VII
full
Chorus
E5open E7sus4 E5open E7sus4 E5open E7sus4 E5open E7sus4 F#5 F#7sus4 F#5 F#7sus4
Gtr. 1
Oh no, they say he's got to go. Go, go God - zil-la. Whoo.
8va
loco
1 1/2
P.M.
F#5 F#7sus4 F#5 F#7sus4 E5open E7sus4 E5open E7sus4 E5open E7sus4 E5open E7sus4
Oh no, there goes To-kyo. Go, go God -

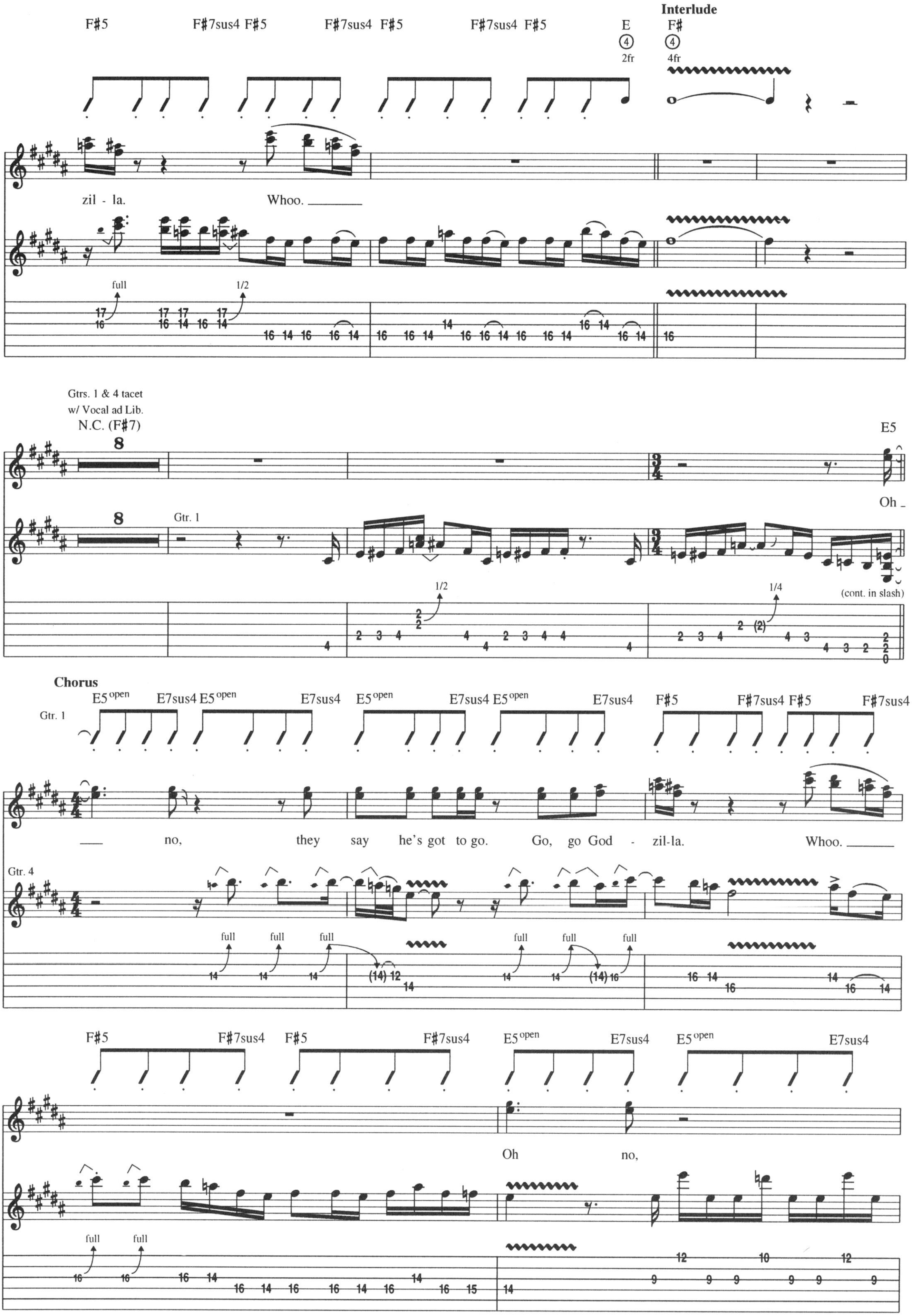
Interlude
F♯5 F♯7sus4 F♯5 F♯7sus4 F♯5 F♯7sus4 F♯5 E F♯
2fr 4fr
zil - la. Whoo.
full 1/2
Gtrs. 1 & 4 tacet
w/ Vocal ad Lib.
N.C. (F♯7)
8
E5
Oh
Gtr. 1
1/2 1/4
(cont. in slash)
Chorus
E5 open E7sus4 E5 open E7sus4 E5 open E7sus4 E5 open E7sus4 F♯5 F♯7sus4 F♯5 F♯7sus4
no, they say he's got to go. Go, go God - zil-la. Whoo.
Gtr. 4
full full full full full full
F♯5 F♯7sus4 F♯5 F♯7sus4 E5 open E7sus4 E5 open E7sus4
Oh no,
full full

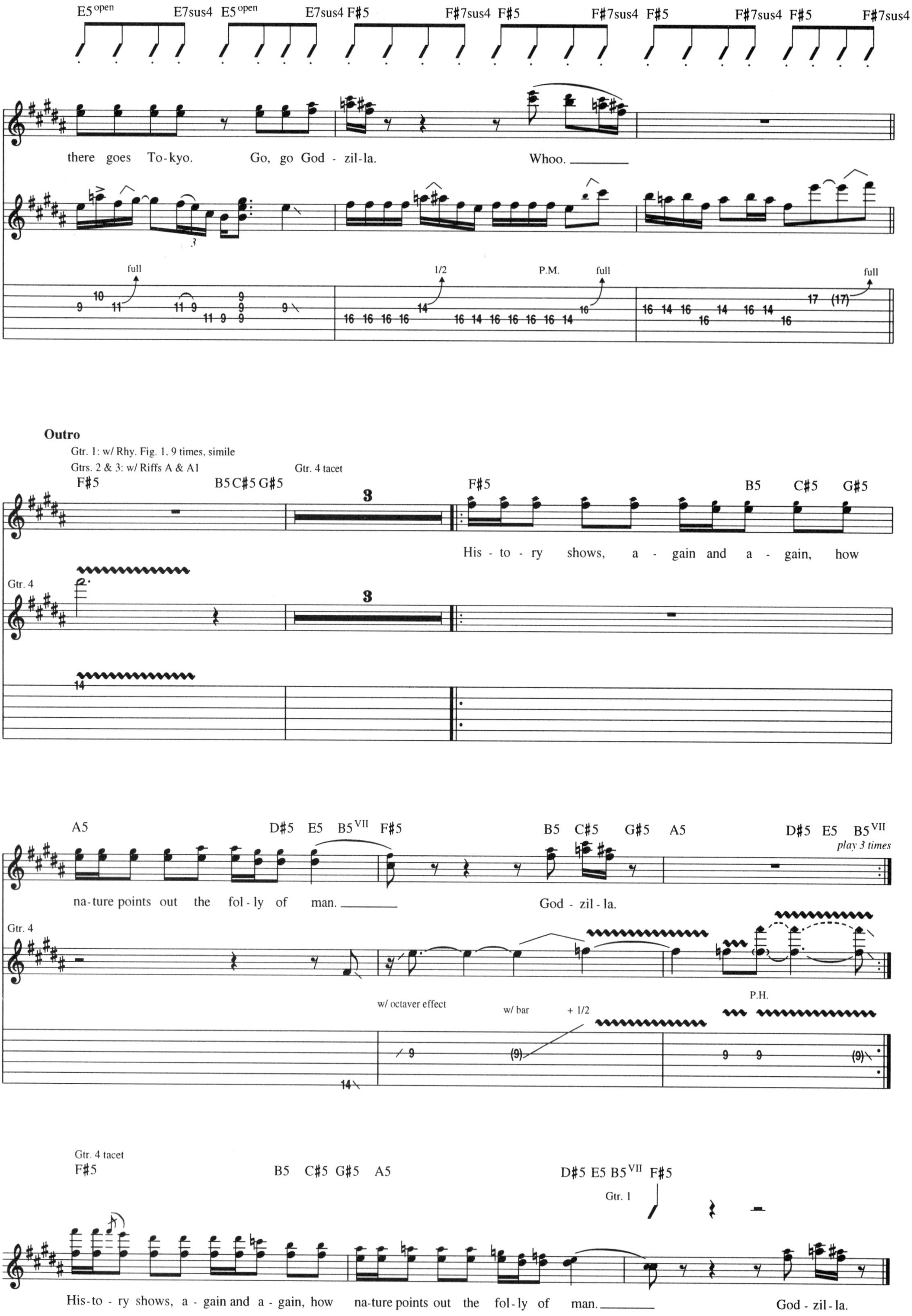
E5open E7sus4 E5open E7sus4 F#5 F#7sus4 F#5 F#7sus4 F#5 F#7sus4 F#5 F#7sus4
there goes To-kyo. Go, go God - zil-la. Whoo.
full
1/2
P.M.
full
full
Outro
Gtr. 1: w/ Rhy. Fig. 1, 9 times, simile
Gtrs. 2 & 3: w/ Riffs A & A1
Gtr. 4 tacet
F#5 B5 C#5 G#5 F#5 B5 C#5 G#5
His - to - ry shows, a - gain and a - gain, how
Gtr. 4
A5 D#5 E5 B5VII F#5 B5 C#5 G#5 A5 D#5 E5 B5VII
play 3 times
na-ture points out the fol-ly of man. God - zil - la.
Gtr. 4
w/ octaver effect
w/ bar
+ 1/2
P.H.
Gtr. 4 tacet
F#5 B5 C#5 G#5 A5 D#5 E5 B5VII F#5
Gtr. 1
His-to - ry shows, a - gain and a - gain, how na-ture points out the fol-ly of man. God - zil - la.

Astronomy

Words and Music by Samuel Pearlman, Albert Bouchard and Joseph Bouchard

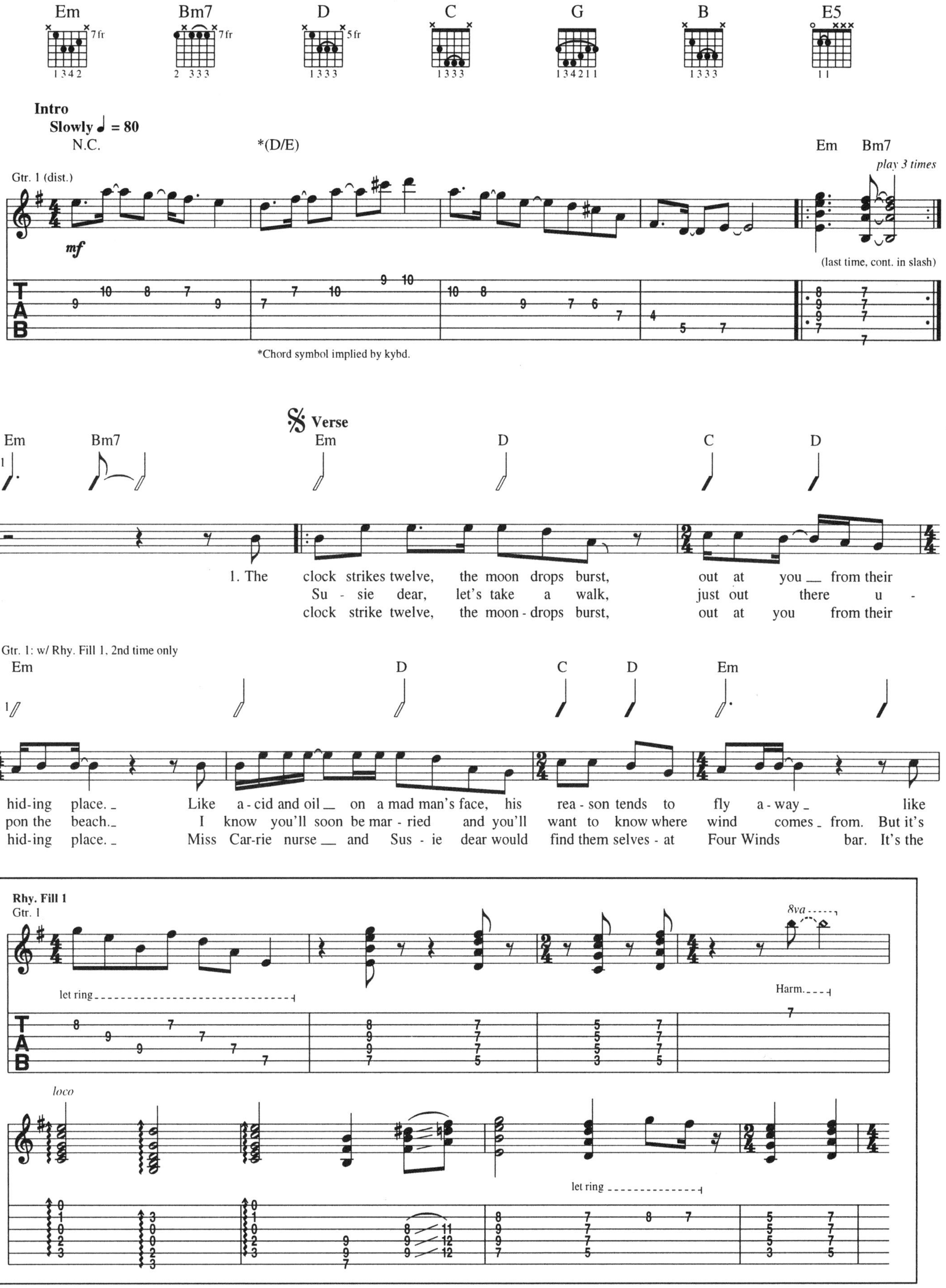
Em Bm7 D C G B E5
7fr 7fr 5fr
Intro
Slowly ♩ = 80
N.C.
*(D/E)
Em Bm7
play 3 times
Gr. 1 (dist.)
mf
(last time, cont. in slash)
*Chord symbol implied by kybd.
Verse
Em Bm7 Em D C D
Gtr. 1
1. The clock strikes twelve, the moon drops burst, out at you from their
Su - sie dear, let's take a walk, just out there u -
clock strike twelve, the moon - drops burst, out at you from their
Gtr. 1: w/ Rhy. Fill 1, 2nd time only
Em D C D Em
Gtr. 1
hid-ing place. Like a - cid and oil on a mad man's face, his rea - son tends to fly a - way like
pon the beach. I know you'll soon be mar - ried and you'll want to know where wind comes from. But it's
hid-ing place. Miss Car-rie nurse and Sus - ie dear would find them selves - at Four Winds bar. It's the
Rhy. Fill 1
Gtr. 1
let ring
8va
Harm.
loco
let ring

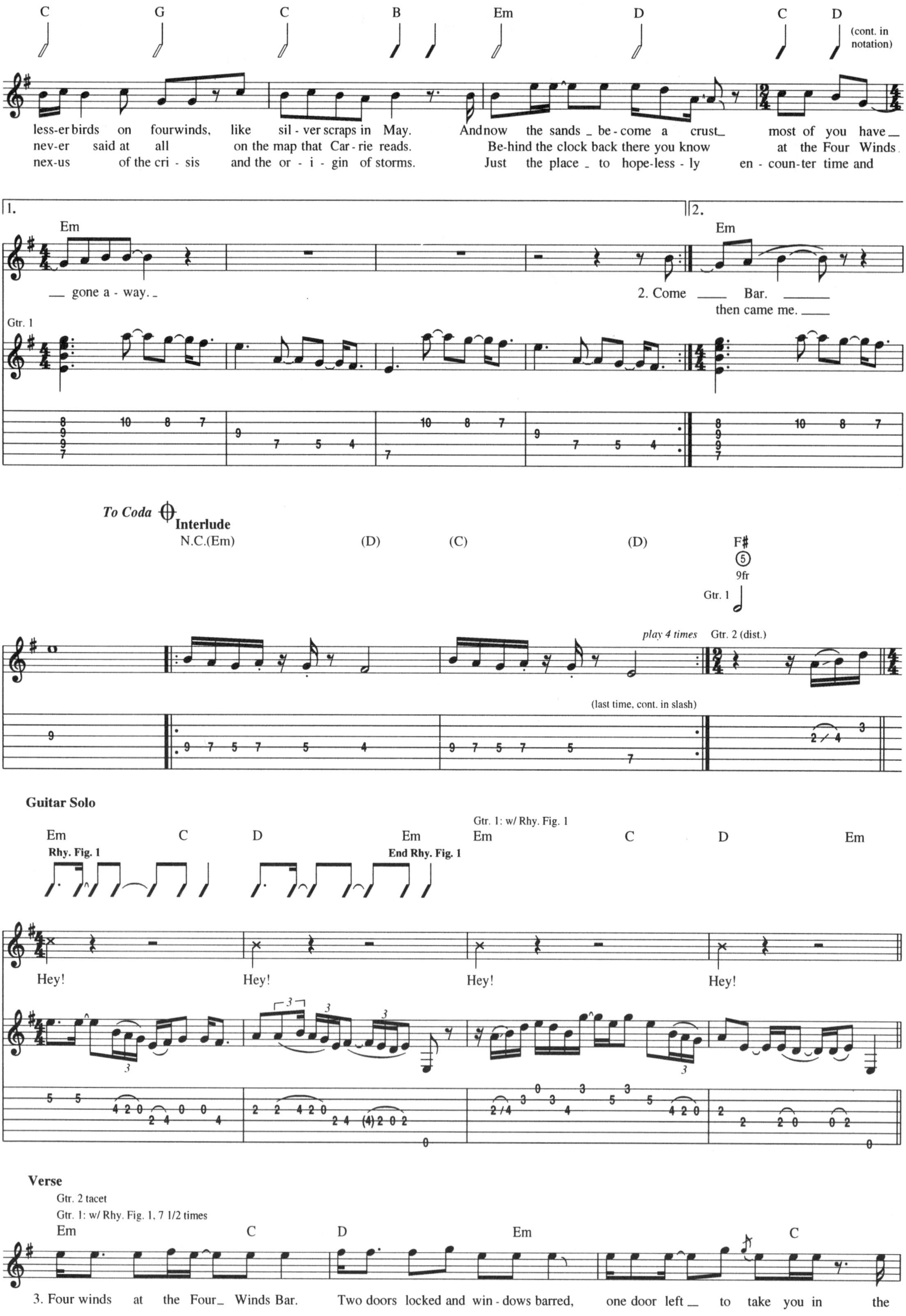
C G C B Em D C D
(cont. in notation)
less-er birds on four winds, like sil - ver scraps in May. And now the sands _ be - come a crust_ most of you have _
nev - er said at all on the map that Car - rie reads. Be-hind the clock back there you know at the Four Winds.
nex - us of the cri - sis and the or - i - gin of storms. Just the place _ to hope-less - ly en - coun - ter time and
1.
Em
_ gone a - way. _
2. Come _ Bar. _
2.
Em
then came me. _
Gtr. 1
To Coda
Interlude
N.C.(Em) (D) (C) (D) F#
9fr
Gtr. 1
play 4 times
Gtr. 2 (dist.)
(last time, cont. in slash)
Guitar Solo
Em C D Em
Rhy. Fig. 1
End Rhy. Fig. 1
Gtr. 1: w/ Rhy. Fig. 1
Em C D Em
Hey! Hey! Hey! Hey!
Verse
Gtr. 2 tacet
Gtr. 1: w/ Rhy. Fig. 1, 7 1/2 times
Em C D Em C
3. Four winds at the Four_ Winds Bar. Two doors locked and win - dows barred, one door left _ to take you in the

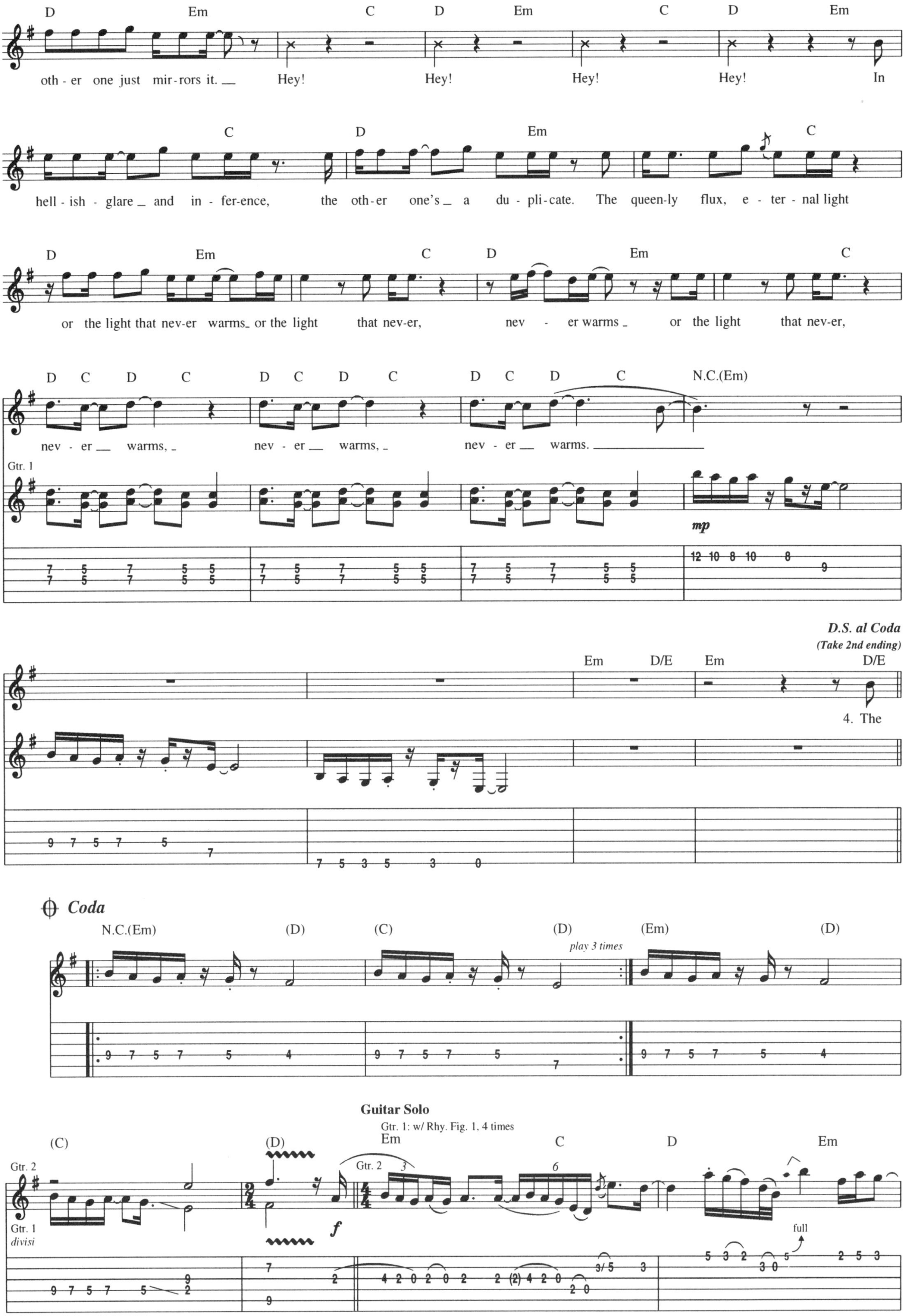
D Em C D Em C D Em
oth - er one just mir-rors it. Hey! Hey! Hey! Hey! In
C D Em C
hell - ish - glare and in - fer-ence, the oth-er one's a du - pli-cate. The queen-ly flux, e - ter - nal light
D Em C D Em C
or the light that nev-er warms or the light that nev-er, nev - er warms or the light that nev-er,
D C D C D C D C D C D C N.C.(Em)
nev - er warms, nev - er warms, nev - er warms.
Gtr. 1
mp
D.S. al Coda
(Take 2nd ending)
Em D/E Em D/E
4. The
Coda
N.C.(Em) (D) (C) (D) (Em) (D)
play 3 times
Guitar Solo
Gtr. 1: w/ Rhy. Fig. 1, 4 times
(C) (D) Em C D Em
Gtr. 2
Gtr. 1
divisi
f
full

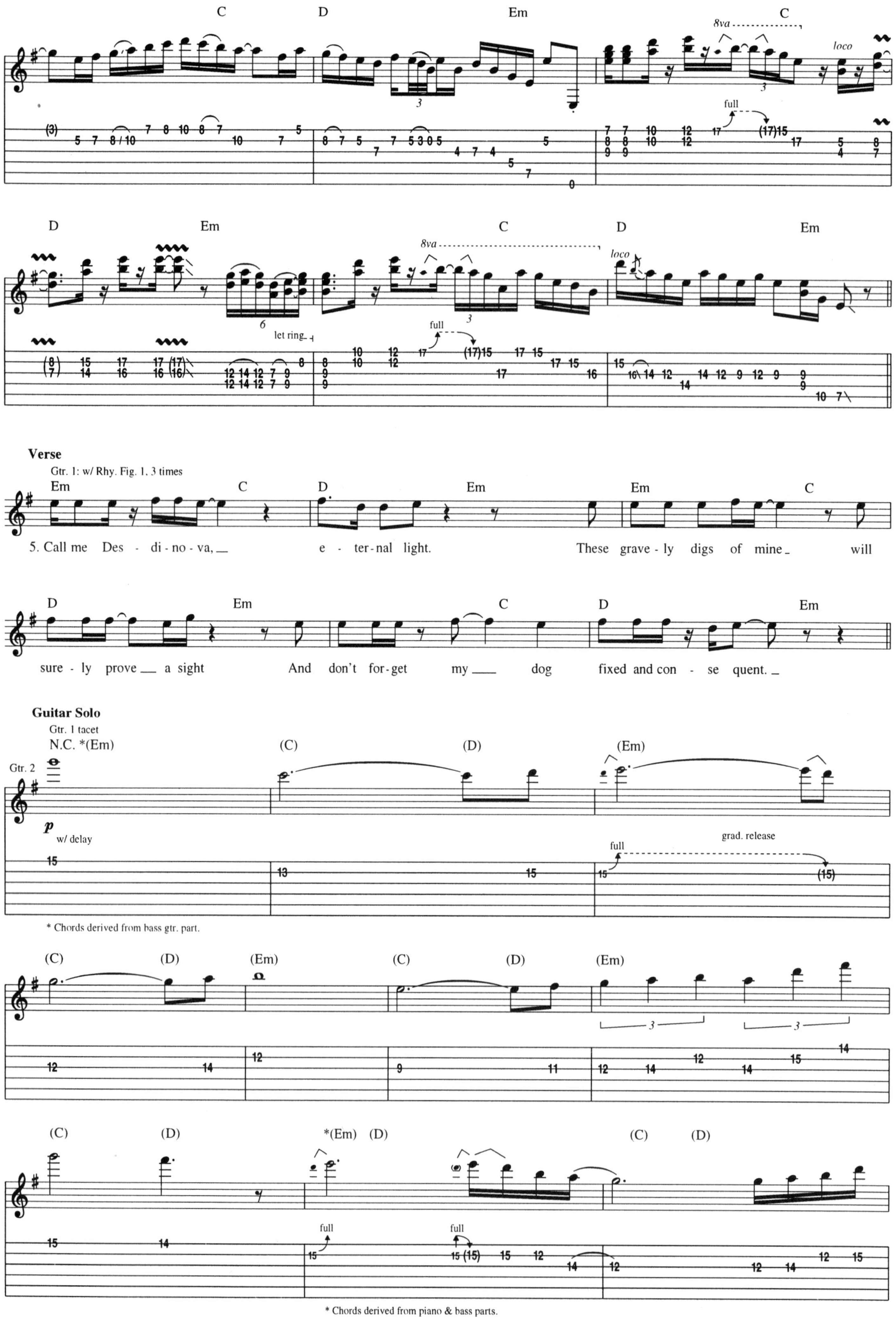
C D Em C
8va
loco
full
D Em C D Em
let ring
Verse
Gtr. 1: w/ Rhy. Fig. 1, 3 times
Em C D Em Em C
5. Call me Des - di - no - va, e - ter - nal light. These grave - ly digs of mine will
D Em C D Em
sure - ly prove a sight And don't for - get my dog fixed and con - se quent.
Guitar Solo
Gtr. 1 tacet
N.C. *(Em) (C) (D) (Em)
Gtr. 2
w/ delay
grad. release
* Chords derived from bass gtr. part.
(C) (D) (Em) (C) (D) (Em)
(C) (D) *(Em) (D) (C) (D)
* Chords derived from piano & bass parts.

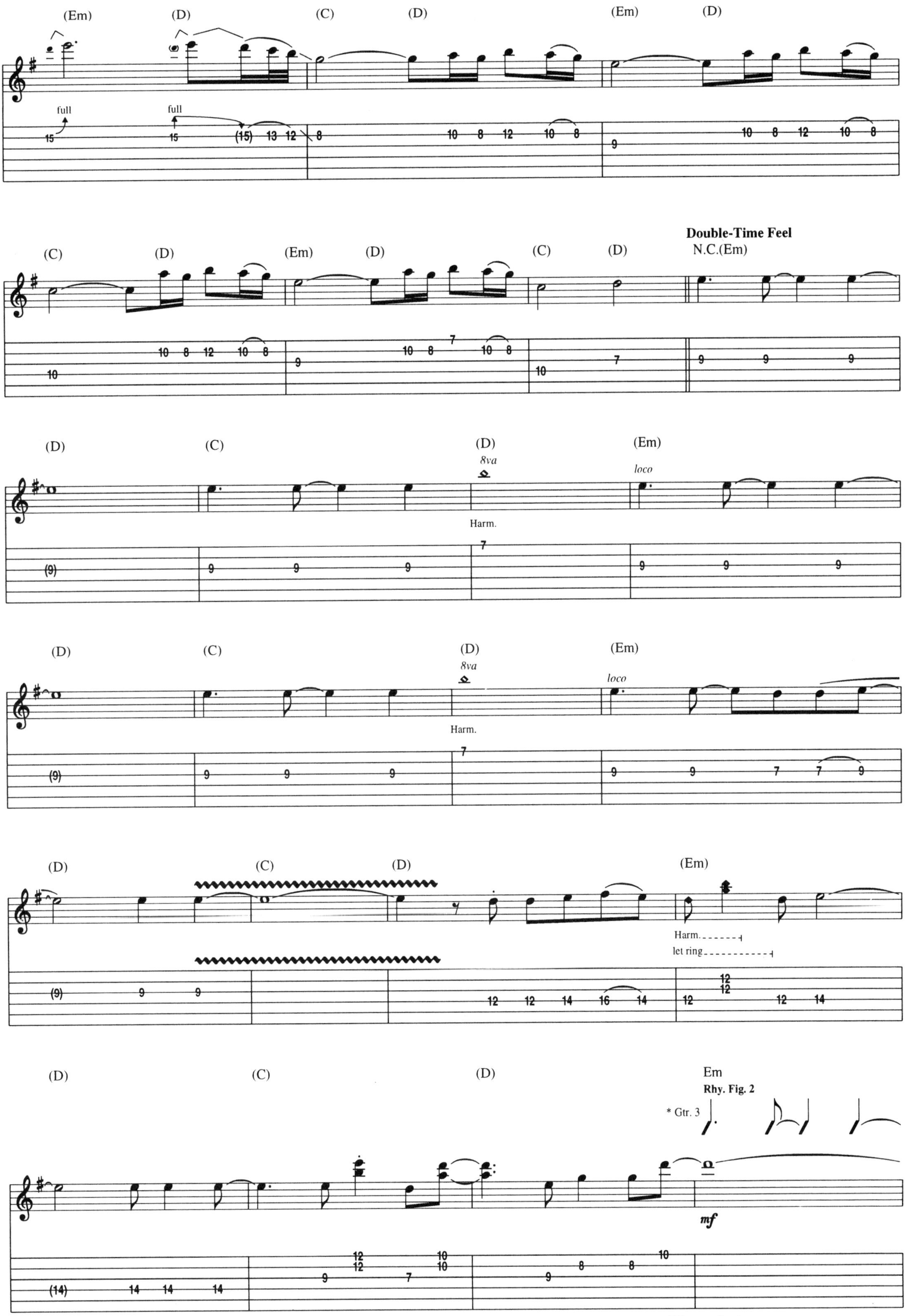

* Piano arr. for gtr.

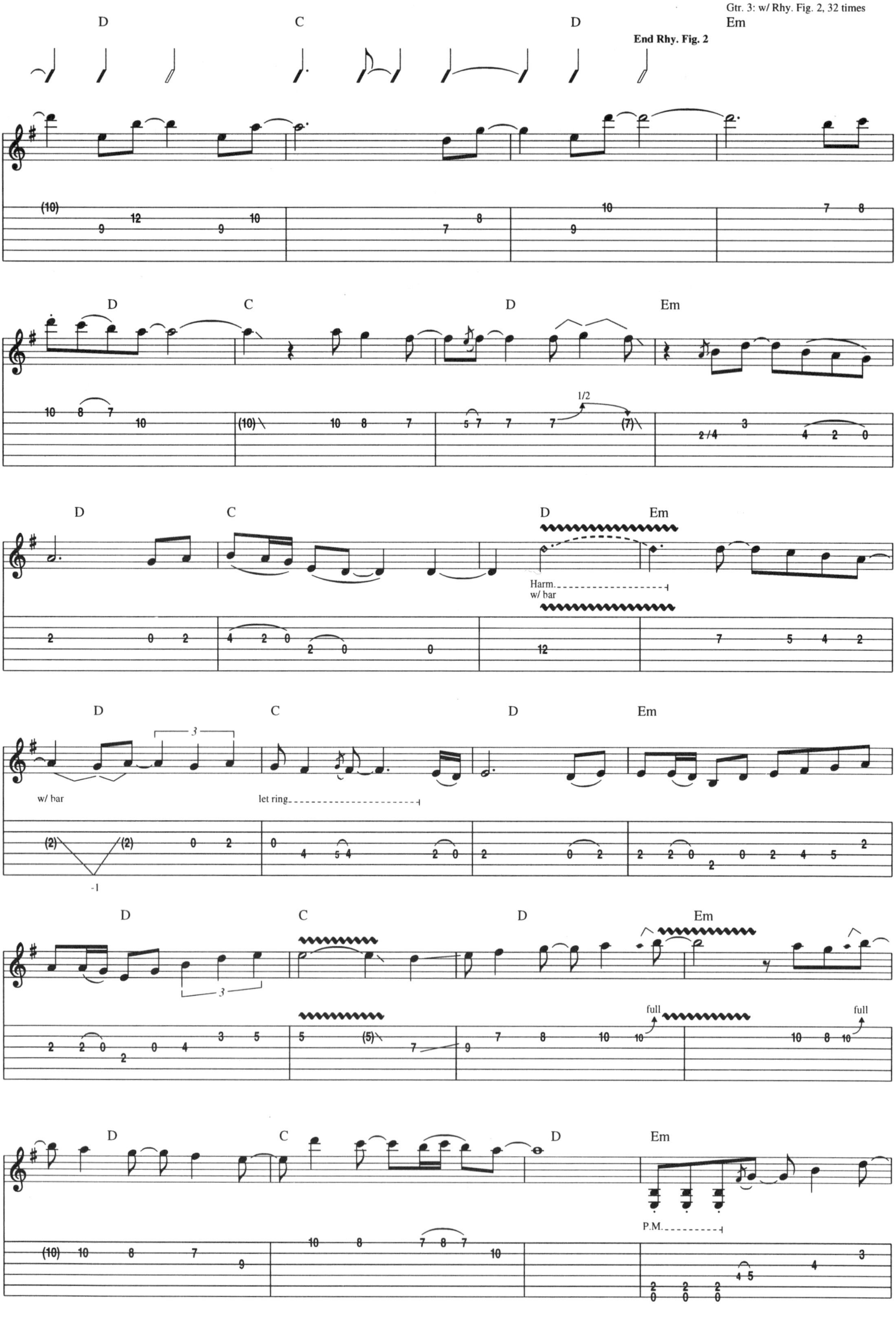
Gtr. 3: w/ Rhy. Fig. 2, 32 times
D
C
D
Em
End Rhy. Fig. 2
1/2
Harm.
w/ bar
w/ bar
let ring
full
P.M.

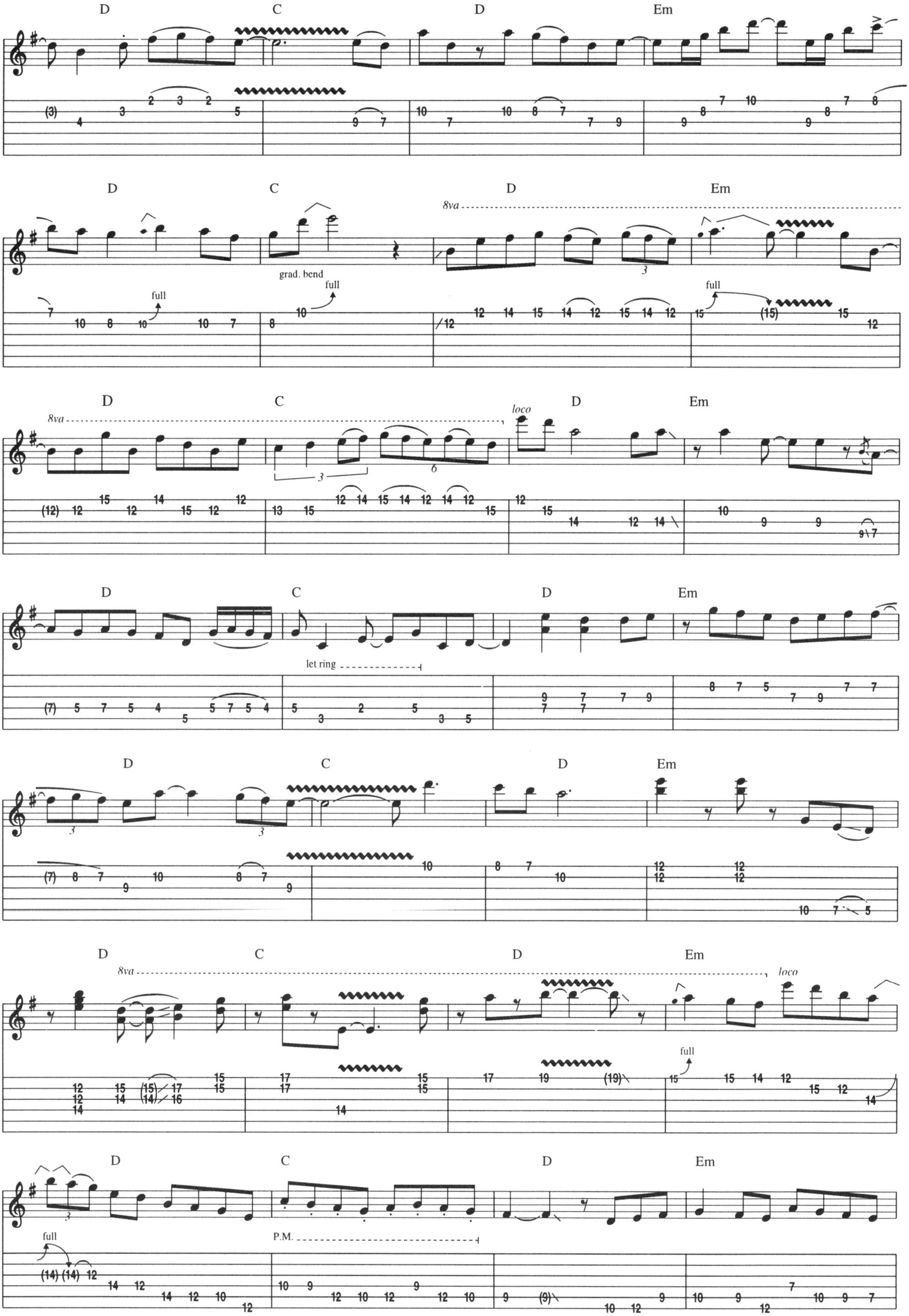
D C D Em
D C D Em
8va
grad. bend
full
D C D Em
8va
loco
D C D Em
let ring
D C D Em
D C D Em
8va
loco
full
D C D Em
full
P.M.

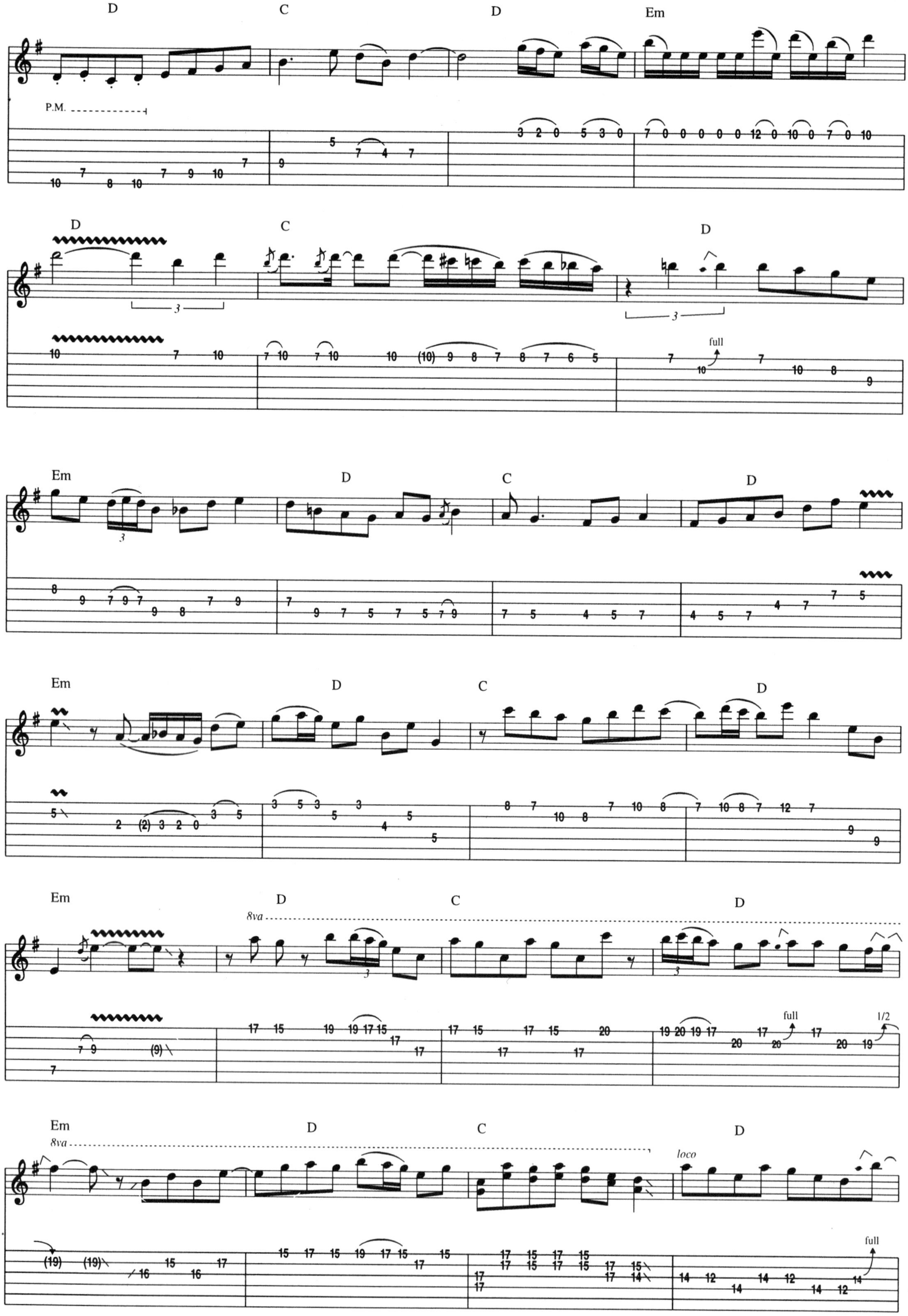
D C D Em
P.M.
D C D
full
Em D C D
Em D C D
Em D C D
8va
full
1/2
Em D C D
8va
loco
full

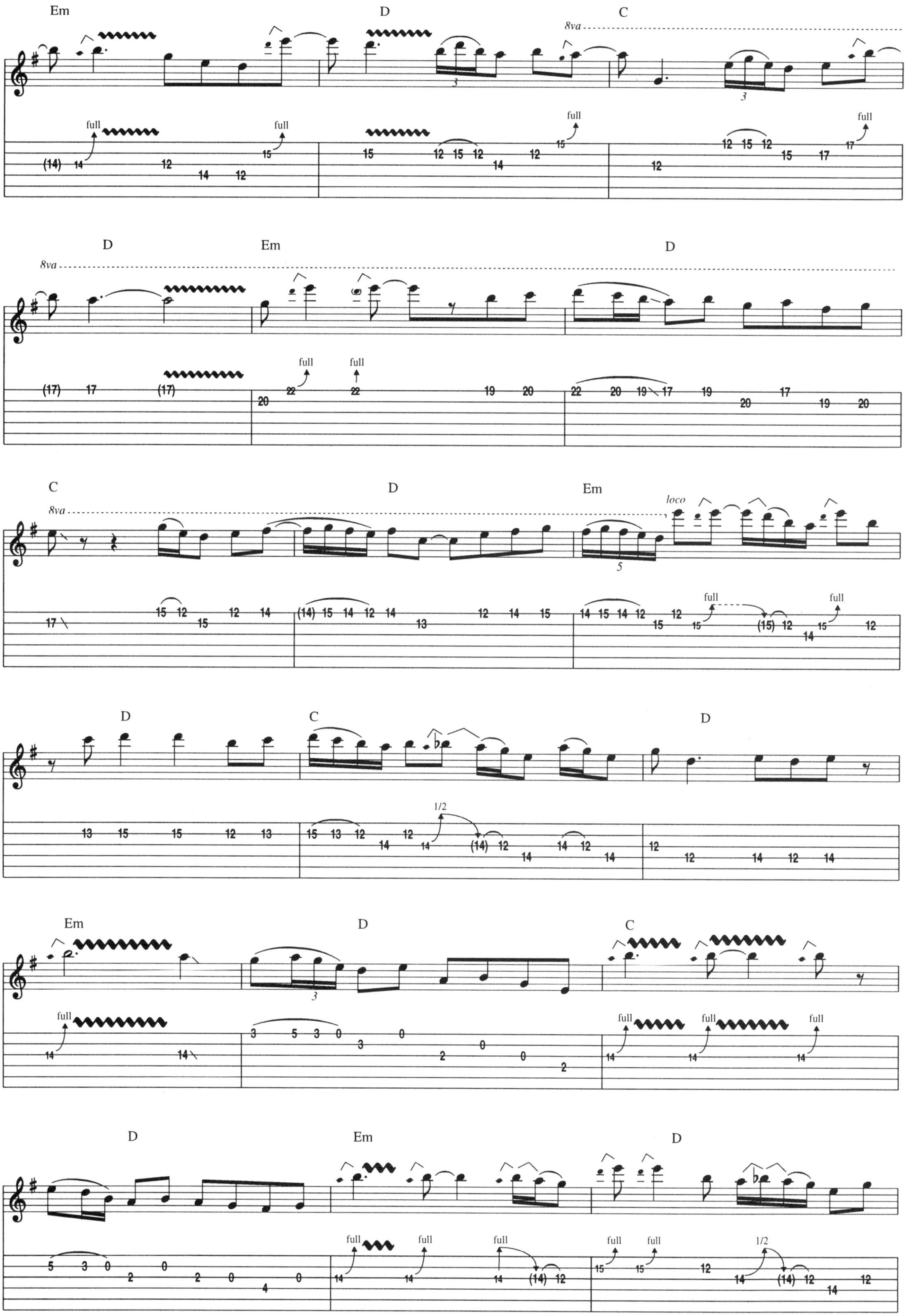
Em D C
8va
full full full full
D Em D
8va
full full
C D Em
8va
loco
full full
D C D
1/2
Em D C
full full full full
D Em D
full full full full full 1/2

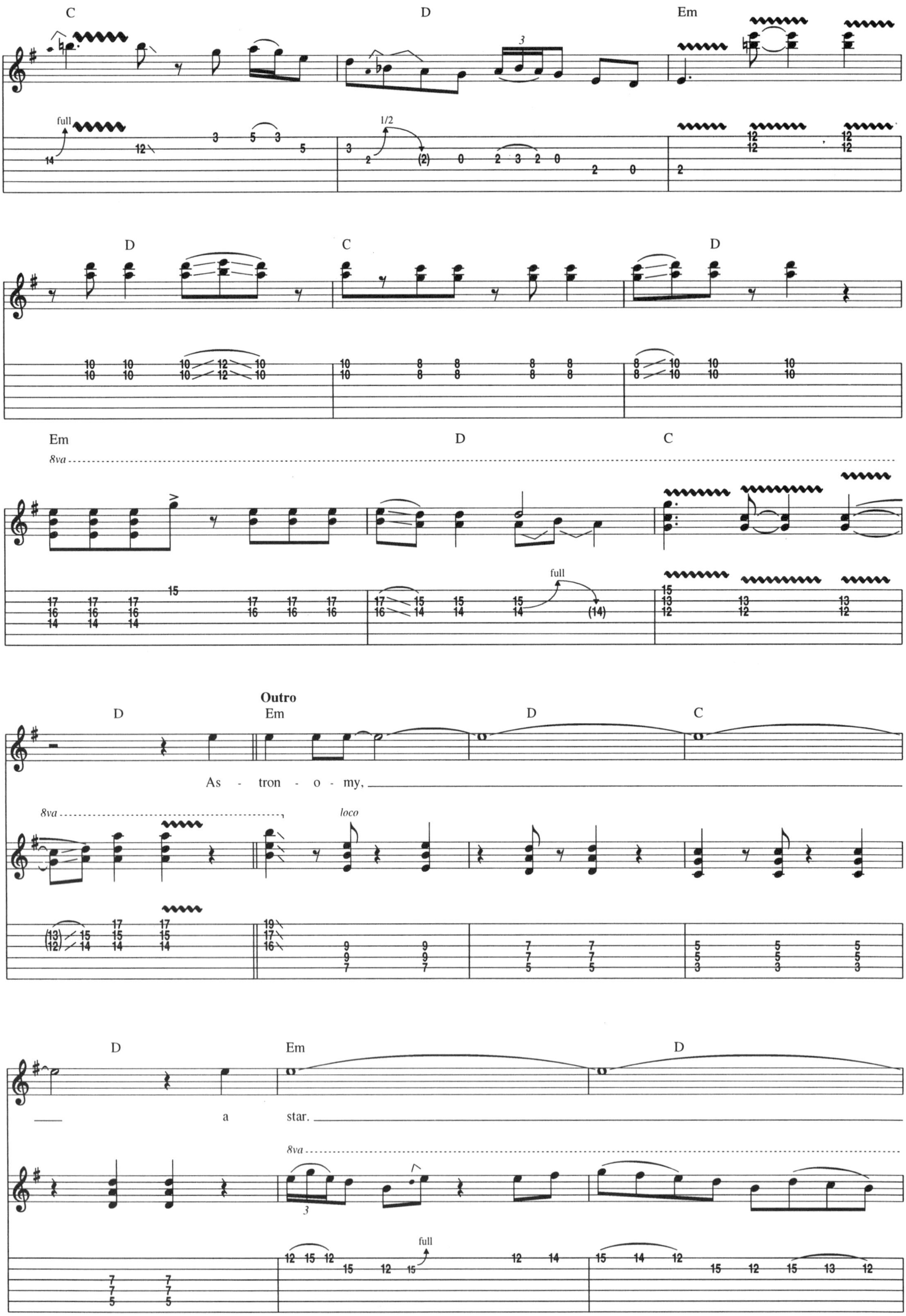
C
D
Em
full
1/2
D
C
D
Em
D
C
8va
full
Outro
D
Em
D
C
As - tron - o - my,
8va
loco
D
Em
D
a star.
8va
full

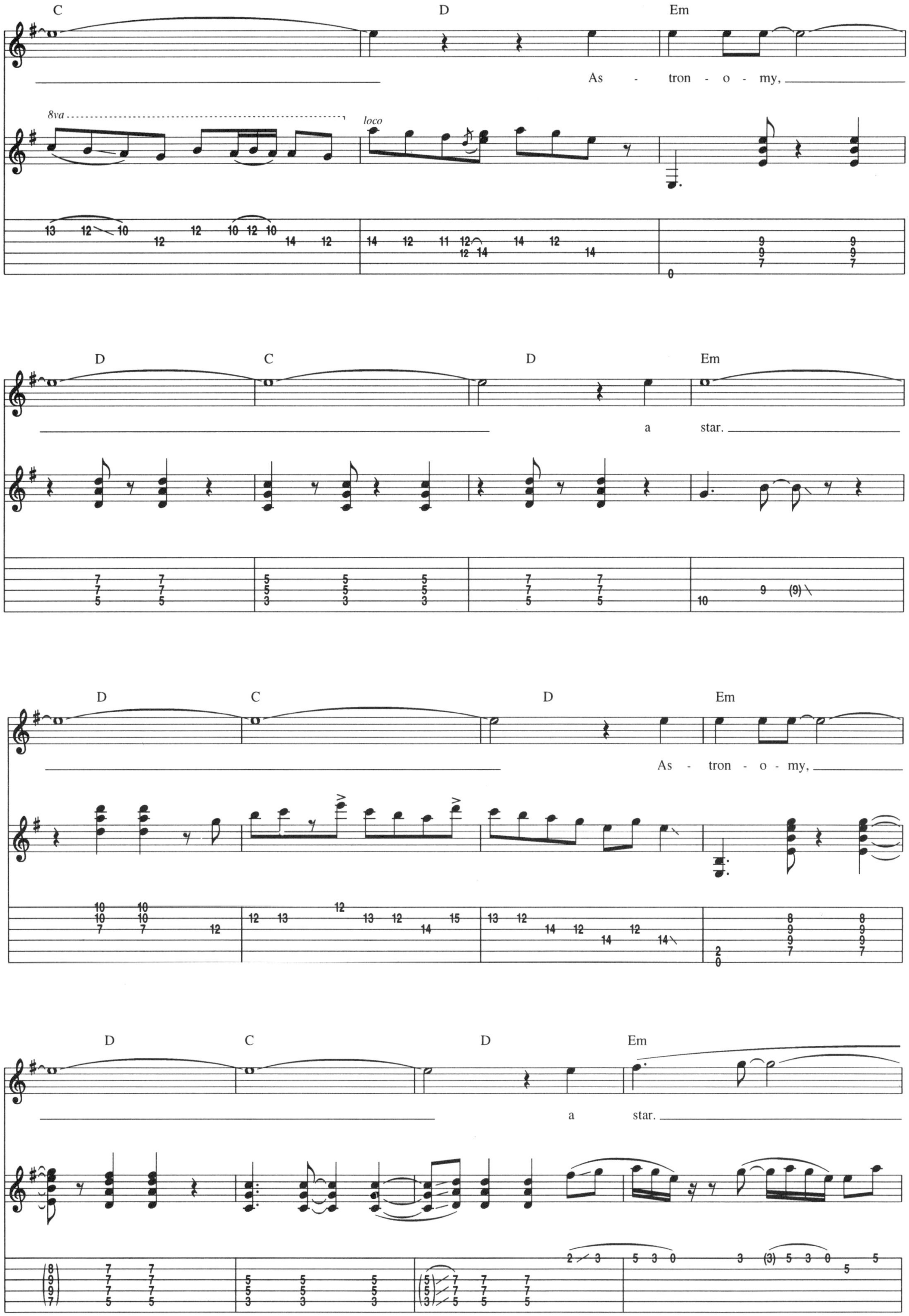
C
D
Em
As - tron - o - my,
8va
loco
D
C
D
Em
a star.
D
C
D
Em
As - tron - o - my,
D
C
D
Em
a star.

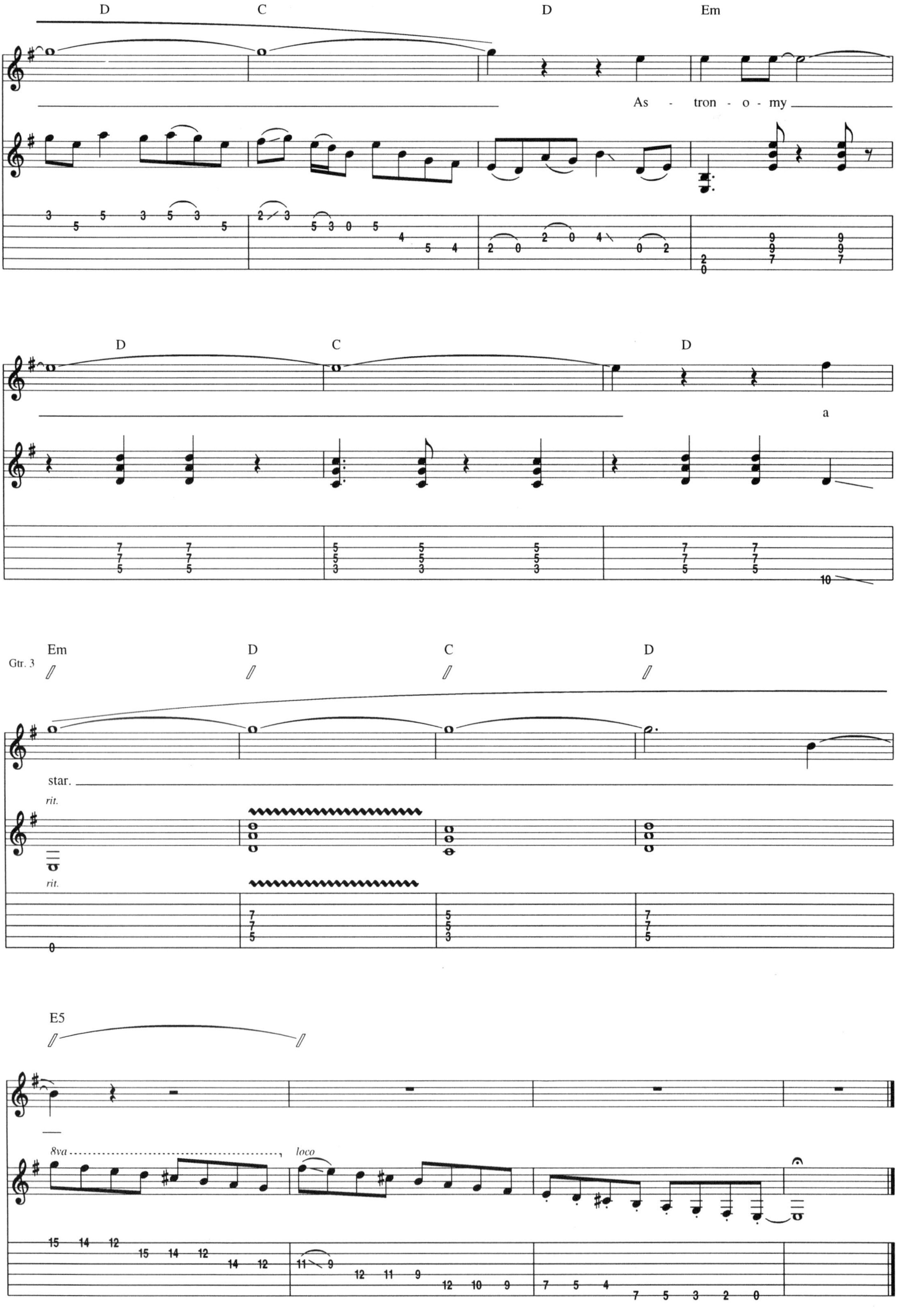
D C D Em
As - tron - o - my
D C D
a
Gtr. 3
Em D C D
star.
rit.
rit.
E5
8va
loco

Cities On Flame With Rock 'N' Roll

Words and Music by Samuel Pearlman, Donald Roeser and Albert Bouchard

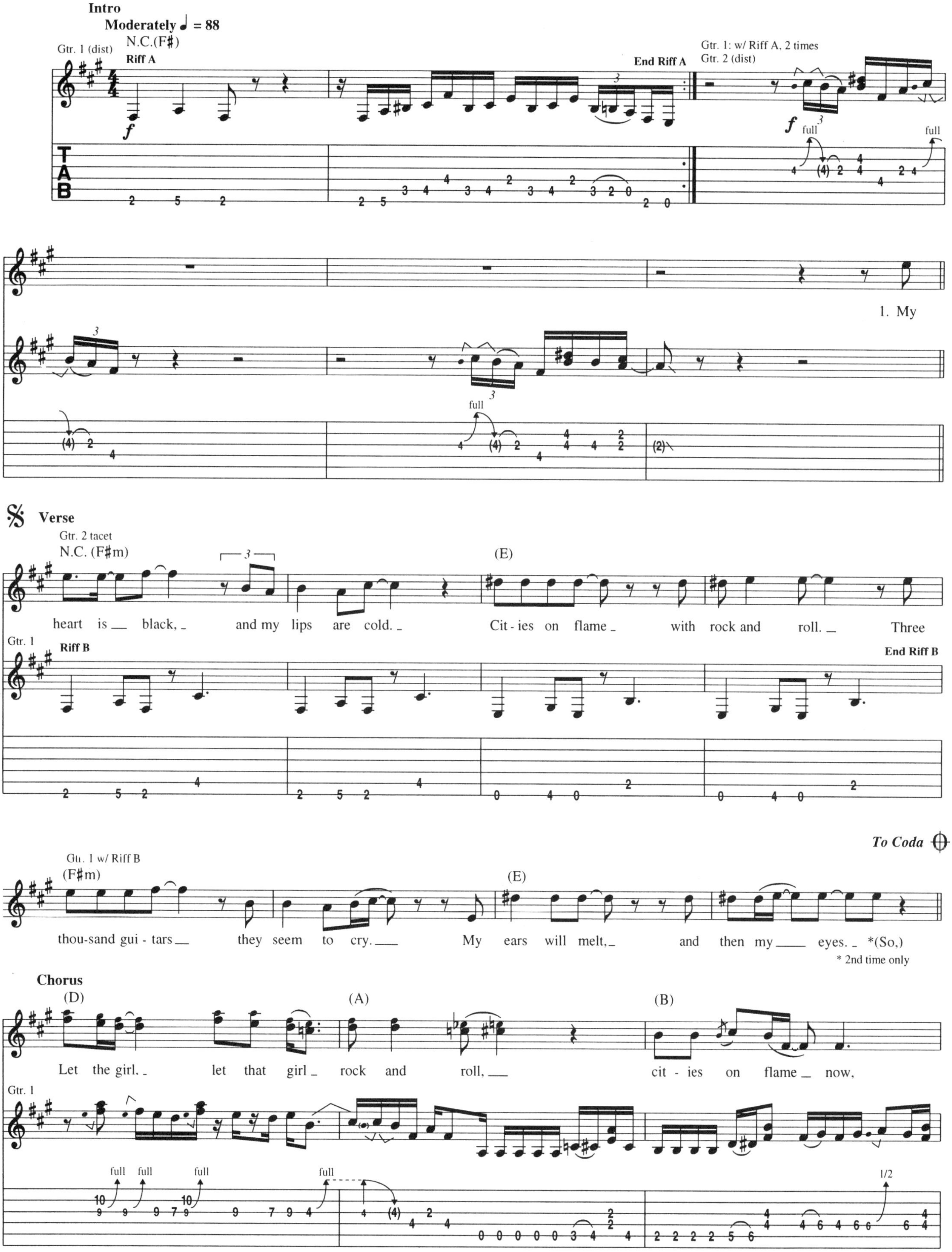

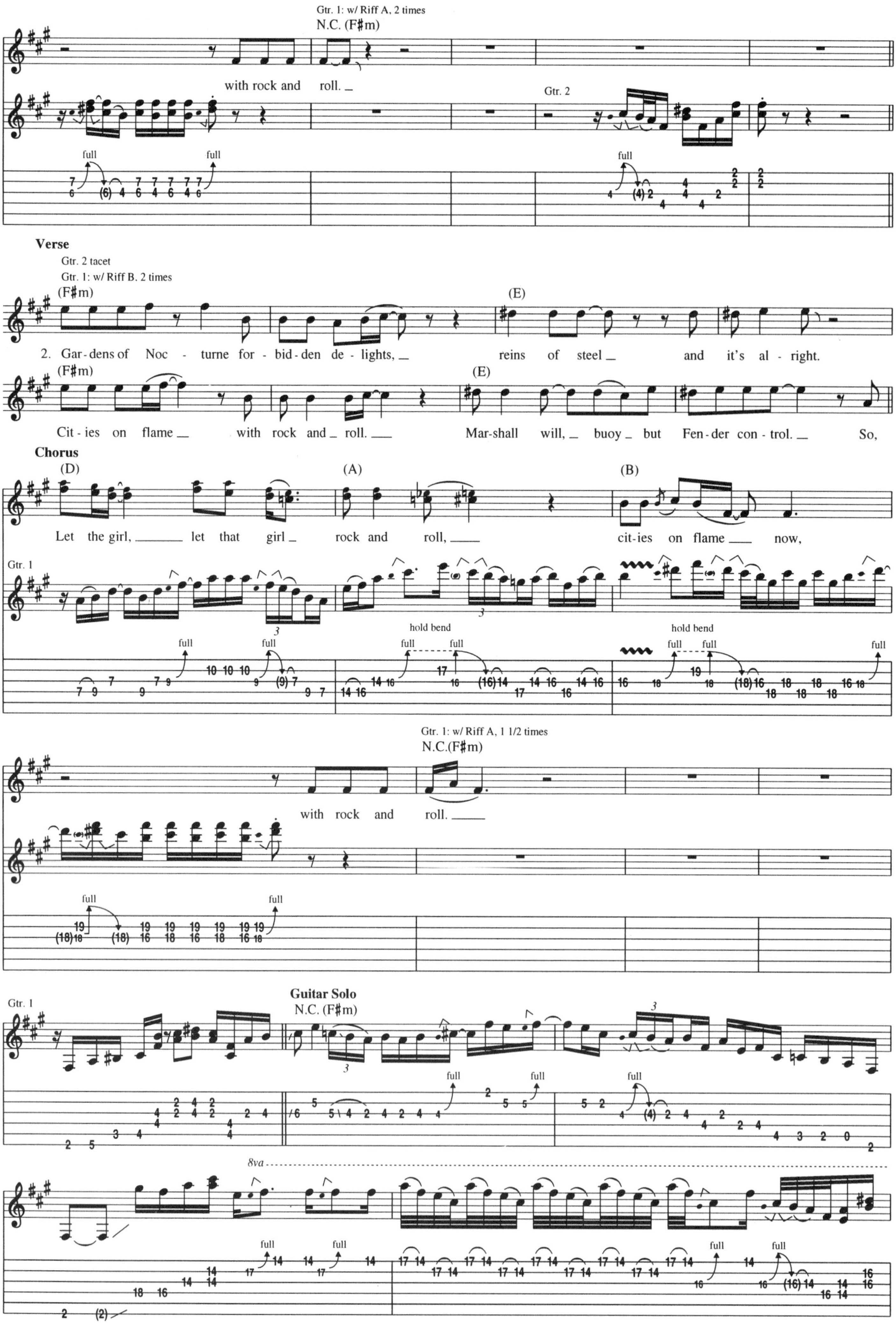
Gtr. 1: w/ Riff A, 2 times
N.C. (F#m)
with rock and roll.
Gtr. 2
full
Verse
Gtr. 2 tacet
Gtr. 1: w/ Riff B, 2 times
(F#m)
(E)
2. Gar-dens of Noc - turne for - bid-den de - lights, reins of steel and it's al - right.
Cit - ies on flame with rock and roll. Mar-shall will, buoy but Fen-der con - trol. So,
Chorus
(D)
(A)
(B)
Let the girl, let that girl rock and roll, cit-ies on flame now,
Gtr. 1
hold bend
Gtr. 1: w/ Riff A, 1 1/2 times
N.C.(F#m)
with rock and roll.
Guitar Solo
N.C. (F#m)
8va

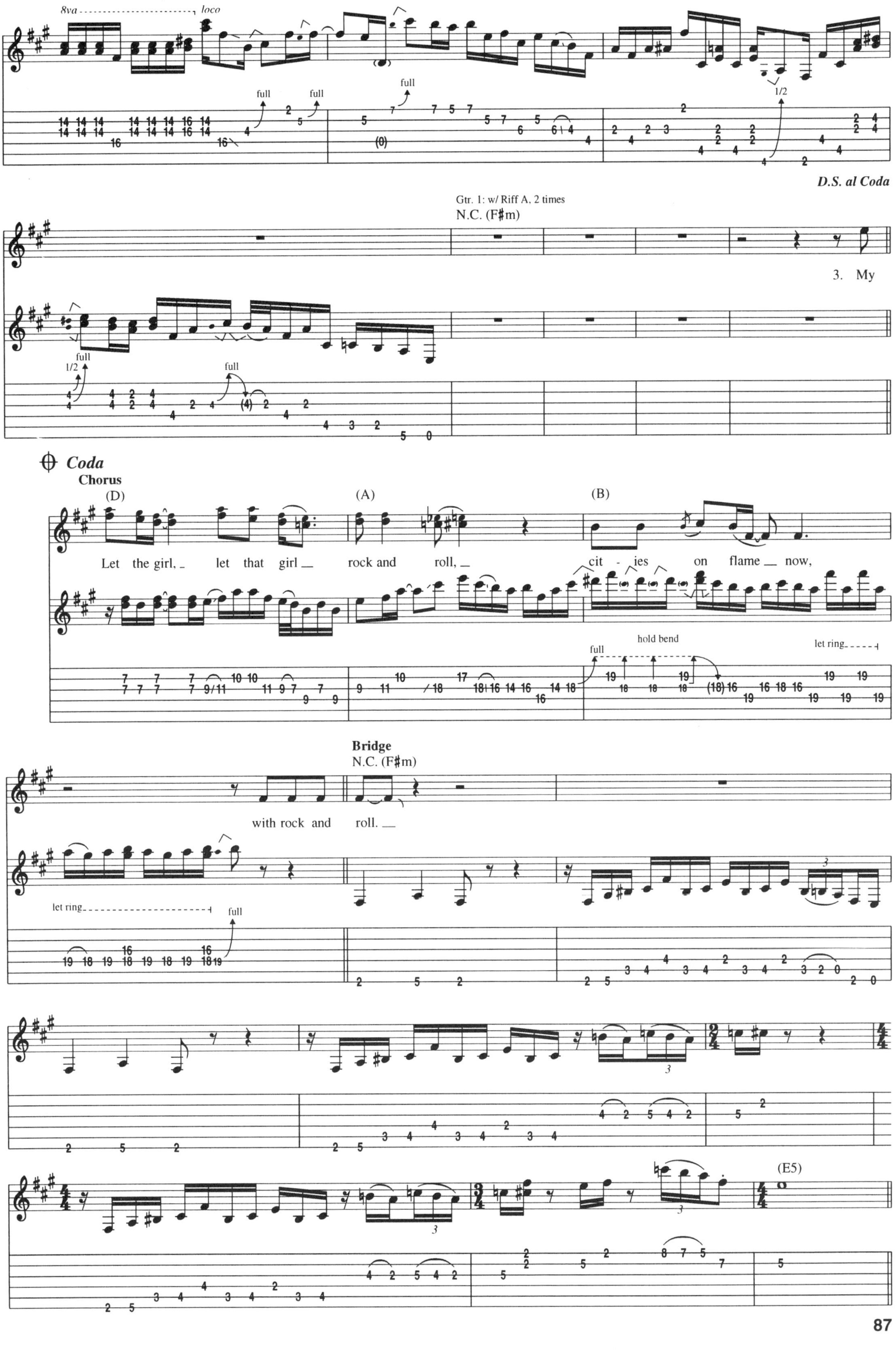
8va
loco
full
full
full
1/2
D.S. al Coda
Gtr. 1: w/ Riff A, 2 times
N.C. (F♯m)
3. My
1/2
full
full
Coda
Chorus
(D)
(A)
(B)
Let the girl, let that girl rock and roll, cit - ies on flame now,
full
hold bend
let ring
Bridge
N.C. (F♯m)
with rock and roll.
let ring
full
(E5)

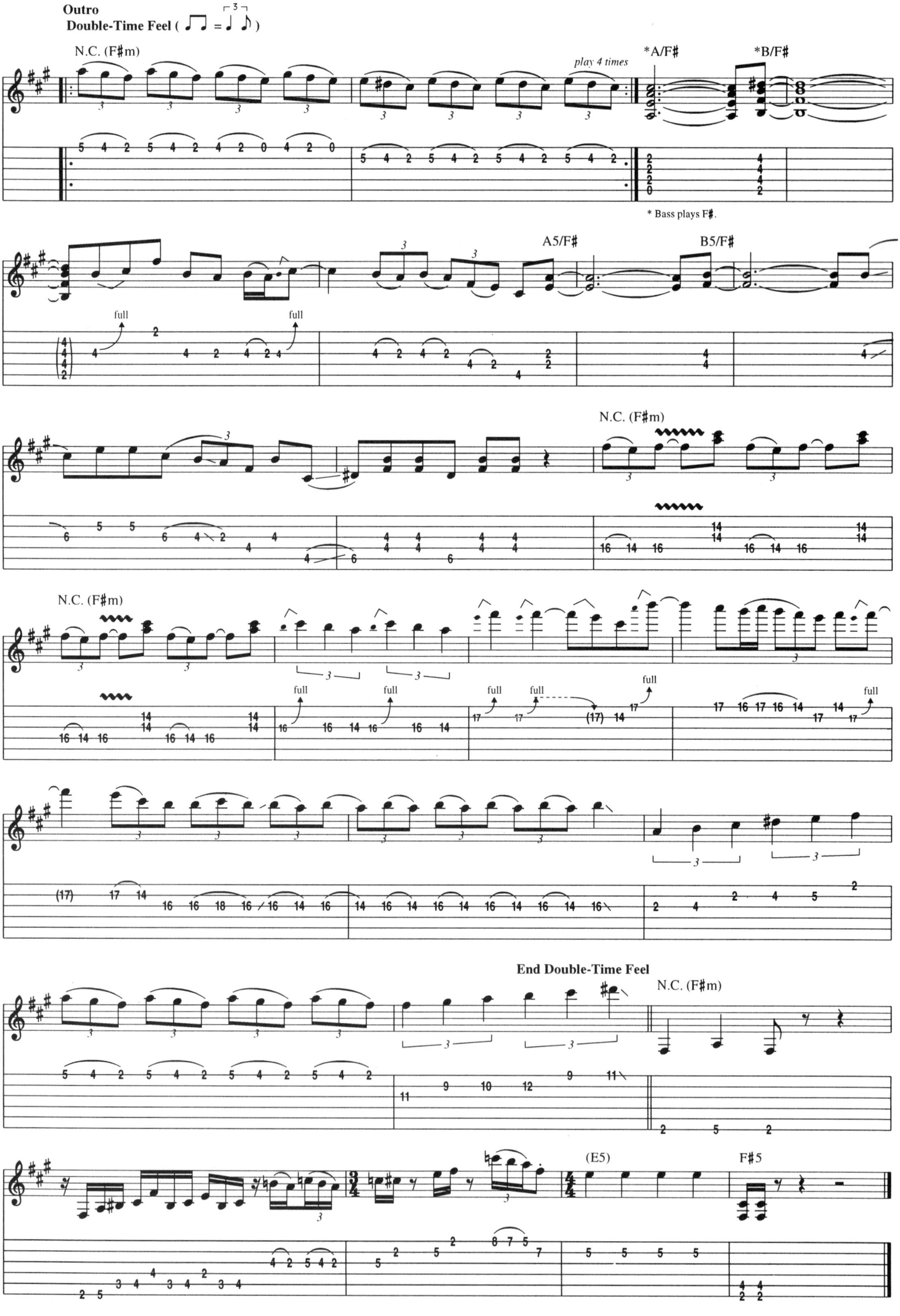
Outro
Double-Time Feel
N.C. (F#m)
play 4 times
*A/F#
*B/F#
* Bass plays F#.
full
A5/F#
B5/F#
N.C. (F#m)
N.C. (F#m)
full
End Double-Time Feel
N.C. (F#m)
(E5)
F#5

Harvester Of Eyes

Words and Music by Donald Roeser, Eric Bloom and R. Meltzer

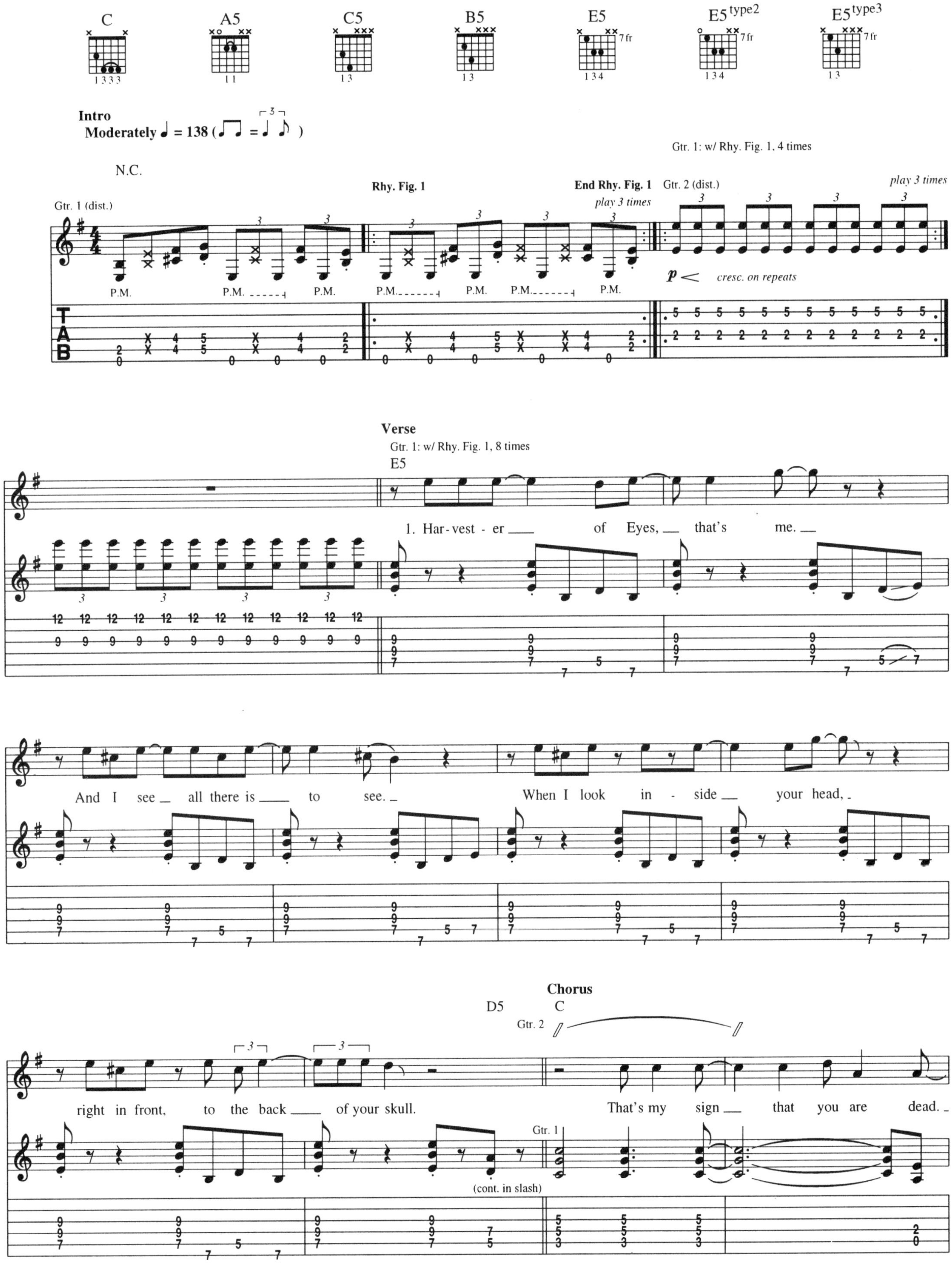

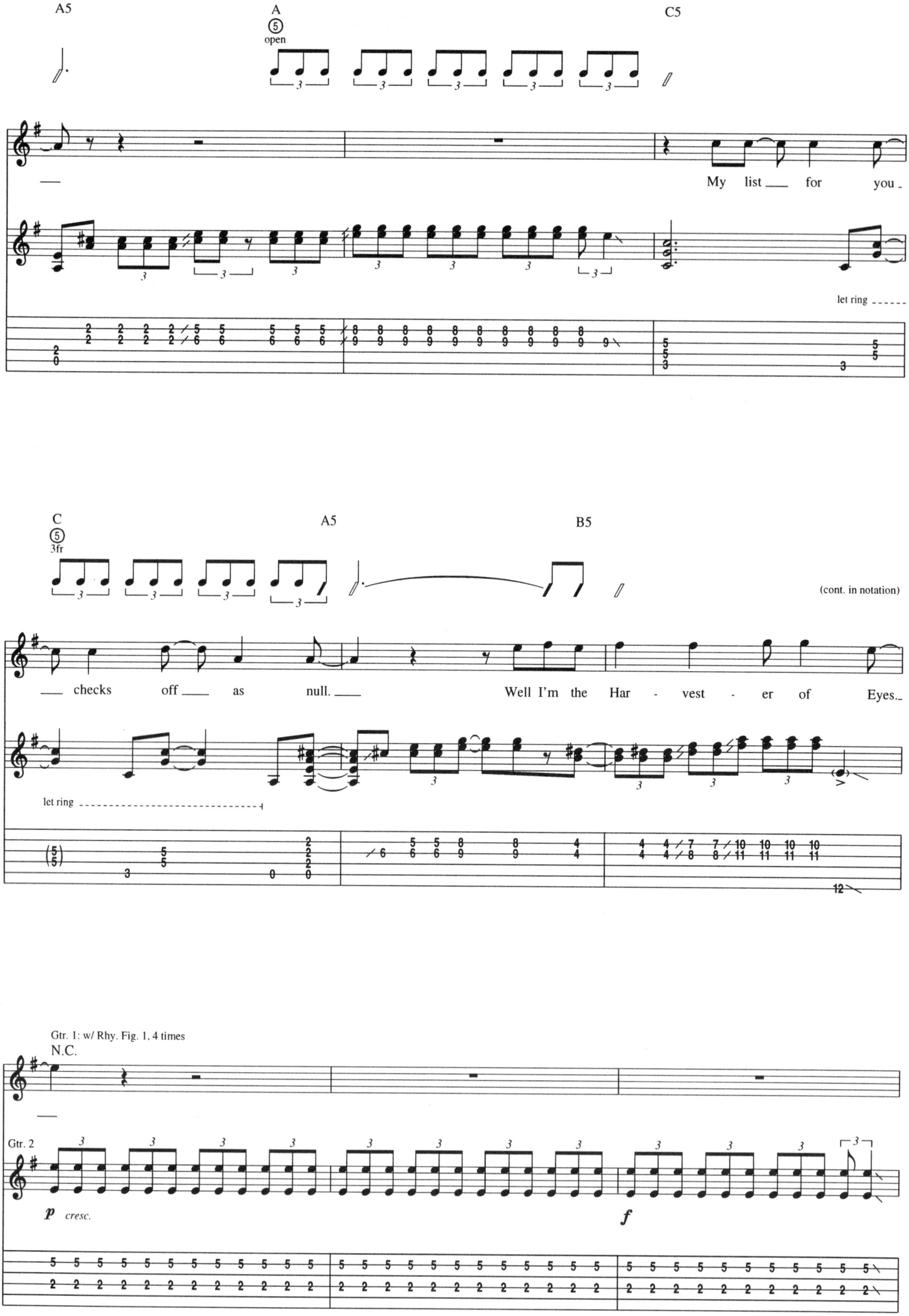
A5
A
open
C5
My list for you
let ring
C
3fr
A5
B5
(cont. in notation)
checks off as null.
Well I'm the Har - vest - er of Eyes.
let ring
Gtr. 1: w/ Rhy. Fig. 1, 4 times
N.C.
Gtr. 2
p cresc.
f

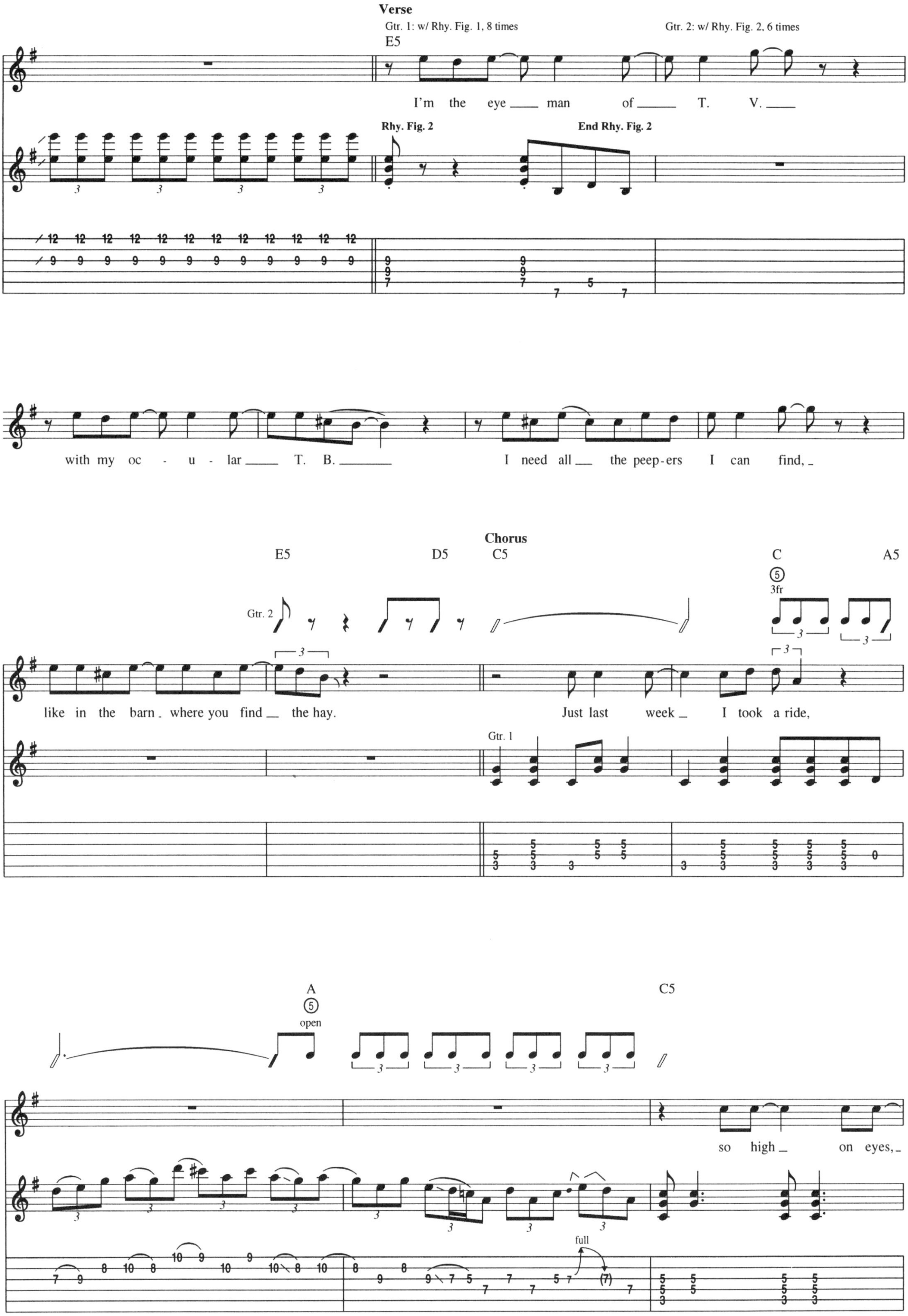
Verse
Gtr. 1: w/ Rhy. Fig. 1, 8 times
Gtr. 2: w/ Rhy. Fig. 2, 6 times
E5
I'm the eye man of T. V.
Rhy. Fig. 2
End Rhy. Fig. 2
with my oc - u - lar T. B.
I need all the peep-ers I can find,
Chorus
E5
D5
C5
C
3fr
A5
Gtr. 2
like in the barn where you find the hay.
Just last week I took a ride,
Gtr. 1
A
open
C5
so high on eyes,
full

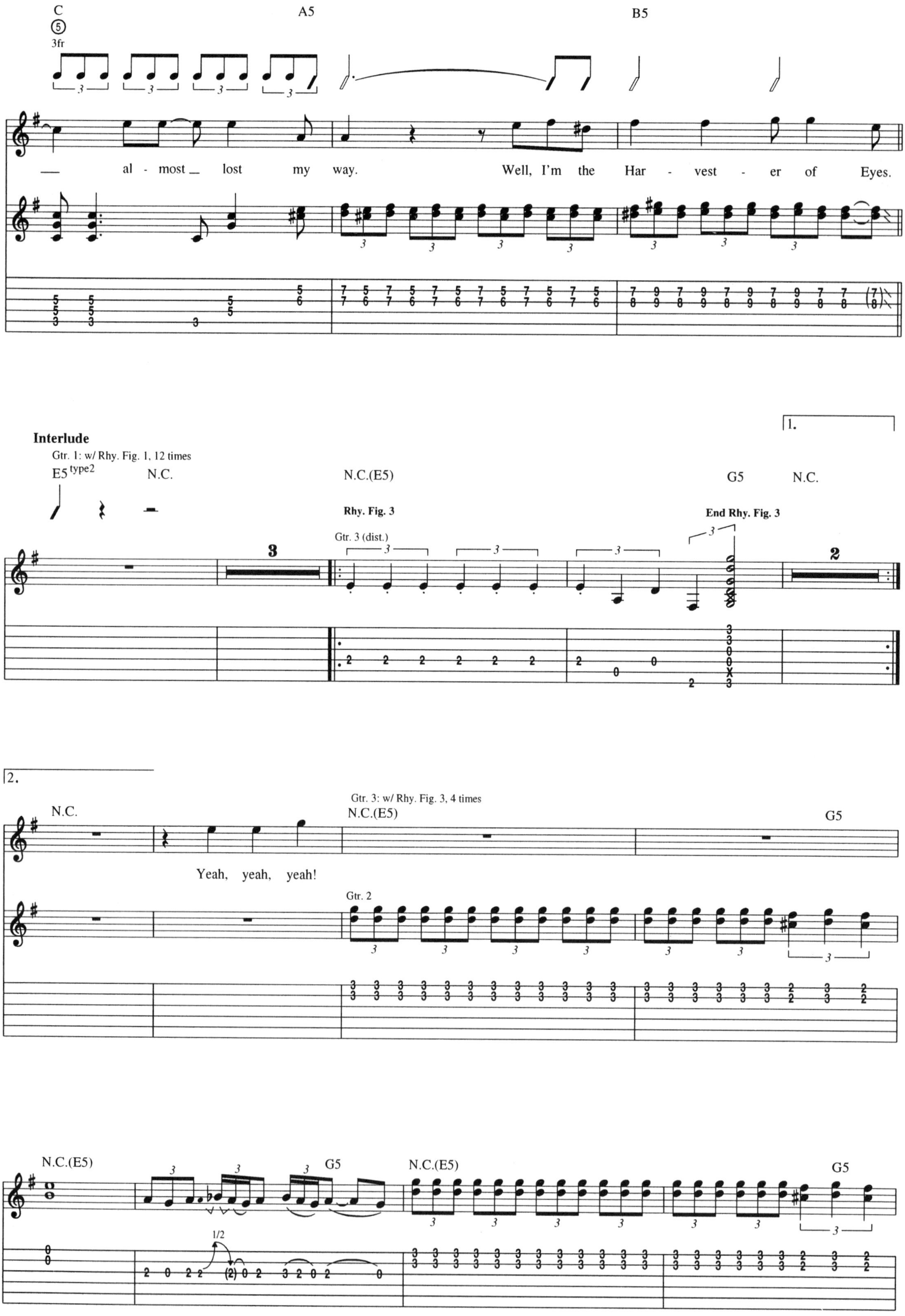
C
3fr
A5
B5
— al - most — lost my way. Well, I'm the Har - vest - er of Eyes.
Interlude
Gtr. 1: w/ Rhy. Fig. 1, 12 times
E5type2
N.C.
N.C.(E5)
Rhy. Fig. 3
Gtr. 3 (dist.)
End Rhy. Fig. 3
G5
N.C.
1.
2.
N.C.
Gtr. 3: w/ Rhy. Fig. 3, 4 times
N.C.(E5)
G5
Yeah, yeah, yeah!
Gtr. 2
N.C.(E5)
G5
1/2
N.C.(E5)
G5

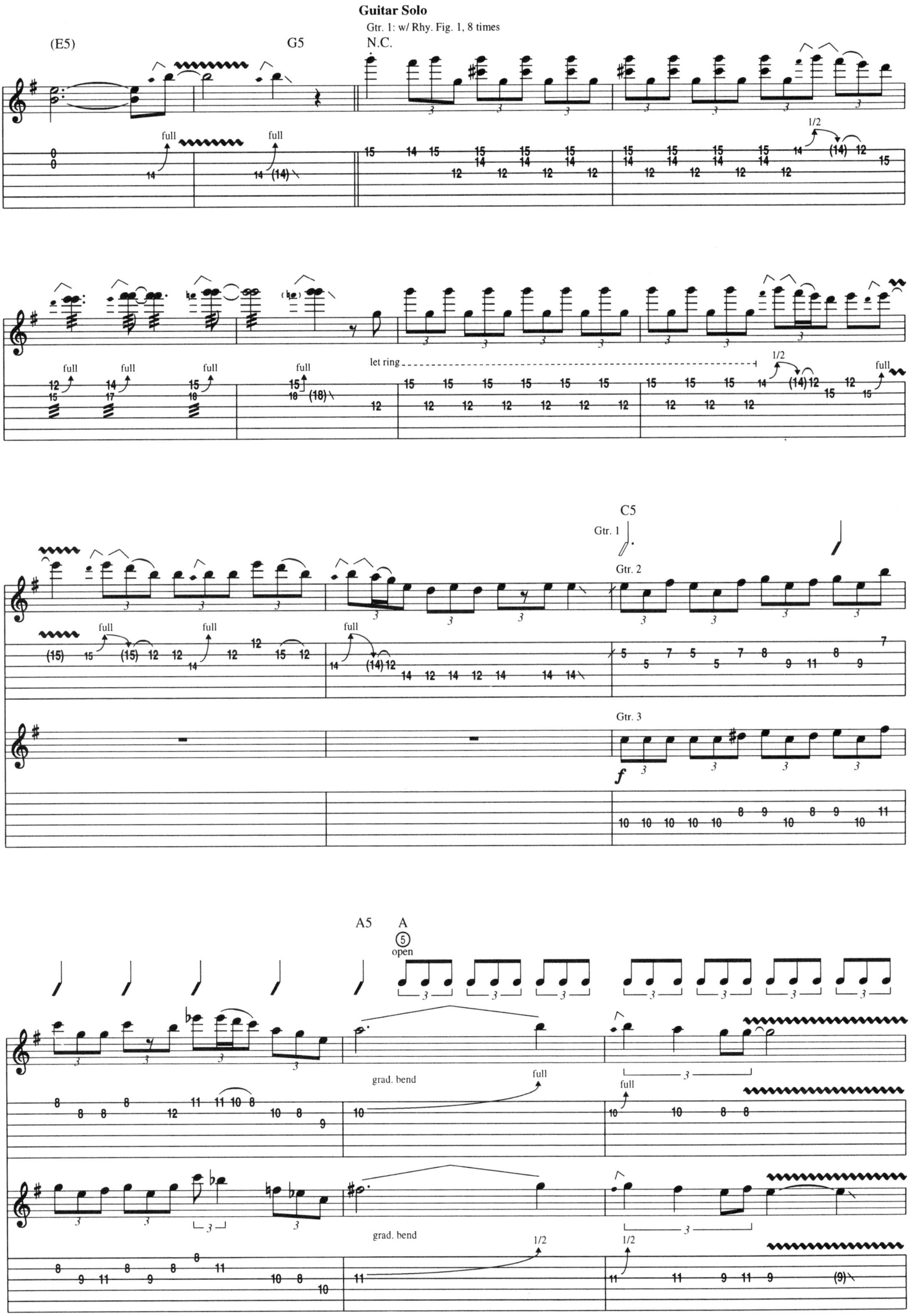
Guitar Solo
Gtr. 1: w/ Rhy. Fig. 1, 8 times
(E5)
G5
N.C.
full
1/2
let ring
C5
Gtr. 1
Gtr. 2
Gtr. 3
A5
A
open
grad. bend

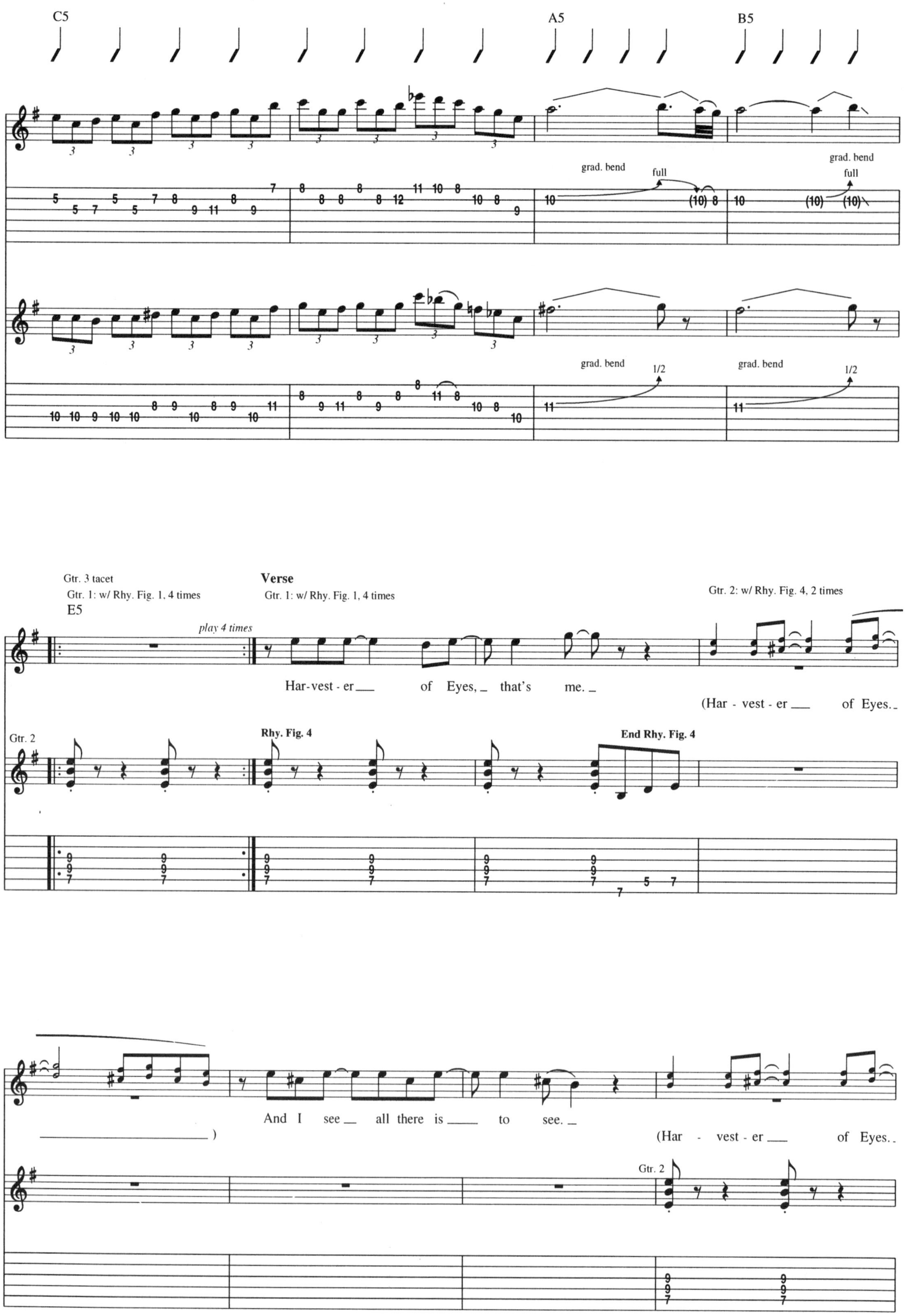
C5
A5
B5
grad. bend
full
grad. bend
full
grad. bend
1/2
grad. bend
1/2
Gtr. 3 tacet
Gtr. 1: w/ Rhy. Fig. 1, 4 times
E5
play 4 times
Verse
Gtr. 1: w/ Rhy. Fig. 1, 4 times
Gtr. 2: w/ Rhy. Fig. 4, 2 times
Har-vest - er of Eyes, that's me.
(Har - vest - er of Eyes.
Gtr. 2
Rhy. Fig. 4
End Rhy. Fig. 4
)
And I see all there is to see.
(Har - vest - er of Eyes.
Gtr. 2

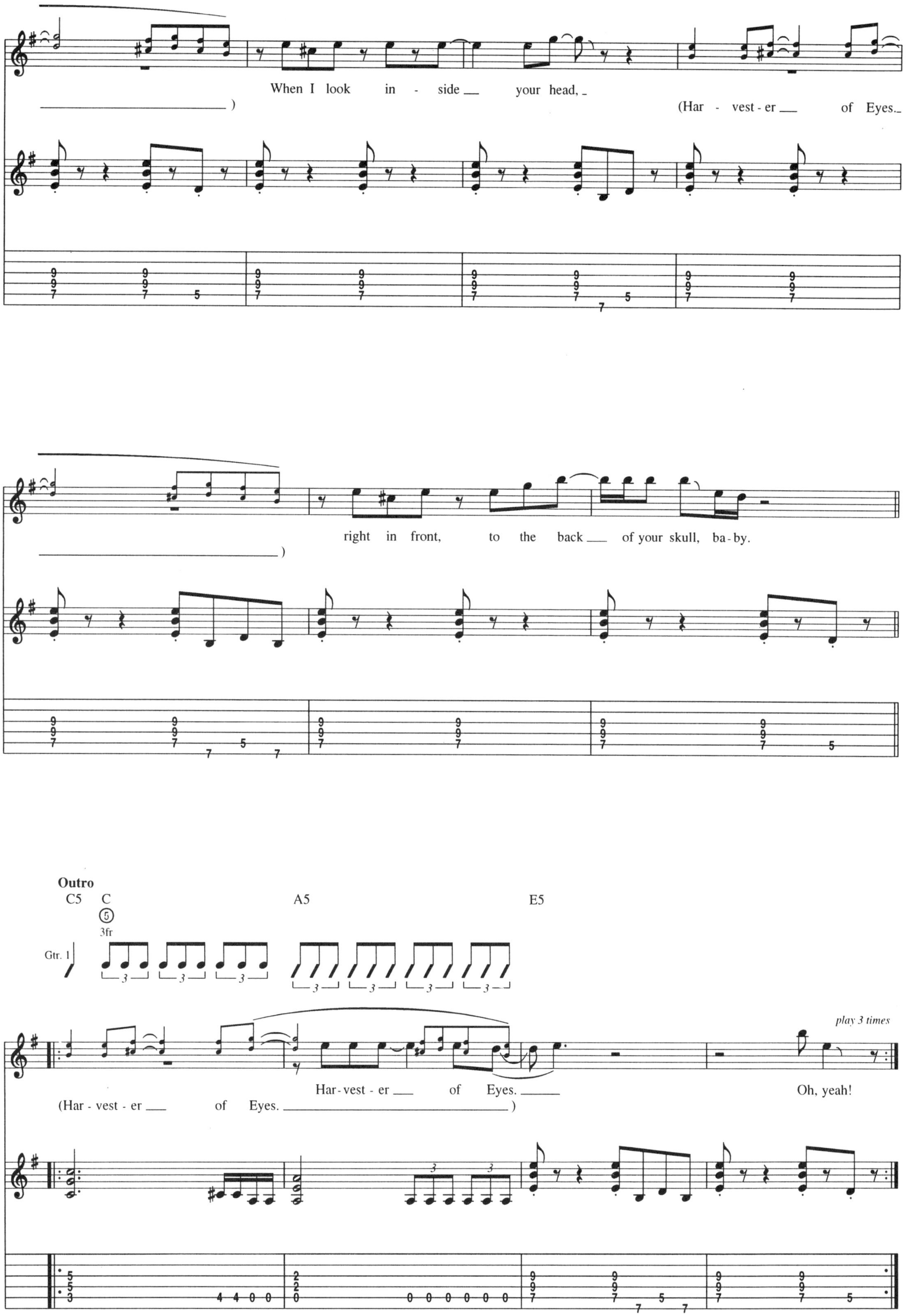
When I look in - side your head,
)
(Har - vest - er of Eyes.
)
right in front, to the back of your skull, ba - by.
Outro
C5 C
5
3fr
A5
E5
Gtr. 1
play 3 times
Har - vest - er of Eyes.
Oh, yeah!
(Har - vest - er of Eyes.
)

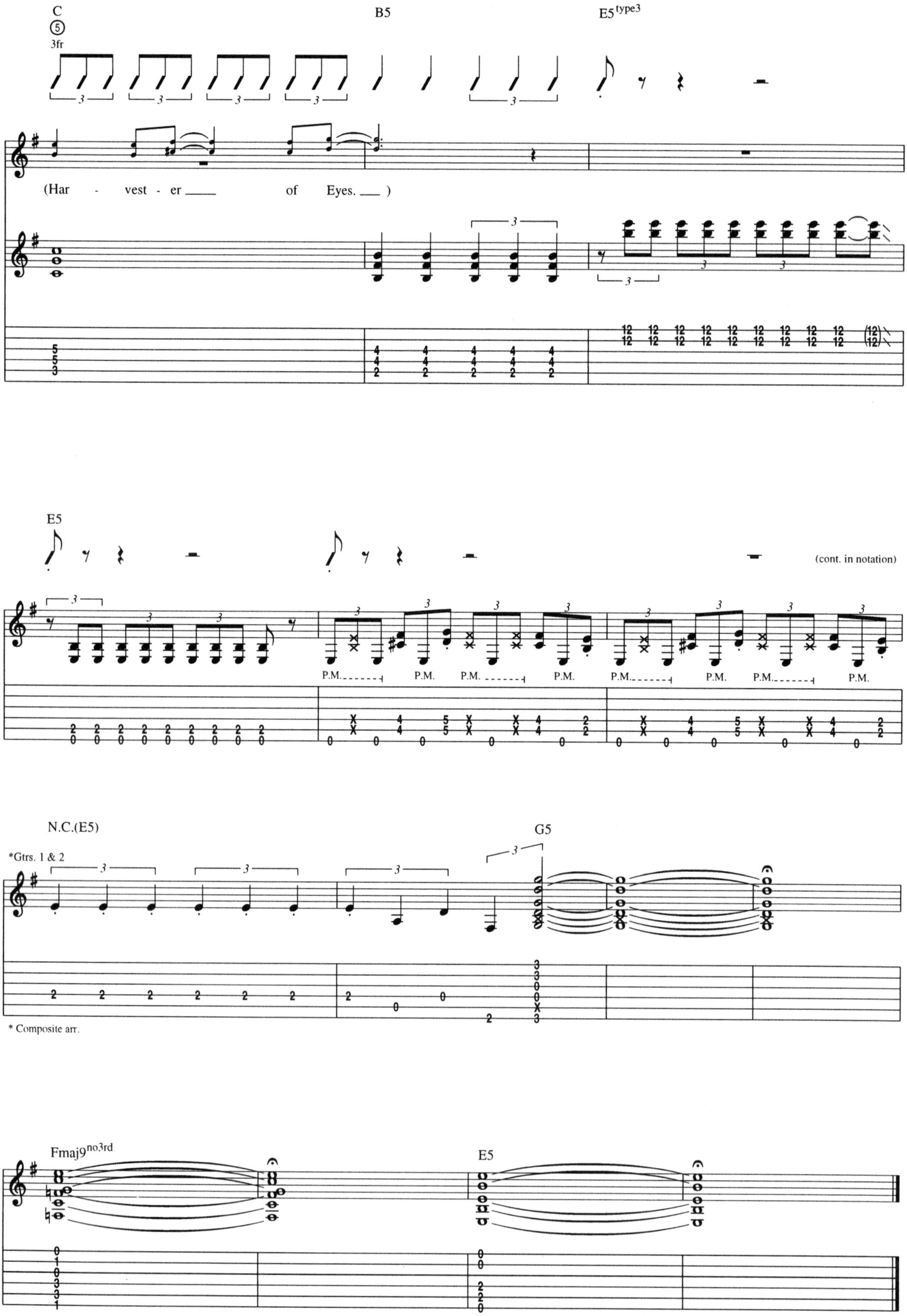
C
3fr
B5
E5type3
(Har - vest - er of Eyes.)
E5
(cont. in notation)
P.M.
N.C.(E5)
*Gtrs. 1 & 2
G5
* Composite arr.
Fmaj9no3rd
E5

Buck's Boogie

Music by Donald Roeser

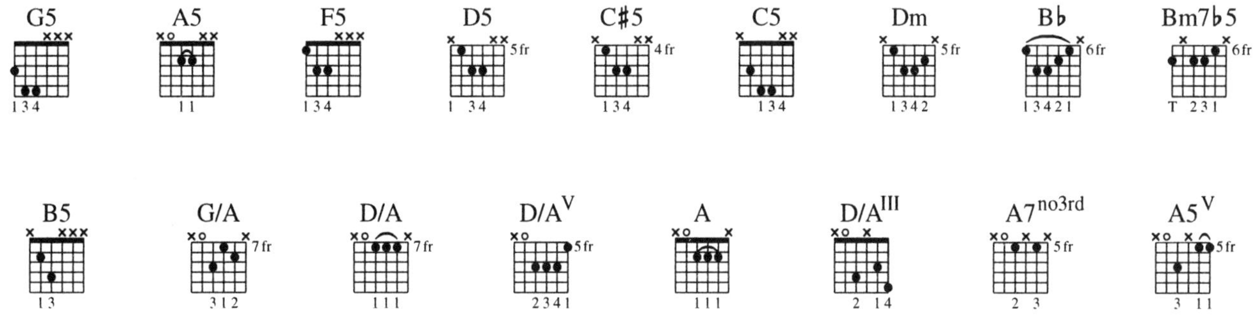

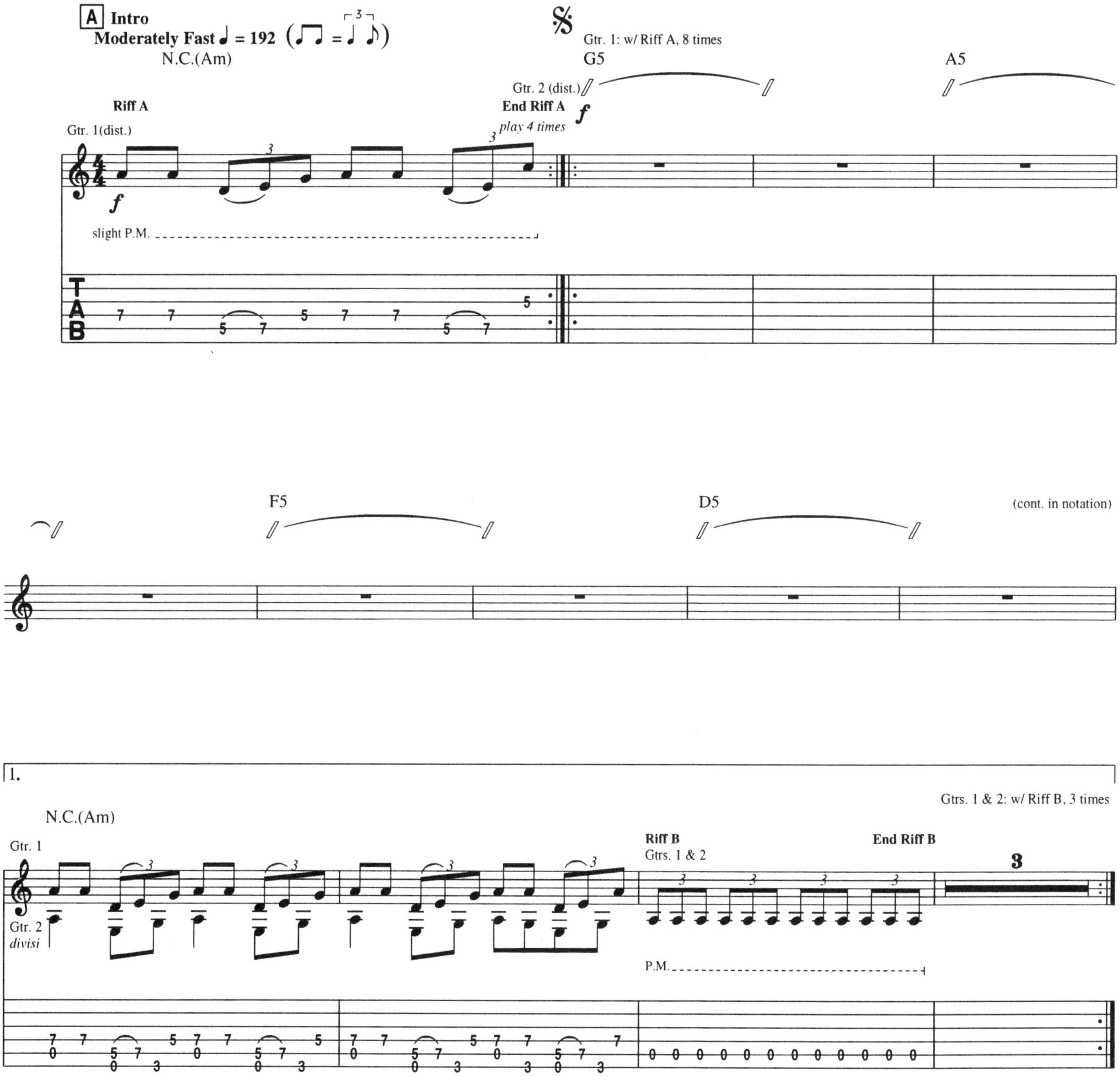

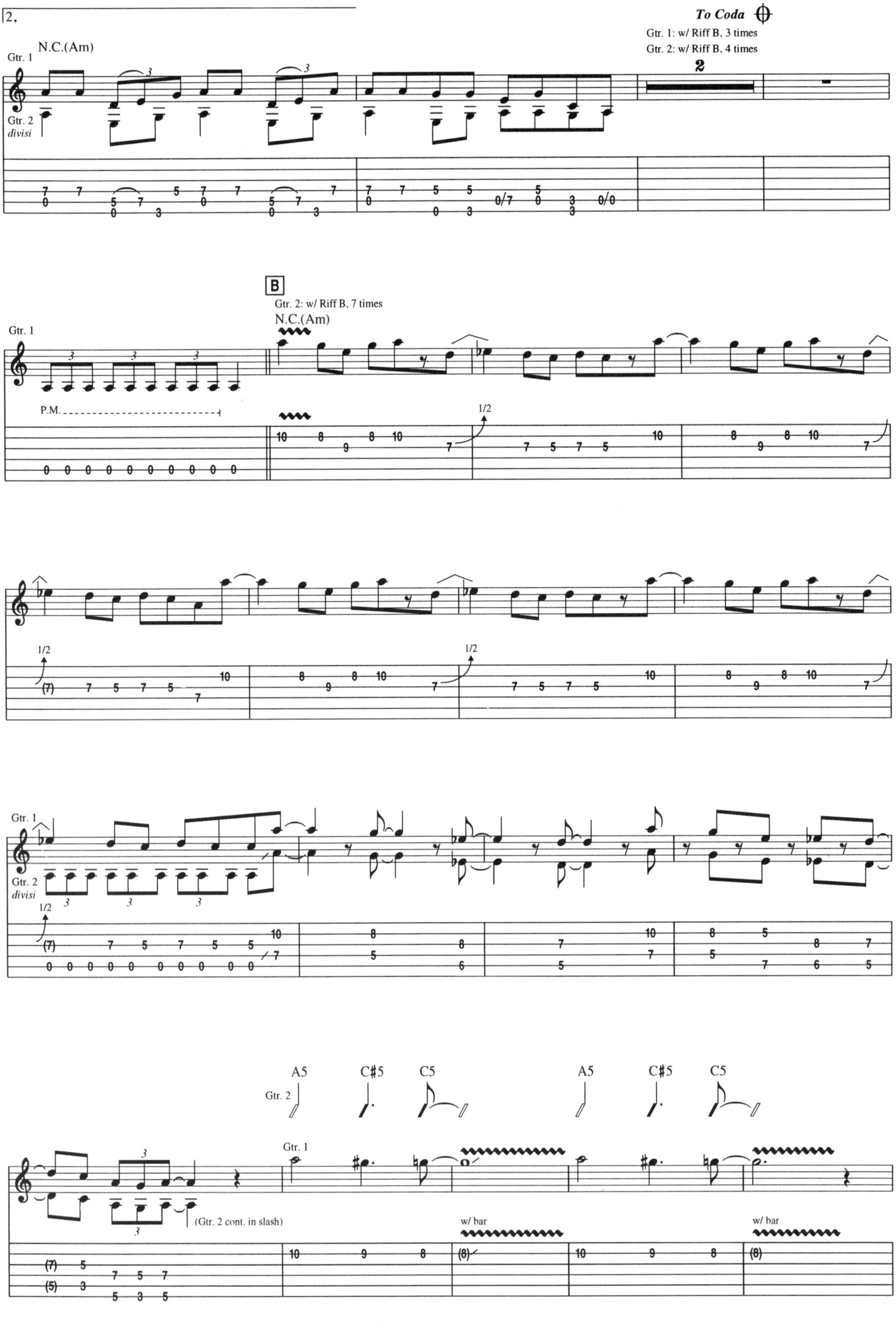
2.
To Coda
Gtr. 1: w/ Riff B, 3 times
Gtr. 2: w/ Riff B, 4 times
N.C.(Am)
Gtr. 1
Gtr. 2 divisi
B
Gtr. 2: w/ Riff B, 7 times
N.C.(Am)
P.M.
1/2
(Gtr. 2 cont. in slash)
A5
C#5
C5
w/ bar

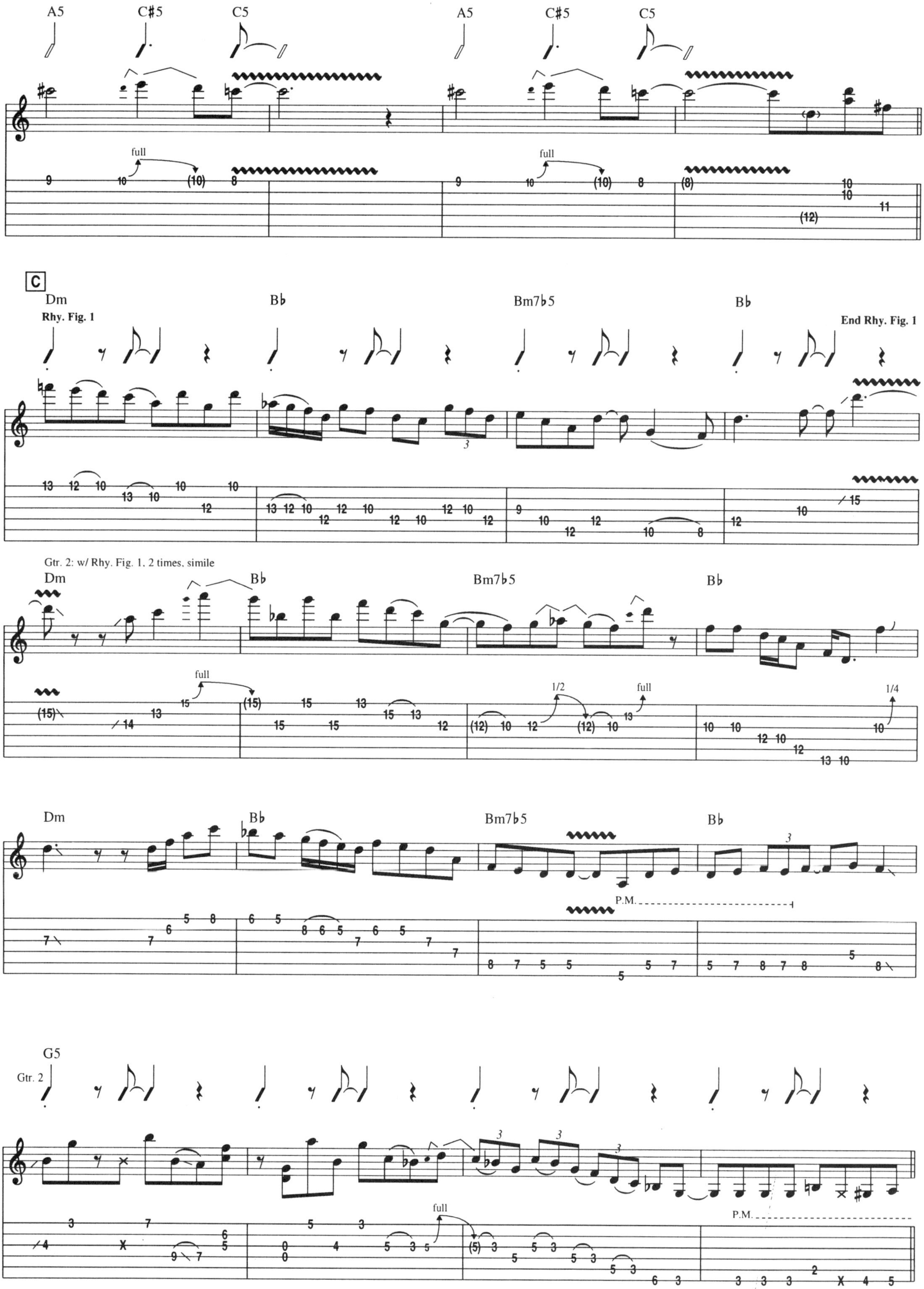

A5
C#5
C5
full
C
Dm
Rhy. Fig. 1
Bb
Bm7b5
End Rhy. Fig. 1
Gtr. 2: w/ Rhy. Fig. 1, 2 times, simile
1/2
1/4
P.M.
G5
Gtr. 2

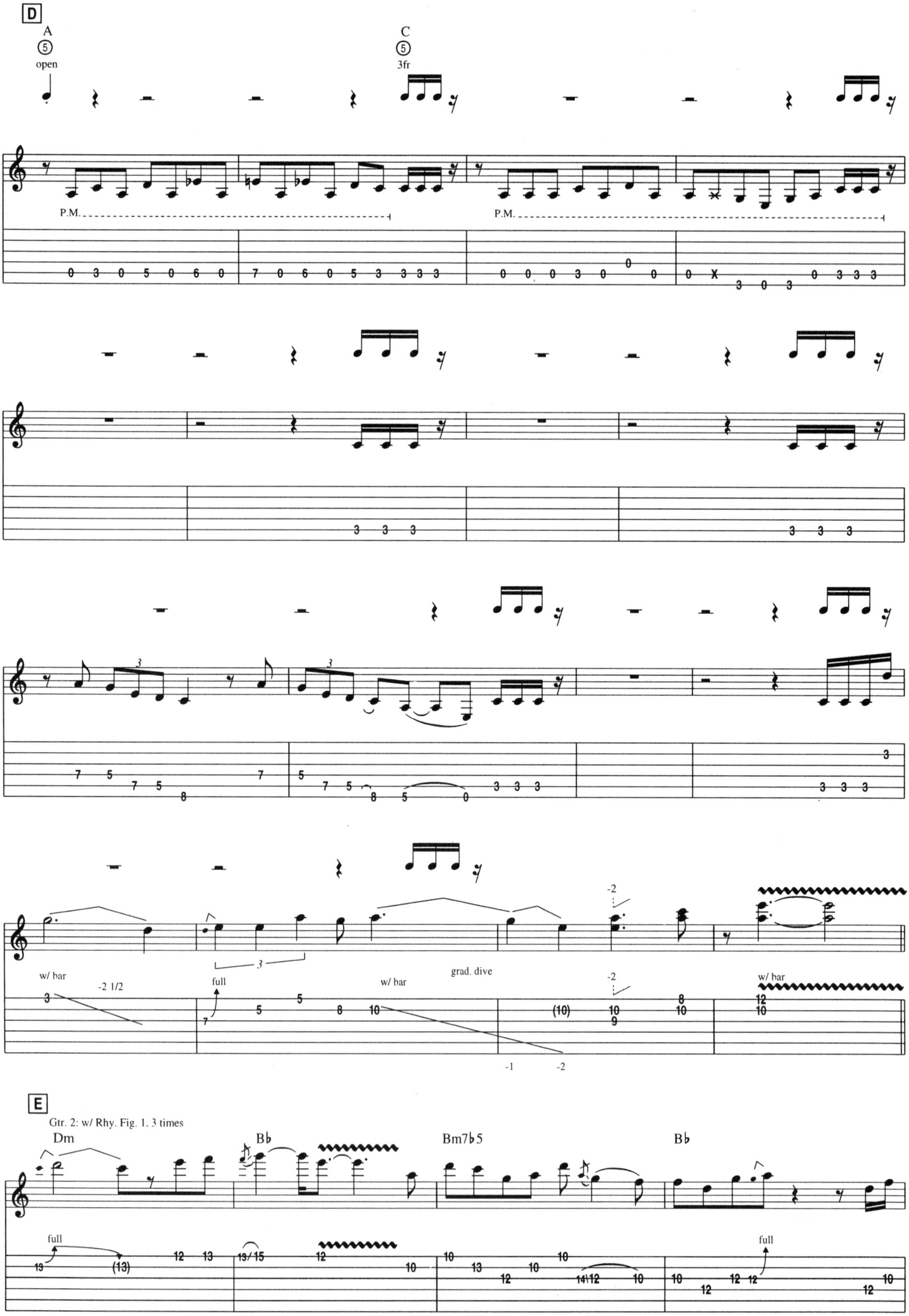
D
A
open
C
3fr
P.M.
w/ bar
-2 1/2
full
grad. dive
-2
-1
E
Gtr. 2: w/ Rhy. Fig. 1. 3 times
Dm
B♭
Bm7♭5

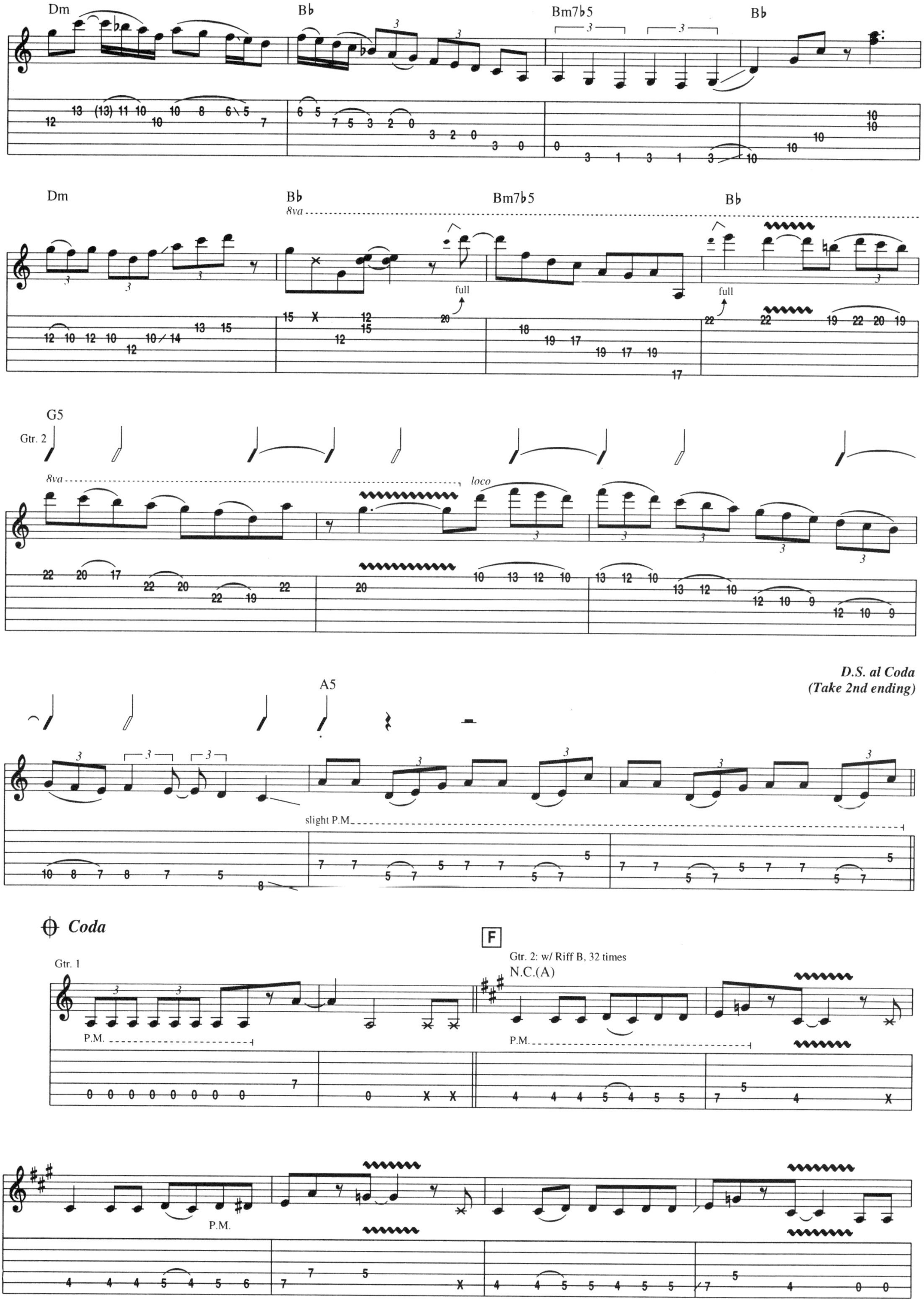
Dm
B♭
Bm7♭5
B♭
Dm
B♭
8va
Bm7♭5
B♭
full
full
G5
Gtr. 2
8va
loco
D.S. al Coda
(Take 2nd ending)
A5
slight P.M.
Coda
F
Gtr. 1
Gtr. 2: w/ Riff B, 32 times
N.C.(A)
P.M.
P.M.
P.M.

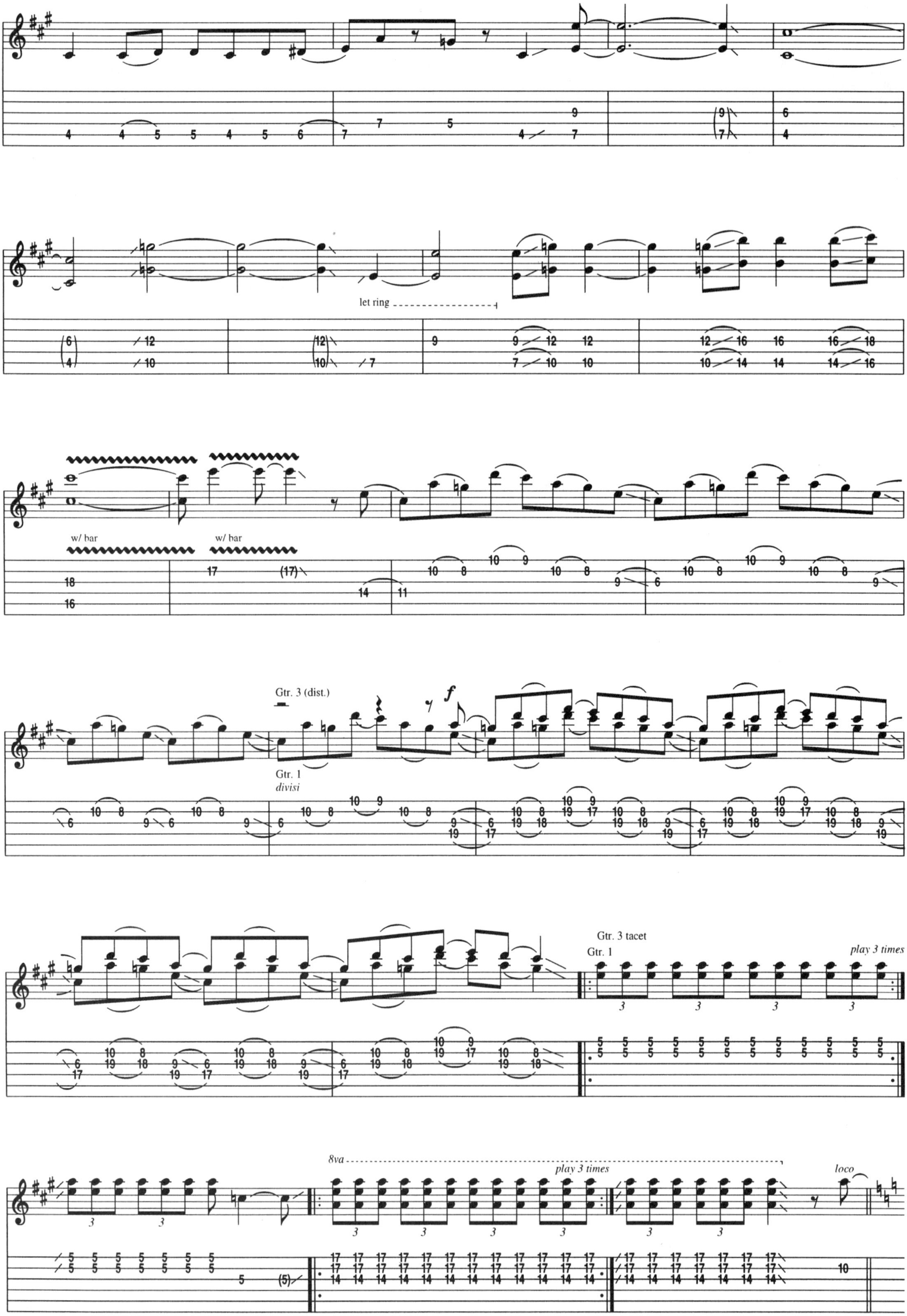
let ring
w/ bar
w/ bar
Gtr. 3 (dist.)
Gtr. 1
divisi
Gtr. 3 tacet
Gtr. 1
play 3 times
8va
play 3 times
loco

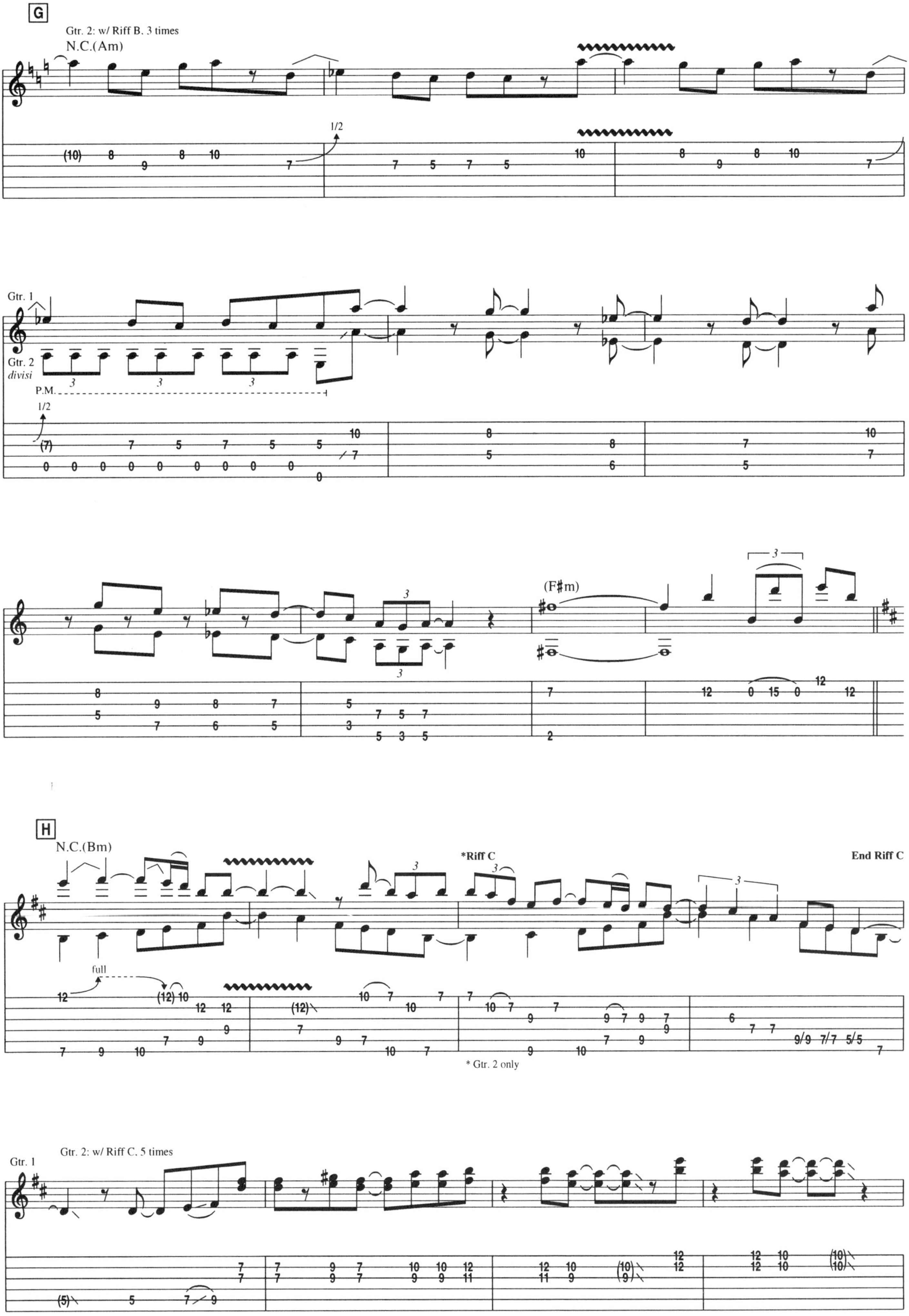
G
Gtr. 2: w/ Riff B, 3 times
N.C.(Am)
1/2
Gtr. 1
Gtr. 2
divisi
P.M.
1/2
(F#m)
H
N.C.(Bm)
*Riff C
End Riff C
full
* Gtr. 2 only
Gtr. 1
Gtr. 2: w/ Riff C, 5 times

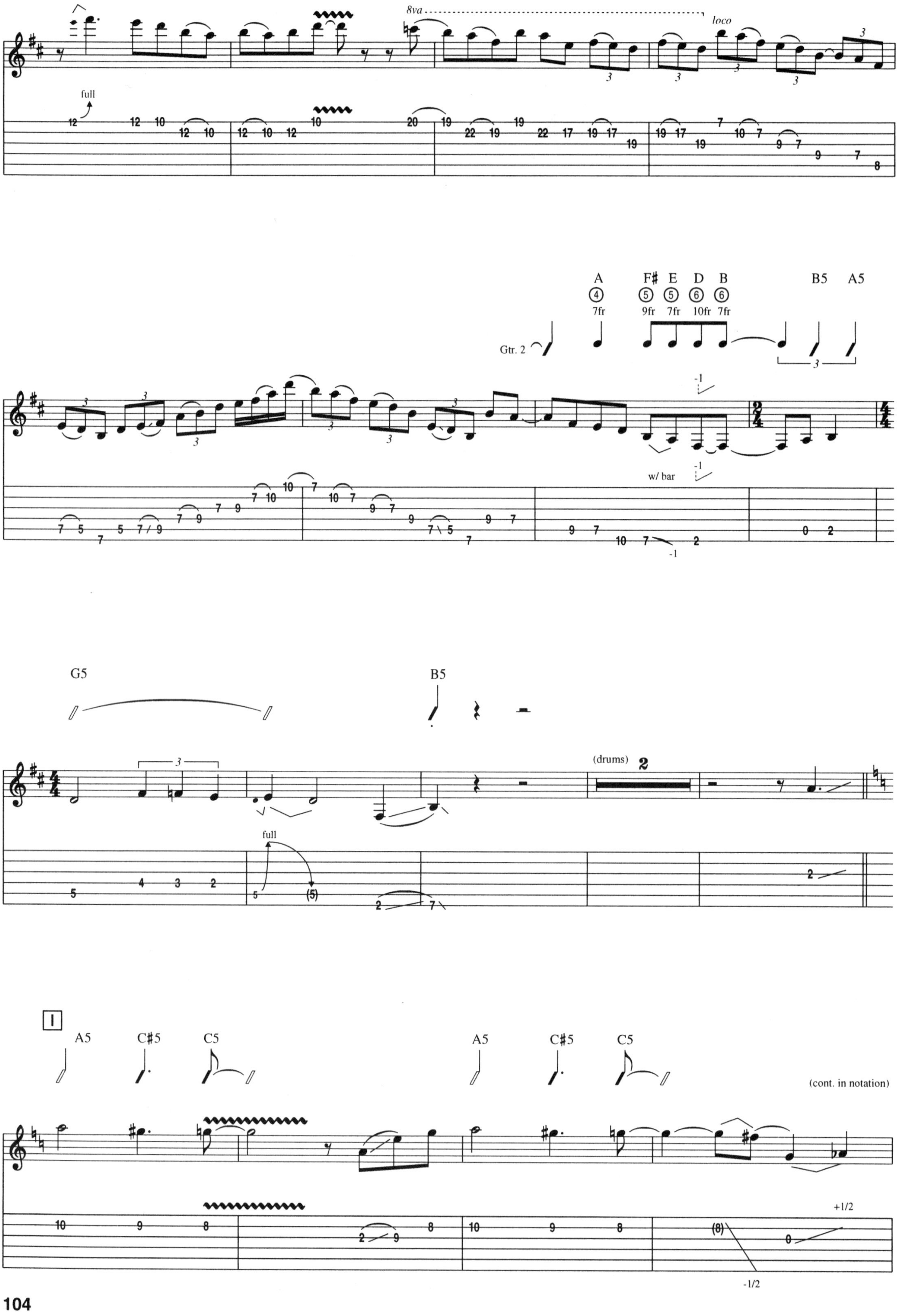
8va
loco
full
A
F♯ E D B
7fr 9fr 7fr 10fr 7fr
Gtr. 2
B5 A5
-1
w/ bar
G5
B5
(drums)
I
A5 C♯5 C5
A5 C♯5 C5
(cont. in notation)
+1/2
-1/2

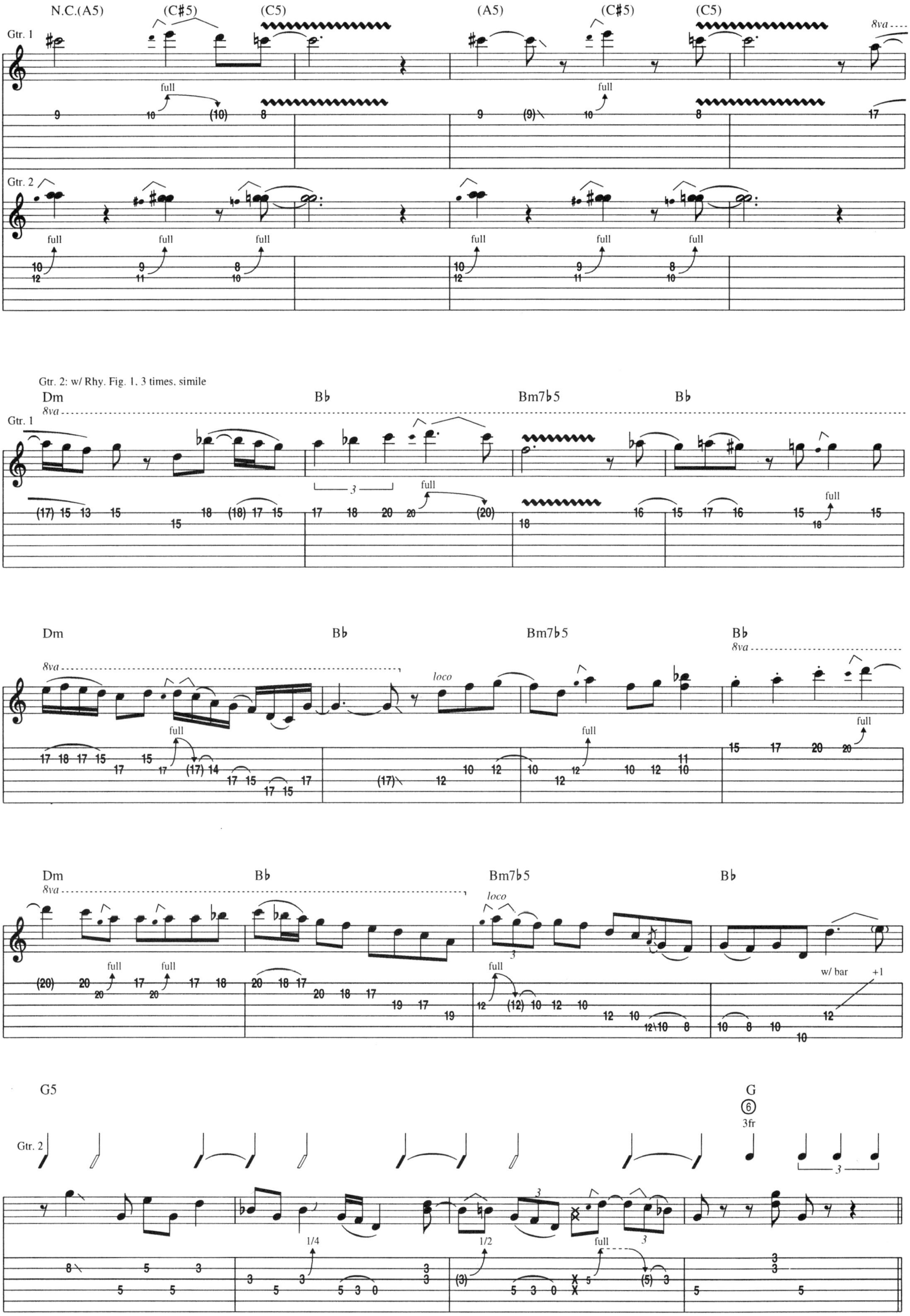
N.C.(A5)
(C#5)
(C5)
(A5)
(C#5)
(C5)
Gtr. 1
Gtr. 2
full
8va
Gtr. 2: w/ Rhy. Fig. 1, 3 times, simile
Dm
Bb
Bm7b5
Bb
loco
w/ bar
+1
G5
G
6
3fr
1/4
1/2

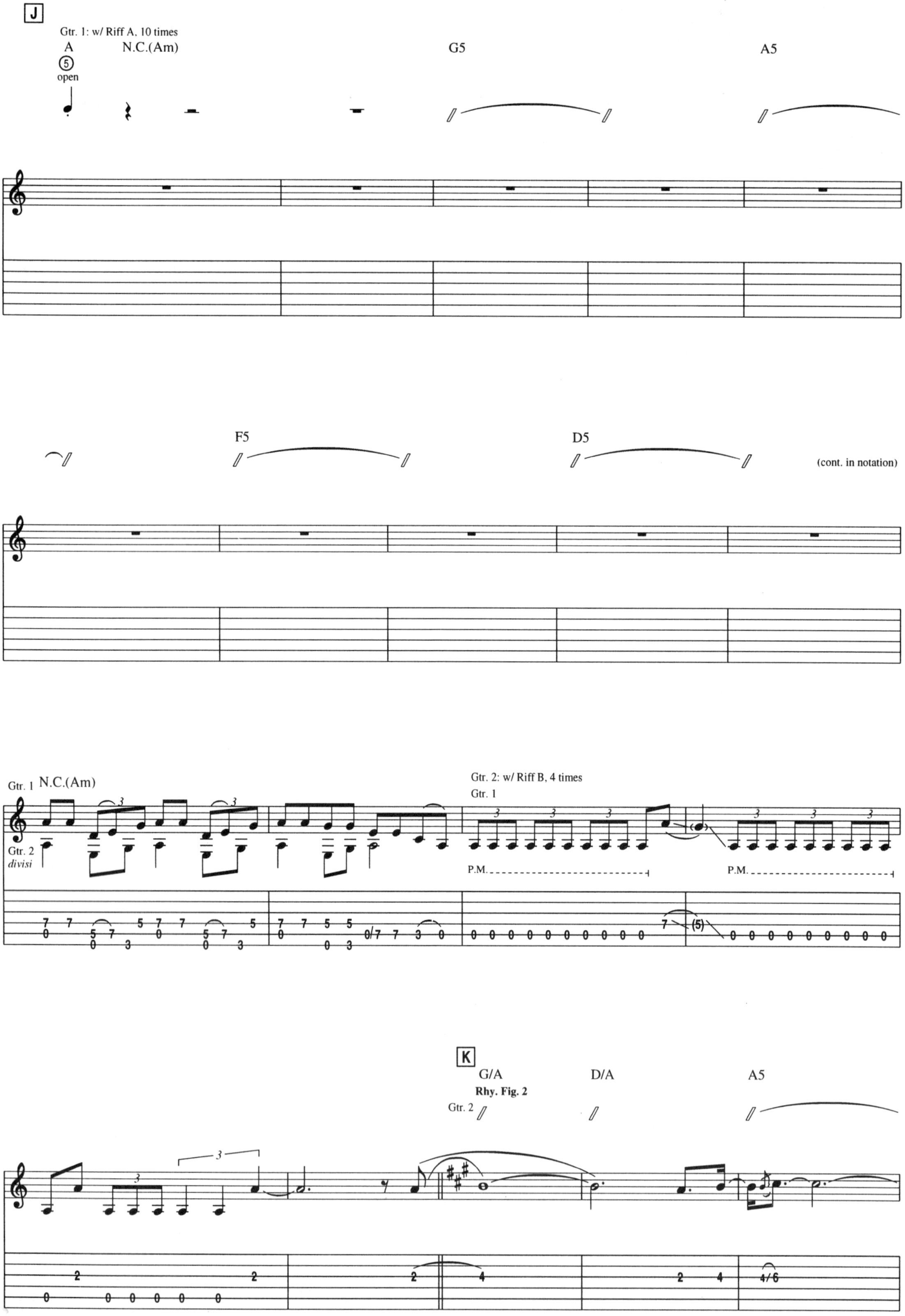
J
Gtr. 1: w/ Riff A, 10 times
A
N.C.(Am)
open
G5
A5
F5
D5
(cont. in notation)
Gtr. 1
N.C.(Am)
Gtr. 2
divisi
Gtr. 2: w/ Riff B, 4 times
Gtr. 1
P.M.
K
G/A
D/A
A5
Rhy. Fig. 2
Gtr. 2

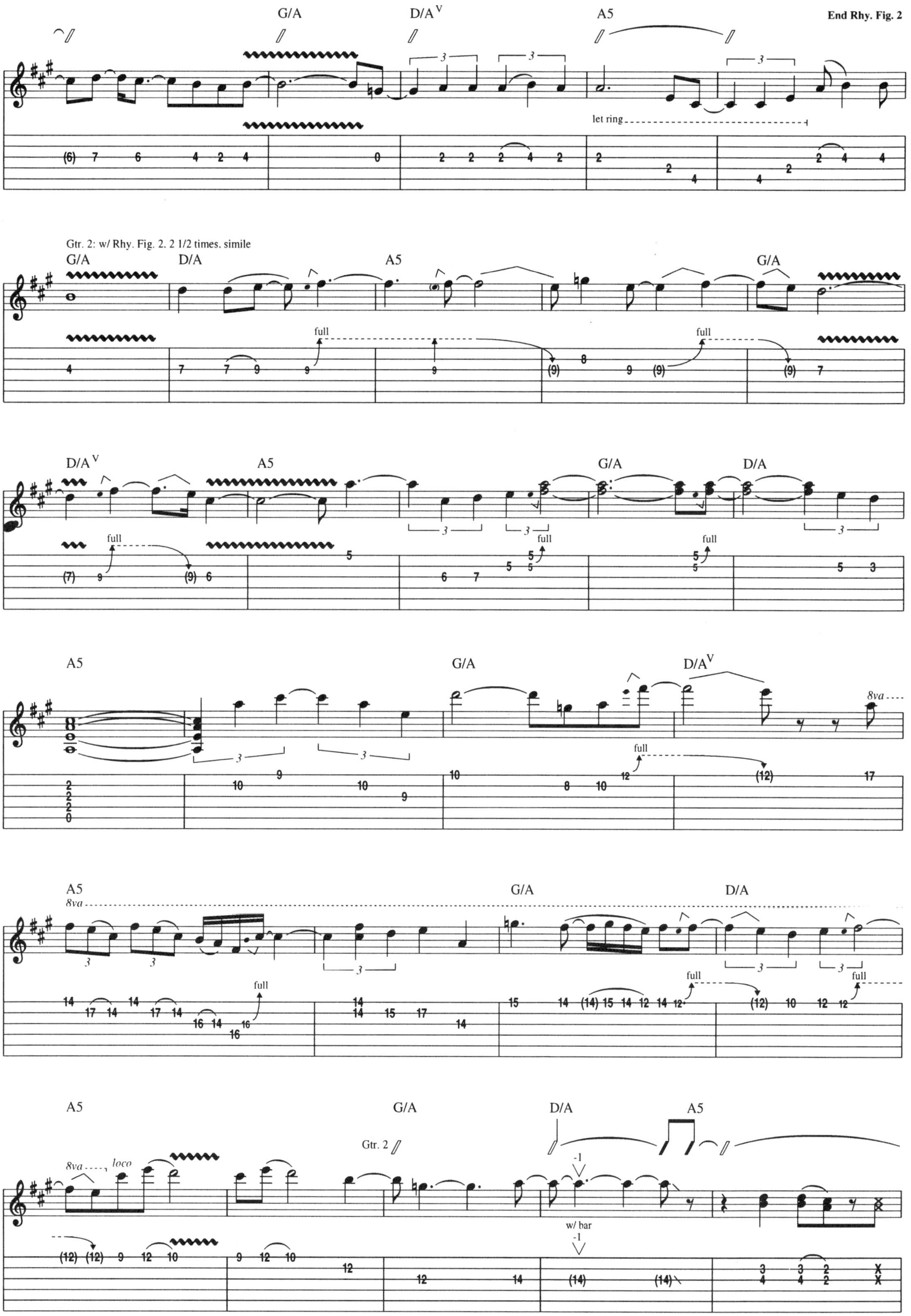
G/A
D/A V
A5
End Rhy. Fig. 2
let ring
Gtr. 2: w/ Rhy. Fig. 2, 2 1/2 times, simile
G/A
D/A
A5
G/A
full
full
D/A V
A5
G/A
D/A
full
full
full
A5
G/A
D/A V
full
8va
A5
8va
G/A
D/A
full
full
full
A5
G/A
D/A
A5
Gtr. 2
8va
loco
-1
w/ bar
-1

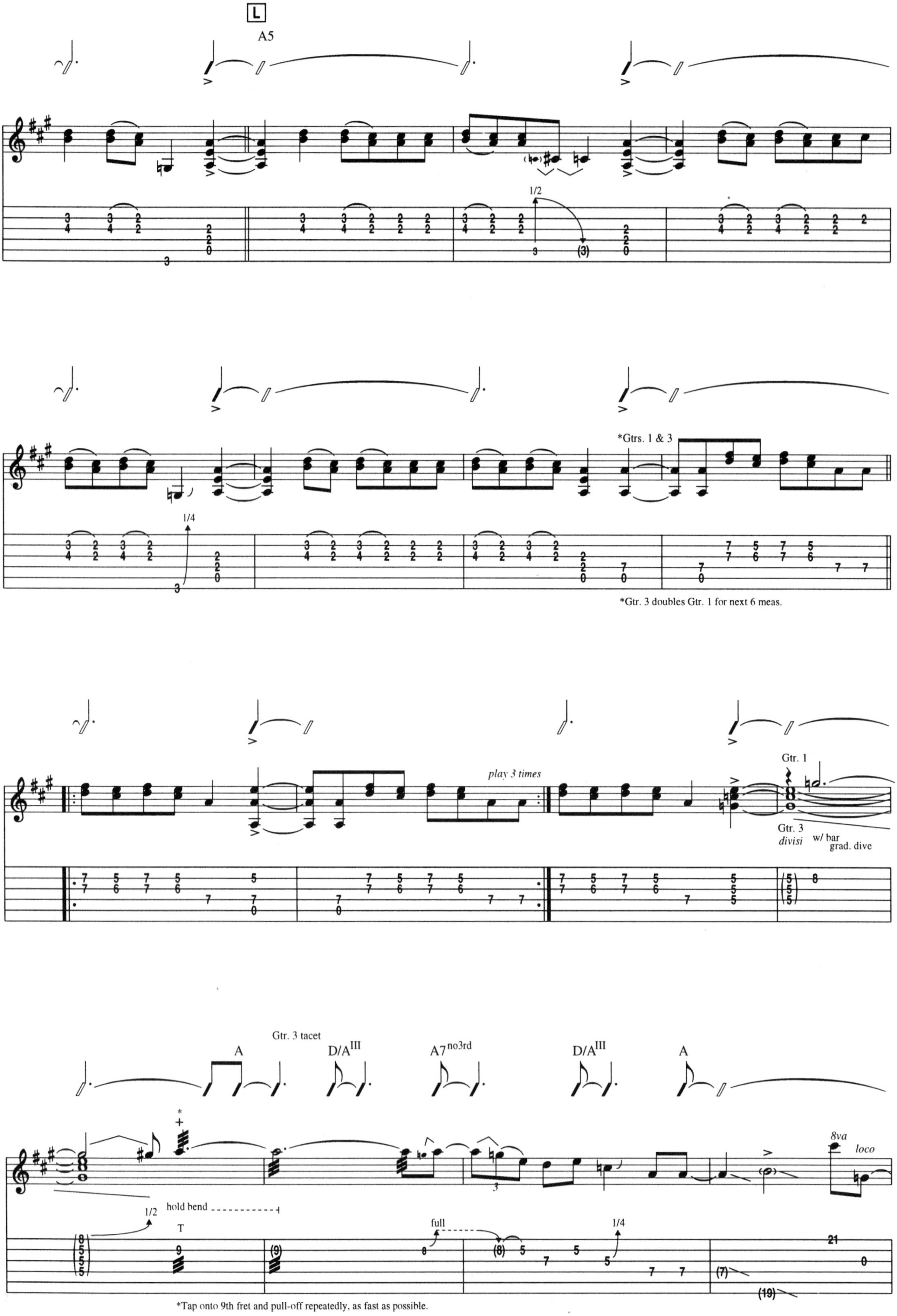

*Tap onto 9th fret and pull-off repeatedly, as fast as possible.

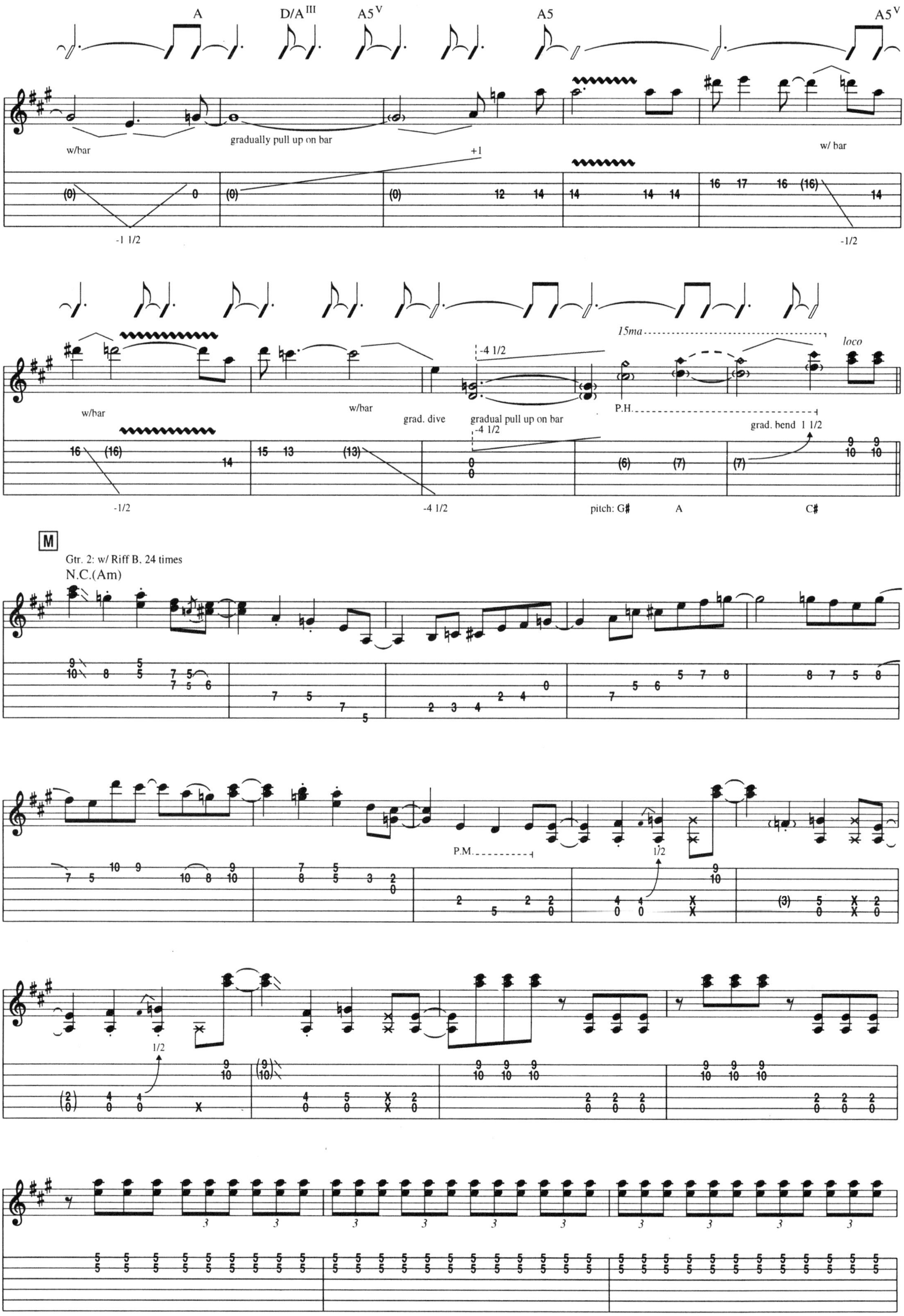
A
D/A III
A5 V
A5
A5 V
w/bar
gradually pull up on bar
+1
-1 1/2
w/ bar
-1/2
w/bar
w/bar
grad. dive
gradual pull up on bar
-4 1/2
15ma
loco
P.H.
grad. bend 1 1/2
pitch: G♯
A
C♯
M
Gtr. 2: w/ Riff B, 24 times
N.C.(Am)
P.M.
1/2

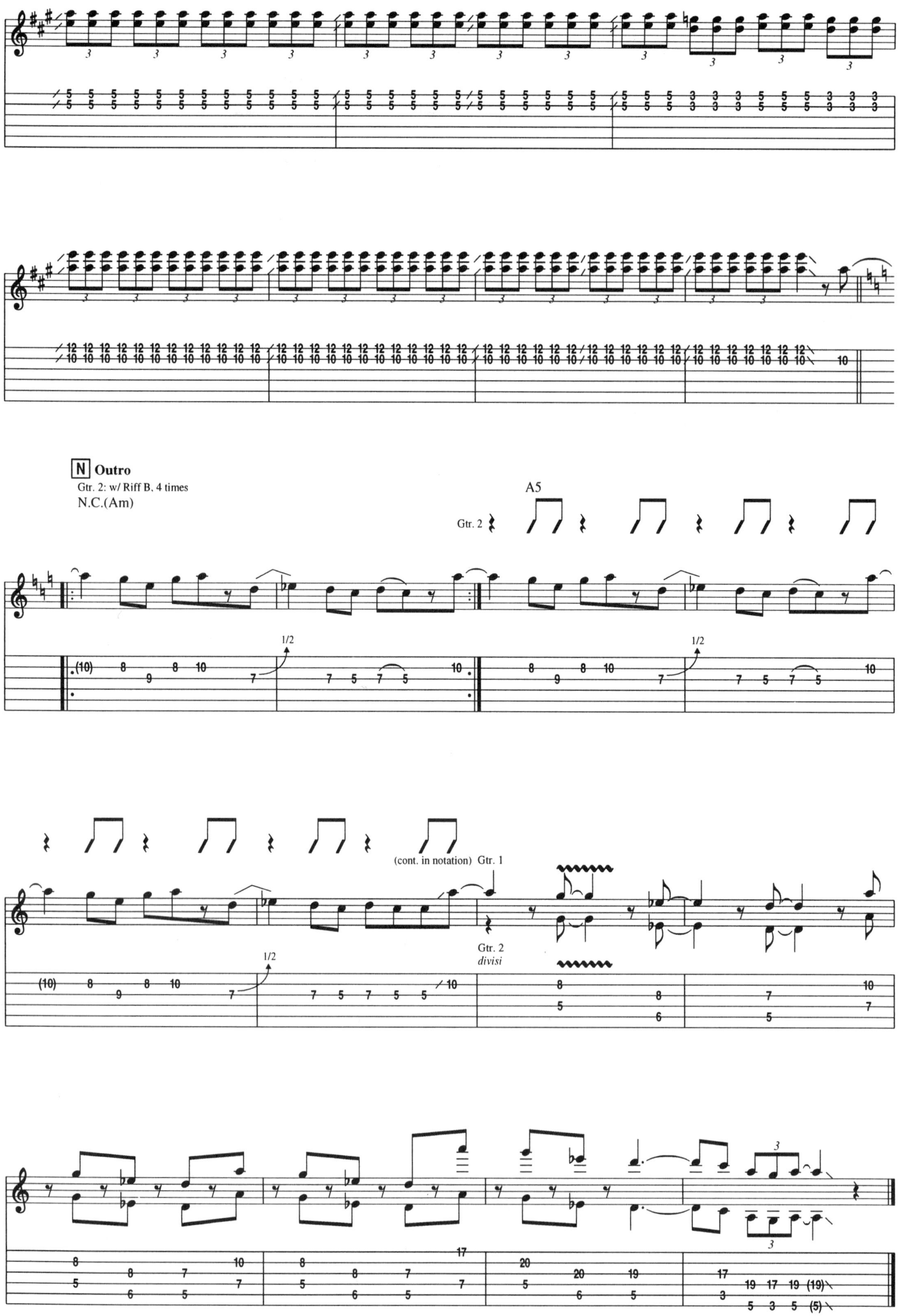
N Outro
Gtr. 2: w/ Riff B, 4 times
N.C.(Am)
A5
Gtr. 2
1/2
(cont. in notation) Gtr. 1
Gtr. 2
divisi

Guitar Notation Legend

Guitar Music can be notated three different ways: on a *musical staff*, in *tablature*, and in *rhythm slashes.*

RHYTHM SLASHES are written above the staff. Strum chords in the rhythm indicated. Use the chord diagrams found at the top of the first page of the transcription for the appropriate chord voicings. Round noteheads indicate single notes.

THE MUSICAL STAFF shows pitches and rhythms and is divided by bar lines into measures. Pitches are named after the first seven letters of the alphabet.

TABLATURE graphically represents the guitar fingerboard. Each horizontal line represents a string, and each number represents a fret.

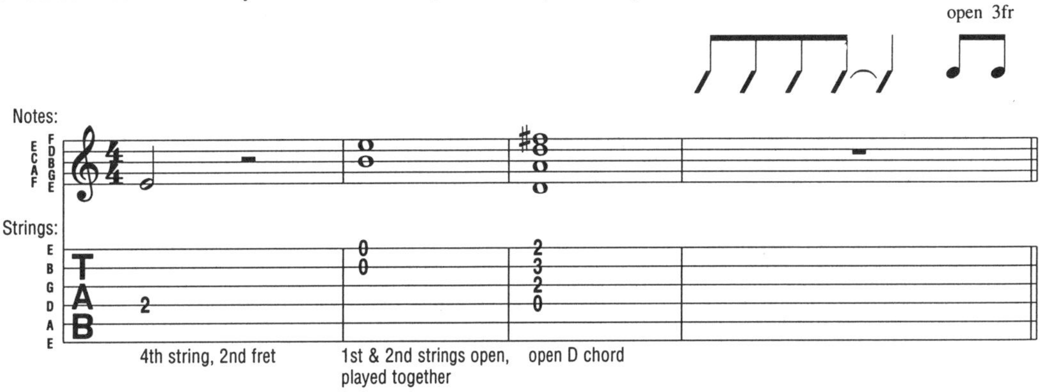

HALF-STEP BEND: Strike the note and bend up 1/2 step.

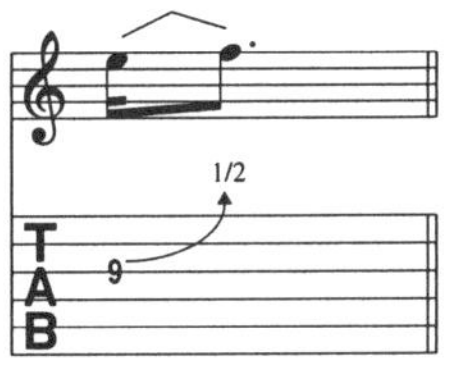

WHOLE-STEP BEND: Strike the note and bend up one step.

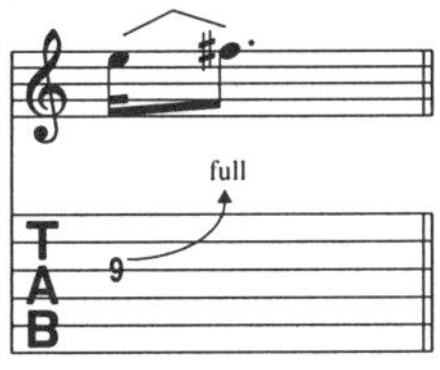

GRACE NOTE BEND: Strike the note and bend up as indicated. The first note does not take up any time.

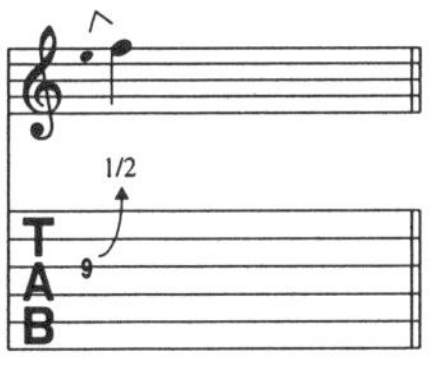

SLIGHT (MICROTONE) BEND: Strike the note and bend up 1/4 step.

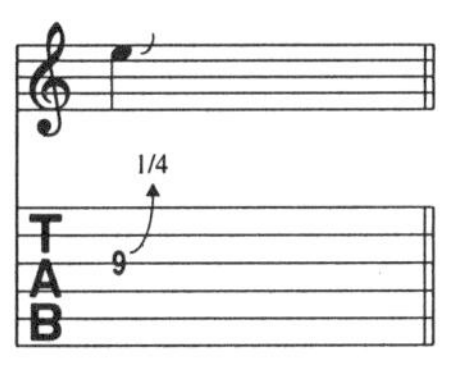

BEND AND RELEASE: Strike the note and bend up as indicated, then release back to the original note. Only the first note is struck.

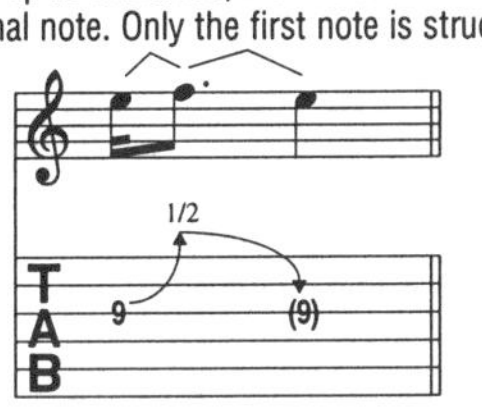

PRE-BEND: Bend the note as indicated, then strike it.

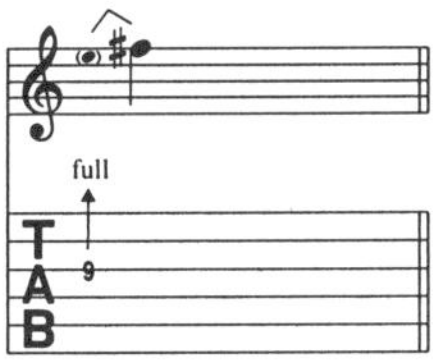

VIBRATO: The string is vibrated by rapidly bending and releasing the note with the fretting hand.

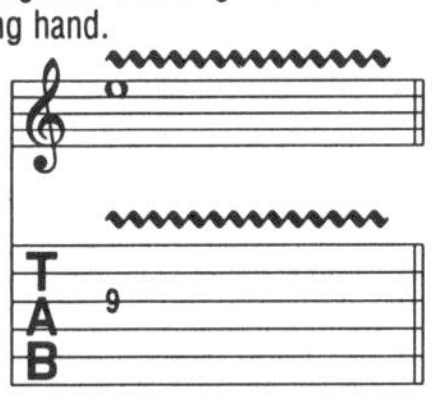

WIDE VIBRATO: The pitch is varied to a greater degree by vibrating with the fretting hand.

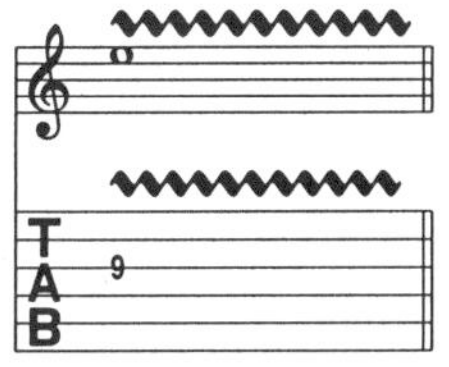

HAMMER-ON: Strike the first (lower) note with one finger, then sound the higher note (on the same string) with another finger by fretting it without picking.

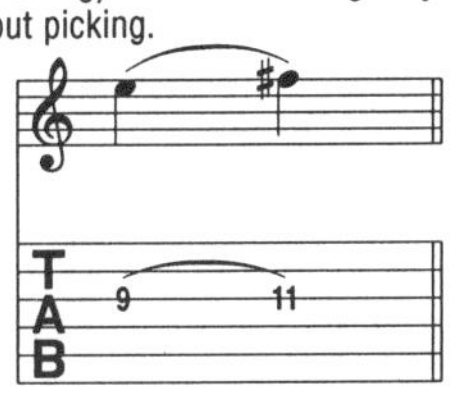

PULL-OFF: Place both fingers on the notes to be sounded. Strike the first note and without picking, pull the finger off to sound the second (lower) note.

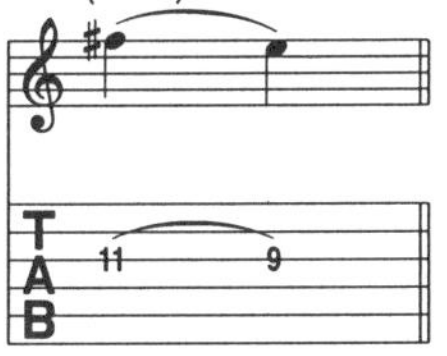

LEGATO SLIDE: Strike the first note and then slide the same fret-hand finger up or down to the second note. The second note is not struck.

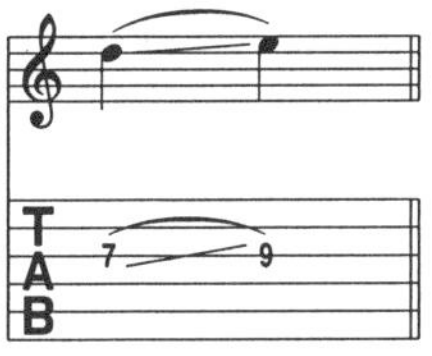

SHIFT SLIDE: Same as legato slide, except the second note is struck.

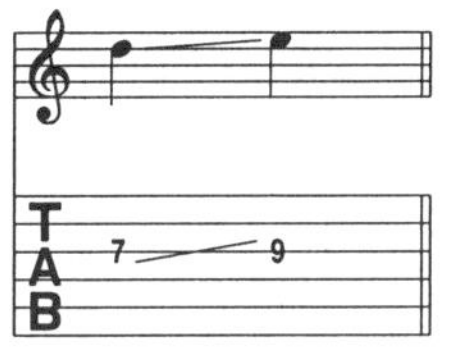

TRILL: Very rapidly alternate between the notes indicated by continuously hammering on and pulling off.

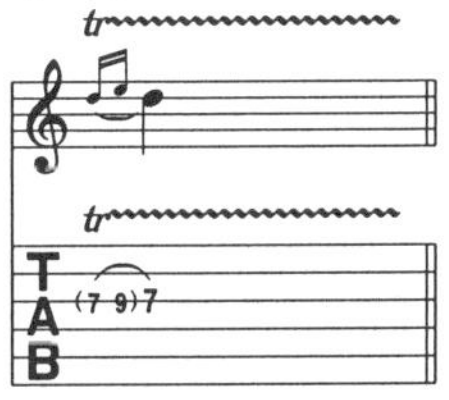

TAPPING: Hammer ("tap") the fret indicated with the pick-hand index or middle finger and pull off to the note fretted by the fret hand.

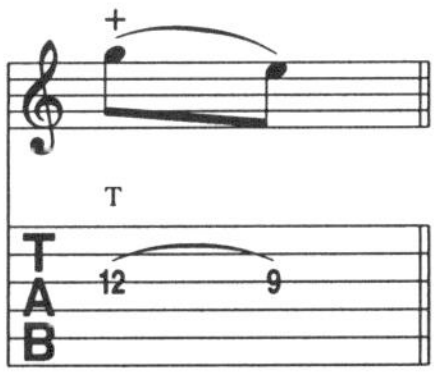

NATURAL HARMONIC: Strike the note while the fret-hand lightly touches the string directly over the fret indicated.

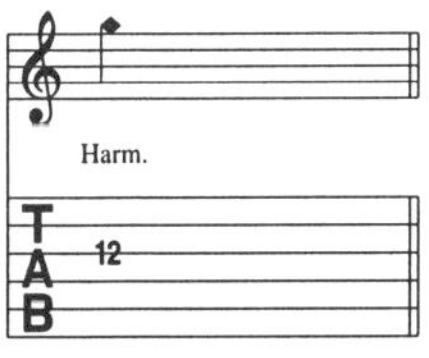

PINCH HARMONIC: The note is fretted normally and a harmonic is produced by adding the edge of the thumb or the tip of the index finger of the pick hand to the normal pick attack.

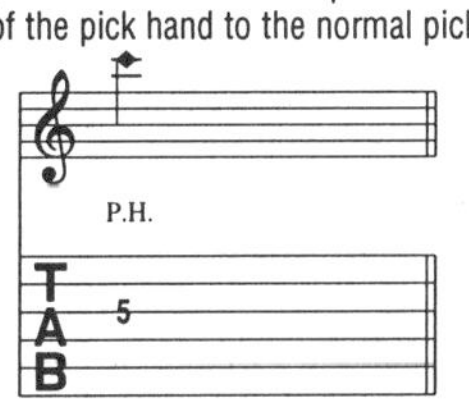

PICK SCRAPE: The edge of the pick is rubbed down (or up) the string, producing a scratchy sound.

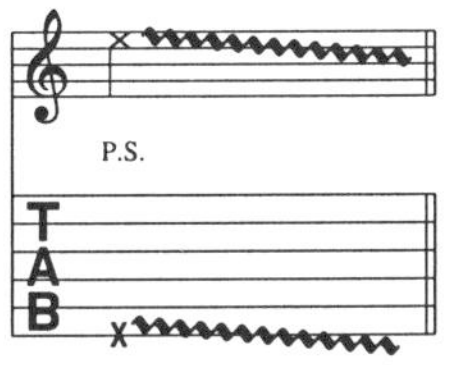

MUFFLED STRINGS: A percussive sound is produced by laying the fret hand across the string(s) without depressing, and striking them with the pick hand.

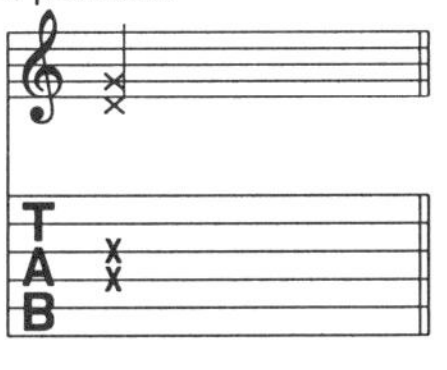

PALM MUTING: The note is partially muted by the pick hand lightly touching the string(s) just before the bridge.

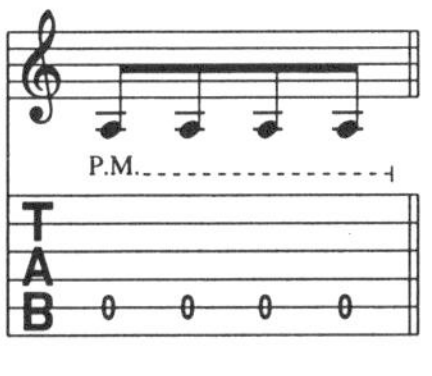

RAKE: Drag the pick across the strings indicated with a single motion.

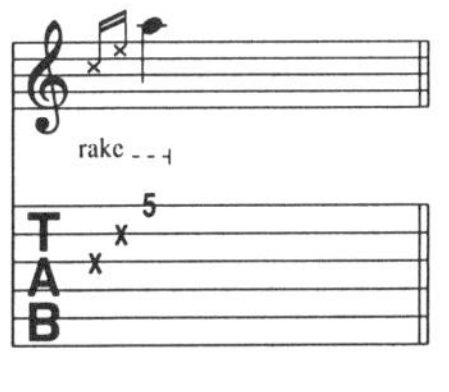

TREMOLO PICKING: The note is picked as rapidly and continuously as possible.

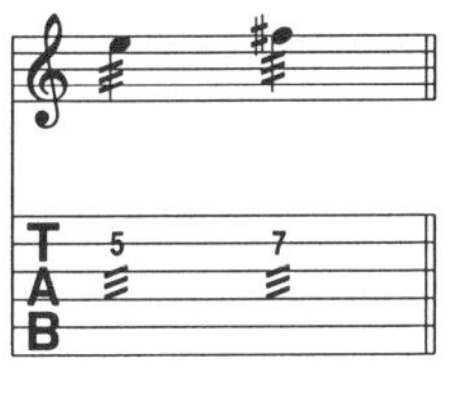

VIBRATO BAR DIVE AND RETURN: The pitch of the note or chord is dropped a specified number of steps (in rhythm) then returned to the original pitch.

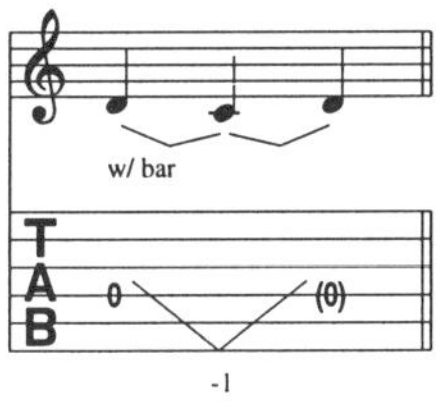

VIBRATO BAR SCOOP: Depress the bar just before striking the note, then quickly release the bar.

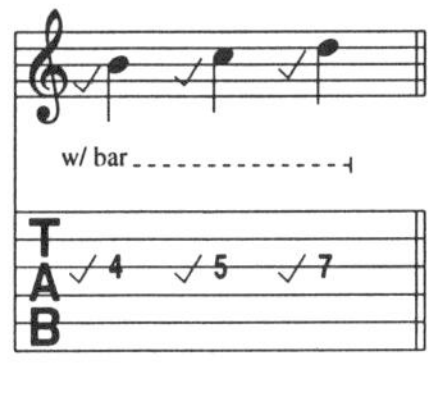

VIBRATO BAR DIP: Strike the note and then immediately drop a specified number of steps, then release back to the original pitch.

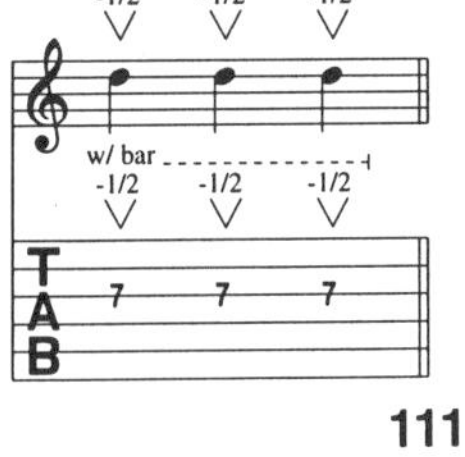

RECORDED VERSIONS

The Best Note-For-Note Transcriptions Available

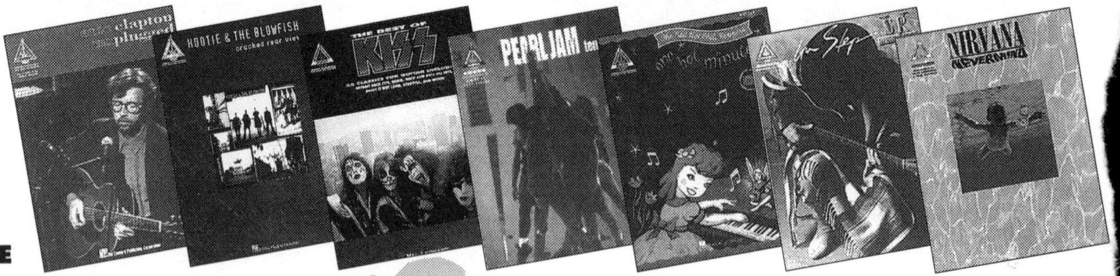

ALL BOOKS INCLUDE TABLATURE

00690002	Aerosmith – Big Ones	$22.95
00694909	Aerosmith – Get A Grip	$19.95
00692015	Aerosmith's Greatest Hits	$19.95
00660133	Aerosmith – Pump	$19.95
00694865	Alice In Chains – Dirt	$19.95
00660225	Alice In Chains – Facelift	$19.95
00694925	Alice In Chains – Jar Of Flies/Sap	$19.95
00694932	Allman Brothers Band – Vol. 1	$24.95
00694933	Allman Brothers Band – Vol. 2	$24.95
00694934	Allman Brothers Band – Vol. 3	$24.95
00694826	Anthrax – Attack Of The Killer B's	$19.95
00694876	Chet Atkins – Contemporary Styles	$19.95
00694877	Chet Atkins – Guitar For All Seasons	$19.95
00694918	The Randy Bachman Collection	$22.95
00694929	Beatles: 1962-1966	$24.95
00694930	Beatles: 1967-1970	$24.95
00694880	Beatles – Abbey Road	$19.95
00694832	Beatles For Acoustic Guitar	$19.95
00660140	Beatles Guitar Book	$19.95
00690044	Beatles – Live At The BBC	$22.95
00694891	Beatles – Revolver	$19.95
00694914	Beatles – Rubber Soul	$19.95
00694863	Beatles – Sgt. Pepper's Lonely Hearts Club Band	$19.95
00694931	Belly – Star	$19.95
00694884	The Best of George Benson	$19.95
00692385	Chuck Berry	$19.95
00692200	Black Sabbath – We Sold Our Soul For Rock 'N' Roll	$19.95
00694770	Jon Bon Jovi – Blaze Of Glory	$19.95
00690008	Bon Jovi – Cross Road	$19.95
00694871	Bon Jovi – Keep The Faith	$19.95
00694775	Bon Jovi – Slippery When Wet	$19.95
00690102	Bon Jovi – These Days	$19.95
00694935	Boston: Double Shot Of Boston	$22.95
00694762	Cinderella – Heartbreak Station	$19.95
00692376	Cinderella – Long Cold Winter	$19.95
00692375	Cinderella – Night Songs	$19.95
00694875	Eric Clapton – Boxed Set	$75.00
00692392	Eric Clapton – Crossroads Vol. 1	$22.95
00692393	Eric Clapton – Crossroads Vol. 2	$22.95
00692394	Eric Clapton – Crossroads Vol. 3	$22.95
00690010	Eric Clapton – From The Cradle	$19.95
00660139	Eric Clapton – Journeyman	$19.95
00694869	Eric Clapton – Unplugged	$19.95
00692391	The Best of Eric Clapton	$19.95
00694896	John Mayall/Eric Clapton – Bluesbreakers	$19.95
00694873	Eric Clapton – Timepieces	$19.95
00694837	Albert Collins – The Complete Imperial Recordings	$19.95
00694862	Contemporary Country Guitar	$18.95
00660127	Alice Cooper – Trash	$19.95
00694941	Crash Test Dummies – God Shuffled His Feet	$19.95
00694840	Cream – Disraeli Gears	$19.95
00690007	Danzig 4	$19.95
00694844	Def Leppard – Adrenalize	$19.95
00660186	Alex De Grassi Guitar Collection	$19.95
00694831	Derek And The Dominos – Layla & Other Assorted Love Songs	$19.95
00660175	Dio – Lock Up The Wolves	$19.95
00660178	Willie Dixon	$24.95
00694920	Best of Free	$18.95
00690089	Foo Fighters	$19.95
00690042	Robben Ford Blues Collection	$19.95
00694894	Frank Gambale – The Great Explorers	$19.95
00694807	Danny Gatton – 88 Elmira St	$19.95
00694848	Genuine Rockabilly Guitar Hits	$19.95
00694798	George Harrison Anthology	$19.95
00690068	Return of The Hellecasters	$19.95
00692930	Jimi Hendrix – Are You Experienced?	$19.95
00692931	Jimi Hendrix – Axis: Bold As Love	$19.95
00694944	Jimi Hendrix – Blues	$24.95
00660192	The Jimi Hendrix – Concerts	$24.95
00692932	Jimi Hendrix – Electric Ladyland	$24.95
00694923	Jimi Hendrix – The Experience Collection Boxed Set	$75.00
00660099	Jimi Hendrix – Radio One	$24.95
00694919	Jimi Hendrix – Stone Free	$19.95
00660024	Jimi Hendrix – Variations On A Theme: Red House	$19.95
00690017	Jimi Hendrix – Woodstock	$24.95
00690038	Gary Hoey – Best Of	$19.95
00660029	Buddy Holly	$19.95
00660200	John Lee Hooker – The Healer	$19.95
00660169	John Lee Hooker – A Blues Legend	$19.95
00690054	Hootie & The Blowfish – Cracked Rear View	$19.95
00694905	Howlin' Wolf	$14.95
00694850	Iron Maiden – Fear Of The Dark	$19.95
00694938	Elmore James – Master Electric Slide Guitar	$14.95
00694833	Billy Joel For Guitar	$19.95
00660147	Eric Johnson	$19.95
00694912	Eric Johnson – Ah Via Musicom	$19.95
00694911	Eric Johnson – Tones	$19.95
00694799	Robert Johnson – At The Crossroads	$19.95
00693185	Judas Priest – Vintage Hits	$19.95
00660050	B. B. King	$19.95
00690019	King's X – Best Of	$19.95
00694903	The Best Of Kiss	$24.95
00690070	Live – Throwing Copper	$19.95
00694954	Lynyrd Skynyrd, New Best Of	$19.95
00694845	Yngwie Malmsteen – Fire And Ice	$19.95
00694756	Yngwie Malmsteen – Marching Out	$19.95
00694755	Yngwie Malmsteen's Rising Force	$19.95
00660001	Yngwie Malmsteen's Rising Force – Odyssey	$19.95
00694757	Yngwie Malmsteen – Trilogy	$19.95
00694956	Bob Marley – Legend	$19.95
00690075	Bob Marley – Natural Mystic	$19.95
00694945	Bob Marley – Songs Of Freedom	$24.95
00690020	Meat Loaf – Bat Out Of Hell I & II	$22.95
00694952	Megadeth – Countdown To Extinction	$19.95
00694951	Megadeth – Rust In Peace	$22.95
00694953	Megadeth – Selections From "Peace Sells... But Who's Buying?" & "So Far, So Good...So What!"	$22.95
00690011	Megadeath – Youthanasia	$19.95
00694868	Gary Moore – After Hours	$19.95
00694849	Gary Moore – The Early Years	$19.95
00694802	Gary Moore – Still Got The Blues	$19.95
00690103	Alanis Morissette – Jagged Little Pill	$19.95
00694958	Mountain, Best Of	$19.95
00694895	Nirvana – Bleach	$19.95
00694913	Nirvana – In Utero	$19.95
00694901	Nirvana – Incesticide	$19.95
00694883	Nirvana – Nevermind	$19.95
00690026	Nirvana – Unplugged In New York	$19.95
00694847	Best Of Ozzy Osbourne	$22.95
00694830	Ozzy Osbourne – No More Tears	$19.95
00694855	Pearl Jam – Ten	$19.95
00693800	Pink Floyd – Early Classics	$19.95
00693864	Police, The Best Of	$18.95
00694967	Police – Message In A Box Boxed Set	$70.00
00692535	Elvis Presley	$18.95
00690032	Elvis Presley – The Sun Sessions	$22.95
00694975	Queen – Classic	$24.95
00694974	Queen – A Night At The Opera	$19.95
00694969	Queensryche – Selections from "Operation: Mindcrime"	$19.95
00694910	Rage Against The Machine	$19.95
00693910	Ratt – Invasion of Your Privacy	$19.95
00693911	Ratt – Out Of The Cellar	$19.95
00690055	Red Hot Chili Peppers – Bloodsugarsexmagik	$19.95
00690090	Red Hot Chili Peppers – One Hot Minute	$22.95
00690027	Red Hot Chili Peppers – Out In L.A.	$19.95
00694968	Red Hot Chili Peppers – Selections from "What Hits!?"	$22.95
00694892	Guitar Style Of Jerry Reed	$19.95
00694899	REM – Automatic For The People	$19.95
00694898	REM – Out Of Time	$19.95
00660060	Robbie Robertson	$19.95
00694959	Rockin' Country Guitar	$19.95
00690014	Rolling Stones – Exile On Main Street	$24.95
00694976	Rolling Stones – Some Girls	$18.95
00694897	Roots Of Country Guitar	$19.95
00694836	Richie Sambora – Stranger In This Town	$19.95
00694805	Scorpions – Crazy World	$19.95
00694916	Scorpions – Face The Heat	$19.95
00694870	Seattle Scene	$18.95
00690076	Sex Pistols – Never The Bollocks, Here's The Sex Pistols	$19.95
00690041	Smithereens – Best Of	$19.95
00694885	Spin Doctors – Pocket Full Of Kryptonite	$19.95
00694962	Spin Doctors – Turn It Upside Down	$19.95
00694917	Spin Doctors – Up For Grabs	$19.95
00694921	Steppenwolf, The Best Of	$22.95
00694801	Rod Stewart, Best Of	$22.95
00694957	Rod Stewart – Unplugged...And Seated	$22.95
00690021	Sting – Fields Of Gold	$19.95
00694824	Best Of James Taylor	$16.95
00694846	Testament – The Ritual	$19.95
00694887	Thin Lizzy – The Best Of Thin Lizzy	$19.95
00690030	Toad The Wet Sprocket	$19.95
00694410	The Best of U2	$19.95
00694411	U2 – The Joshua Tree	$19.95
00690039	Steve Vai – Alien Love Secrets	$24.95
00660137	Steve Vai – Passion & Warfare	$24.95
00694904	Vai – Sex and Religion	$24.95
00690023	Jimmy Vaughan – Strange Pleasures	$19.95
00690024	Stevie Ray Vaughan – Couldn't Stand The Weather	$19.95
00694879	Stevie Ray Vaughan –In The Beginning	$19.95
00660136	Stevie Ray Vaughan – In Step	$19.95
00660058	Stevie Ray Vaughan – Lightnin' Blues 1983 – 1987	$24.95
00690036	Stevie Ray Vaughan – Live Alive	$24.95
00694835	Stevie Ray Vaughan – The Sky Is Crying	$19.95
00690015	Stevie Ray Vaughan – Texas Flood	$19.95
00690025	Stevie Ray Vaughan – Soul To Soul	$19.95
00694776	Vaughan Brothers – Family Style	$19.95
00660196	Vixen – Rev It Up	$19.95
00694789	Muddy Waters – Deep Blues	$24.95
00690071	Weezer	$19.95
00694888	Windham Hill Guitar Sampler	$18.95

Prices and availability subject to change without notice. Some products may not be available outside the U.S.A.

FOR MORE INFORMATION, SEE YOUR LOCAL MUSIC DEALER, OR WRITE TO:

HAL•LEONARD™